Alex Pettes

Praise for *S.U.R.E.-Fire Direct Response Marketing*

—BY RUSSELL KERN

"This book takes the guesswork out of planning, strategizing, and implementing effective direct marketing campaigns and provides a step-by-step answer to the questions direct marketers frequently ask. After reading this book you can improve response rates, reduce your marketing risk, increase lead quality and sales revenue, and maximize relationships with your customers."

BOB ARMSTRONG, *Co-Chairman*
Direct Marketing School Programs
Los Angeles Direct Marketing Association

"Russell Kern has captured the essence of successful direct marketing! His S.U.R.E.-Fire process is incredibly effective at reducing the risks of our marketing campaigns and measurably improving our sales results."

JEFFREY P. GAIA, *President*
Business Banking Group
Bank One Corporation

"*S.U.R.E.-Fire Direct Response Marketing* provides a practical and truly comprehensive approach to successful direct marketing for companies large and small. Kern combines time honored techniques with important, evolving innovations in such areas as E-mail marketing and banner advertising. I found his discussion of CRM and data mining particularly valuable. This book will prove highly useful to the direct marketing novice and experienced practitioner alike."

ALISA S. MACLIN, *Program Director*
Solutions Marketing
IBM

S.U.R.E.-Fire®
Direct Response Marketing

S.U.R.E.-Fire® Direct Response Marketing

GENERATING BUSINESS-TO-BUSINESS SALES LEADS FOR BOTTOM-LINE SUCCESS

Russell M. Kern
President/CEO of Kern Direct Marketing

McGraw-Hill

New York   Chicago   San Francisco   Lisbon   London   Madrid   Mexico City   Milan
New Delhi   San Juan   Seoul   Singapore   Sydney   Toronto

Library of Congress Cataloging-in-Publication Data

Kern, Russell, M.
    Sure-fire direct response marketing : generating business-to-
business sales leads for bottom-line success / Russell M. Kern.
        p.   cm.
    Includes index.
    ISBN 0-658-00622-3
    1. Advertising, Direct-mail.   2. Direct marketing.   I. Title.

HF5861 .K47   2001
658.8'4—dc21   00-48066

McGraw-Hill

A Division of The **McGraw-Hill** *Companies*

1 2 3 4 5 6 7 8 9 0 HPC/HPC 0 9 8 7 6 5 4 3 2 1

ISBN 0-658-00622-3

This book was set in Minion by Hespenheide Design
Printed and bound by Hamilton Printing

McGraw-Hill books are available at special quantity discounts to use as premiums
and sales promotions, or for use in corporate training programs. For more
information, please write to the Director of Special Sales, Professional Publishing,
McGraw-Hill, Two Penn Plaza, New York, NY 10121-2298. Or contact your local
bookstore.

Portions of this book were excerpted by permission from previously published
works. **Page 2** From "Strategic Planning for the Small Business" by Craig Rice.
Adams Media Corp; **113** Best Software Inc; **122, 123** From "My Life in Advertising
and Scientific Advertising" by Claude Hopkins, 1996. Used with permission from
NTC/Contemporary Publishing Group; **128, 150** From "Managing Sales Leads"
by Donath, Dixon, Crocker, Obermayer, 1995. Used with permission from
NTC/Contemporary Publishing Group; **129** From "Care and Feeding of Sales
Channels: An Inquiry Management Approach." M. H. "Mac" McIntosh. Published by
Cahners Business Information, 1996; **129** James Obermayer, Sales Leakage
Consulting, www.salesleakage.com; **144** M. H. "Mac" McIntosh, The Mac McIntosh
Company, Inc. www.salesleadexperts.com 800-944-5553; **150** From "Managing
Sales Leads" by Donath, Dixon, Crocker, Obermayer, 1995. Used with permission
from NTC/Contemporary Publishing Group; **147** Saligent, Inc; **196, ch. 12**
Reprinted with permission from *Direct Mail & Mail Order Handbook*, 3rd edition.
Copyright 1980 by Dartnell Corporation, 360 Hiatt Drive, Palm Beach Gardens,
Florida 33418. All rights reserved. For more information on this or other products
published by Dartnell, please call (800) 621-5463, ext. 564; **210** Program details
courtesy of Chordiant Software, Inc; **225** Throckmorton, Joan. *Winning Direct
Response Advertising*, 2nd edition. Lincolnwood, IL, NTC Publishing Group, 1997:
pp. 185–212.

This book is printed on acid-free paper.

I dedicate this book to my wife, Lynne, and to our children. Lynne, thank you for your love, support, and constant encouragement. Your love of writing and creativity is a constant torch of inspiration to me. Thank you for standing by and making this journey a success.

Michelle, Sean, and Hillary, thank you for putting up with my constant writing (even on our ski trip). I hope you will always believe in your dreams. You can make them come true, if you consistently chip away at them. And, of course: go slow, stay calm, and write neatly.

I love each one of you deeply.

CONTENTS

ACKNOWLEDGMENTS

My thanks go first to Danielle Egan-Miller, business editor, for her vision with regard to this book and its value to the direct marketing community.

Thanks also to my support team for their hard work and dedication to this project. In particular, I would like to acknowledge Rhonda Vinton, of Vinton Marketing & Associates, Thousand Oaks, California, for her commitment and support in making this the best book possible. Her professionalism and knowledge of direct marketing is unquestionable. I also extend thanks to Barbara Ketchum, who was an invaluable source of support to Rhonda and me. I thank Barbara for focusing on the thousands of details required to make this book a reality.

In addition, I would like to thank:

Kate Bertrand, for her invaluable writing assistance. She believed in me and in the value of this book from its inception to its completion.

Jim Obermayer, for his contributions and guidance. Jim's knowledge of response management systems, the lead generation process, and sales management was vital to this project.

Rhonda Vinton and Rachel Taylor, for working closely with me in defining and refining the S.U.R.E.-Fire research process.

The entire staff of Kern Direct, for their support in the development of this book. In particular, I would like to recognize Kassie Gavrilis, Elaine Benditson, Inna Stone, Brad Pagano, Ruby Carrillo, Emily Orozco, Stacey Bartholomew, Julia Miller, Jonathan Eun, Jay Jacobesen, Maria Spear, and Katie Morris for their hard work and extra effort in bringing this project to fruition.

This book would never have been written without the experience I have gained over the years from my direct marketing peers and colleagues, particularly: John Coe, Bernie Goldberg, Vic Hunter, Tracy Emerick, Bob Hacker, Richard Rosen, Ray Jutkins, Ruth Stevens, Michael Brown, Mike Wallen, Dennis McGuire, David Bell, Mac McIntosh, Robert Bly, Bob Stone, Ed Nash, David Ogilvy, Joan Throckmorton, Les Morris, Phil Herring, Craig Walker, Steve Colich, Jim Pratt, Jack Daly, Louise Guryan, Glen Freidman, Laura McQuire, Lester Wunderman, Stan Rapp, Doug Drew, Jerry Mathai, and my first agency partner, Carl Parsons.

Finally, in my twenty-plus years in this business, I have found that there are no better teachers than my clients. I must thank all the people who have given me the opportunity to create direct marketing programs or implement the S.U.R.E.-Fire process on their behalf. These people include but are not limited to: Tina Babbi, Doron Aspitz, Ofer Matan, Shannon Hughes, Deborah Henken, Joe Williams, Tom Grant, Maddy Ginsberg, Susan Zykoski, Linda Haury, Eric Morley, Zarnez Arlia, Cori Kaylor, Joanne Urbanik, Tom Toperczer, Dan Carmel, Jennifer Saunders, Tracy Groves, Peter Soderberg, Matt Hill, Bill Middleton, Debbie Erickson, Jane King, Jennifer Harper, Lisa Hiatt, Loren Zeller, Lori Kaplan, Susan Albano, Ross Goldberg, Lori Harmon, Bobbi Maselli, Scott Anderson, Terry Rosson, Andy Chase, Geri Cohen, Jackie Rutkowitz, Lou Ryan, Mary Culley, Frank Jones, Chris Grejtak, Judy Laine, Nancy Stinettet, Tracey Mustacchio, Alyce Menton, Jeff Gaia, Hanna Irwin, Kristen Burke, Cheryl Spekhardt, Mike Collett, Paul Stout, Dave Campbell, Mary Ludloff, Susan Cassella, Raj Jaswa, Rathi Almaula, Rose Maugeri, Alley Neal, Jacqueline Meaney, and Alexis Kim.

Finally, I thank my mother, brothers, and sister for pushing me to complete the big stuff and always supporting my business endeavors and my father, who I will always remember for teaching me the love of learning. I want to thank Marty and Audrey Appel for their encouragement and support. Paul, Allen, Lenny, and Dave your friendship counts. And many thanks to Bill Pasnau for his unwavering friendship and continued guidance in my development of a repeatable process that has the potential to change an industry.

INTRODUCTION

Communication is not just words, paint on canvas, math symbols, or the equations and models of scientists; it is the interrelation of human beings trying to escape loneliness, trying to share experience, trying to implant an idea.

—WILLIAM M. MARSTELLER
Advertising executive

The Direct Marketing Association predicts business-to-business direct marketing expenditures will grow 7.4 percent annually, to $118.3 billion by 2003. The DMA also predicts that fully 56 percent of this $118.3 billion will be used to generate sales leads. Technologies and tools such as personal computers, teleconferencing, marketing automation software, and, of course, the Internet are catalyzing this growth in business-to-business marketing. The new technologies are making lead generation marketing strategies possible in cases in which they were not cost-effective in the past. Now you, as a business-to-business direct marketer, can deliver personal messages at a very low cost, obtain instant result measurements, and change campaign elements (such as offers or messages) on the fly.

Yet even with the Internet and all the new high-technology software applications, the fundamentals of direct marketing have not changed. Campaign planning, creative writing, advertising design, and production management are central. Knowing the fundamentals of direct marketing and how to manage the direct marketing process remain crucial for your programs to succeed. The Internet is the biggest and greatest direct marketing medium ever. However, its users, your potential customers, are just people—people who react based on their own human situations. They respond or do not respond to your marketing messages based on their personal needs and desires. To maximize the return on marketing investments, you will have to strategically plan, research, implement, and manage your direct marketing programs with the goal of tapping into these emotions. Excellence in all parts of the process is the key to making that happen.

This book is for both seasoned and novice business-to-business direct marketing professionals—anyone responsible for generating sales leads and converting them to revenue. If you are a seasoned professional, you will find a comprehensive approach to the direct marketing process and valuable reminders of the fundamentals, which can be used to evaluate campaigns or train others. If you are a novice, you will learn the basics of lead generation in a framework that is easy to understand, remember, and implement. All readers will learn how to use printed and electronic direct response advertising to generate sales inquiries. You will also learn how to use advanced print and electronic direct marketing strategies to convert inquiries into customers.

The S.U.R.E.-Fire direct response planning process—unique to this book—is designed to give you more marketing confidence by providing you with a comprehensive, four-phase approach to business-to-business sales lead generation and inquiry nurturing. The S.U.R.E.-Fire process will help you reduce your marketing risk whether you are a business-to-business direct marketer at a large company or a small one. The process will help you stop making assumptions about market wants, stop selecting creative by guesswork, and stop failing to anticipate crucial implementation details. If you were trained to rely solely on "in-field live" testing, this book will encourage you to try some of the research methods used by your peers in general advertising as a way to avoid costly test failures.

Business-to-business direct marketers are under pressure to produce results, so they shy away from up-front planning. They also are budget conscious and believe they cannot afford market research. All too often, they rely on ad hoc methods to manage campaigns. Such seat-of-the-pants approaches to lead generation campaign development need not be standard operating procedure. This book offers an alternative to crapshoot marketing. Just like the professional portfolio manager who invests a client's money based on proper planning and financial research, business-to-business direct marketing professionals must do the appropriate work up front. The four phases of the S.U.R.E.-Fire process lead to proper planning, research, and implementation of sales lead generation campaigns. This process will improve your overall campaign effectiveness. It will help you increase your lead quality and quantity—and your sales.

Introducing the S.U.R.E.-Fire Direct Response Planning Process

The S.U.R.E.-Fire planning process is based on a review of over five hundred direct marketing campaigns that produced more than nine hundred thousand sales leads for more than forty-three companies in twenty-two industries. These campaigns produced by Kern Direct Marketing represent a combined advertising investment of more than $40 million, made on behalf of my clients during a twenty-year period. The day-to-day, hands-on, in-field experience I have gained by implementing lead generation programs and closely monitoring their results has enabled me to create the S.U.R.E.-Fire process. The S.U.R.E.-Fire acronym stands for:

Strategic planning
Understanding for empathy
Response management
Execution excellence

The S.U.R.E.-Fire planning process will help you accomplish two direct marketing objectives: First, the process will improve the quantity and quality of sales leads by identifying messages and offers that appeal most to potential buyers. Second, the process will help to convert more prospects to sales faster. This is accomplished using best-business practices to capture sales leads, separate hot buyers from tire-kickers, and implement relationship marketing strategies to stay in contact with prospects until they buy.

S: Strategic Planning Before Implementation

Engaging in comprehensive discussions about program goals, objectives, strategies, and tactics before a single word is written or picture drawn is key to a program's success. During planning meetings, all members of the marketing and sales teams have a chance to express their concerns and opinions so these factors can be considered up front. Strategic planning is the first phase of the S.U.R.E.-Fire process. In this phase, you use analytical tools such as SWOT analysis, media- and market-opportunity analysis, financial analysis, sales-process analysis, and unique sales proposition definition to give your marketing team a foundation for the direct marketing process. In Chapters 1 through 3, you will learn how and when to do strategic planning and use these analytical tools.

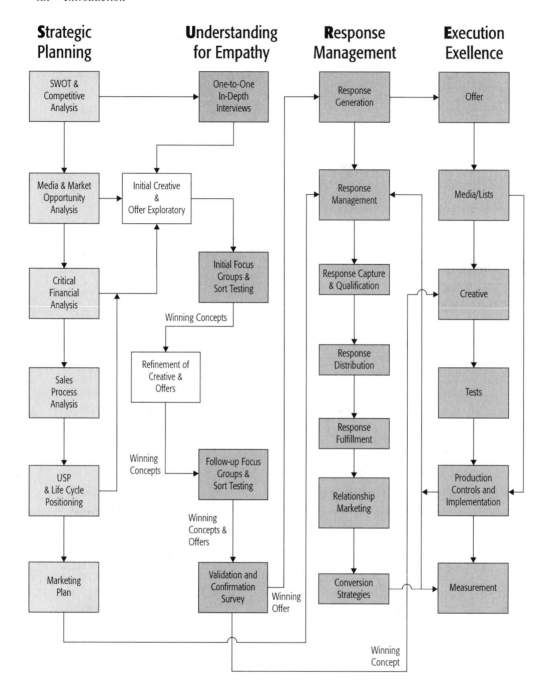

S.U.R.E.-Fire® Direct Response Planning A four-phase process to generate sales leads and quickly convert them to revenue. Copyright 2000. Kern Direct Marketing, Inc. All rights reserved.

U: Understanding Customers and Their Issues

To conceive and write effective direct response advertising, you must know what your prospective customers worry about, what their opinions are, and how they think. Developing empathy for your prospective buyer is the foundation for the second phase of the process. In this second phase, you will learn how to use qualitative and quantitative market research to conduct in-depth one-to-one interviews, develop a message map, evaluate creative ideas, rank offers, and identify concepts that have the most interest to your target audience. In Chapters 4 and 5, you will learn how to integrate three market research methods to reduce your marketing risk and stop the guesswork of campaign concept selection.

R: Response Management—Generation and Conversion

Response management is an essential part of the S.U.R.E.-Fire process. It includes generating and capturing responses and developing a relationship with the prospect to make the sale. The first part of response management is response generation. This requires a self-qualifying offer that appeals to the personal interests of prospective buyers. The stronger the offer—the better it solves the problems of prospective buyers—the greater response will be. In Chapter 6, you will learn about the power of offers, including how to structure direct response offers and how to promote them to maximize response.

The second part of response management is converting sales inquiries into buyers. This requires a robust response management system that works in concert with the buying process of customers and with the selling system of your organization. A response management system needs to capture sales inquiries, qualify them, and distribute them automatically to the sales organization. In addition, it must recognize that converting sales inquiries into customers takes time. The second part of response management focuses on the latest permission-based relationship marketing methods for staying in contact with prospects until they are ready to buy. In Chapters 7 and 8, you will gain insight into best-business practices of response management, see the statistics that validate the importance of long-term lead nurturing, and learn the techniques involved in customer relationship management.

E: Execution Excellence—Implementing the Marketing Fundamentals

The fundamentals—media selection, creative development, testing procedures, results analysis, and production controls—will never go out of style. Developing compelling graphics, writing clear copy with precisely targeted messages, organizing marketing tests, and managing the details of direct marketing are the central themes of the fourth phase of the S.U.R.E.-Fire process. In Chapter 9, you will examine media selection, ranking, and planning. You will also learn how to manage the details of testing strategies. In Chapters 10 and 11, you will learn about creative excellence, including how to integrate findings from the earlier phases of the process into final implementation. These chapters also explain how to evaluate and manage the creative process of direct response print advertising, direct mail packages, E-mail, and banner advertising.

It is my hope that this book will serve as a valuable reference for you—one you will use for every lead generation campaign you manage.

A Note on Use of Terms To help your reading, I have used the word *products* to represent both products and services. You will find the words *suspect, prospect,* and *customer* throughout the book. *Suspect* refers to a person or company that has not initiated a sales dialog with you. A *prospect* is anyone who has responded or inquired about getting more information. For example, a Web inquirer, a direct mail responder, and a person who requested information at your trade show booth would all be considered prospects. A *customer* is someone who has made a purchase from your company. The phrase *direct marketing* is used as the umbrella term for the concept of generating response from advertising communications, capturing that response, and nurturing the respondent. I use the term *direct response advertising* to describe ads designed to solicit immediate response from readers. E-mail, banner ads, print ads, and direct mail packages are examples of direct response advertising.

STRATEGIC PLANNING

All men can see these tactics whereby I conquer, but what
none can see is the strategy out of which victory is evolved.

—Sun-tzu
Chinese military strategist

Strategic planning is one of the most-discussed aspects of business marketing. If you ask ten marketers to define strategic planning, you will inevitably receive eleven opinions. For our purposes, strategic planning is the process of collecting marketing intelligence on your company and your competitors, analyzing that information, and then formulating an action plan to achieve your stated objectives.

Consider the philosophy of General George S. Patton on strategic planning and the study of the competition:

> *I have studied the enemy all my life. I have read the memoirs of his generals and his leaders. I have even read his philosophers and listened to his music. I have studied in detail the account of every damned one of his battles. I know exactly how he'll react under any given set of circumstances. And he hasn't the slightest idea what I'm going to do. So when the time comes, I'm going to whip the hell out of him.*

When business direct marketers apply the best practices of strategic planning before implementing their business-to-business lead generation campaigns, they dramatically reduce their risk and increase their odds of success. Why? Because a structured planning process enables them to examine and evaluate the factors that will influence the short- and long-term success of their campaigns—before campaign investments.

Consider these facts, from *Strategic Planning for the Small Business*, by Craig Rice:

- Many managers prefer to guess, to prove they are macho.
- Most failed projects occur through ignorance or mistakes.
- Management is right only 50 percent of the time.
- Most failures occur because managers are too impatient to gather necessary information.
- The cost of getting facts is much less than the cost of failure.
- In business, war, and poker, knowledge really is power.

The first phase in creating S.U.R.E.-Fire direct response marketing, therefore, is the implementation of comprehensive strategic planning. This strategic planning process focuses on collecting information—facts—to determine how you can meet business goals through lead generation and lead-conversion programs.

To win at chess, you must understand how to play the game, how each of the pieces can move, how to check and checkmate your opponent, as well as know your opponent's strengths and weaknesses. So too in marketing. Those who succeed start with a sense of what it takes to get to marketing checkmate. Like a chess player, a marketer requires knowledge of the industry (the board), the competition (the opponent), and the tools at hand (pawns, knights, bishops, and other pieces). Finally, great chess players know the psychology of their opponents—how they think and how they will react to offensive or defensive moves. In marketing, we need to know not only how competitors think, but also how customers think. This is fundamental to selling and to creating customers.

Gaining Insight into Your Situation

Thus, the first step in developing an effective business-to-business lead generation program is to gain deep insight into your company, your product or service, the marketplace, and your competition. Effective campaigns result when you have a complete understanding of the following:

- Marketing challenges. What are the key obstacles to success?
- Product attributes. What are both the positive and negative features?
- Product positioning in comparison to the competition. How do your product and your advertising stack up against the competition? Are you a leader or a laggard? Why?
- Short- and long-term sales opportunities. Where can you have the most immediate impact?
- Threats from changes in the marketplace or competition. Where are your company and your product vulnerable to market forces?

To answer these fundamental marketing questions, the S.U.R.E.-Fire direct response planning process begins with an in-depth information-gathering technique called a SWOT analysis. Specifically, a SWOT analysis determines the current state of the market and outlines the challenges that lie ahead. Businesses often use a SWOT analysis for overall strategic and marketing planning. I suggest that as a business-to-business direct marketer, you also use this methodology for specific campaign development:

Strengths: What do we have that gives us a competitive advantage?
Weaknesses: Where can we be attacked? What don't we have?
Opportunities: Where are the best markets to g enerate successful results?
Threats: What do we need to look out for that would have negative impact on results?

A SWOT analysis helps you understand the product's attributes, the competition, and sales opportunities. It helps you develop consensus on the scope of the marketing project required to achieve desired sales goals, and to understand the marketing and financial resources available to do the job. In addition, a SWOT analysis gives you valuable input from your management team about key messages and issues that will need to be tested in the second phase of the S.U.R.E.-Fire planning process, Understanding for Empathy. Another benefit of a campaign-specific SWOT analysis is that it brings out the painful truth about how much or how little marketers, salespeople, and top management know about their product, the competition, sales goals, and market threats. This might seem less than positive, but it is quite valuable. A SWOT analysis reveals the marketing assumptions made within the walls of the organization and reduces false beliefs about how marketing and sales success can be achieved.

SWOT Analysis for a Lead Generation Campaign

A SWOT analysis conducted for a business-to-business lead generation campaign has a narrower focus than a SWOT analysis meant to support a companywide strategic plan. Instead of taking days, it generally takes only four to six hours. Data gathering is best conducted in a room where all members of marketing, sales, and management who are invested in the program's success can sit comfortably. It is valuable to have two people conducting the session, a moderator to facilitate the meeting and a scribe to take notes. If people are geographically dispersed, a SWOT session can be conducted via a conference call. Because a SWOT is the first—and likely the only—chance a direct marketer has to bring together the entire marketing and sales team, it is important to invite all individuals responsible for lead generation or with a perspective about the role lead generation plays in making sales. Typically, that includes the vice president of marketing, marketing manager, advertising manager, direct marketing manager, product manager, research director, vice president of sales, sales manager, fulfillment manager, telemarketing unit managers, telemarketing personnel, executive staff, key sales representatives, and key distributors.

The following questions provide an effective guide to moderating a SWOT meeting. The word *product* is used to represent the product or service that you and your company want to promote.

Assess Your *Strengths*

In the first part of the SWOT session, the goal is to identify the most important attributes of the product. Begin by asking about the product's strengths, focusing on its three most important or unique strengths in the marketplace. This helps participants narrow their thinking and focus on the top characteristics of your product: Is it the least expensive, the highest quality, the most durable, the most flexible, the most powerful? After determining the top three strengths, it is valuable to ask what other characteristics or benefits the product offers. This gives participants permission to expand their thinking and generate additional ideas.

In addition, ask in what way the product or service is superior to that of the competition. This question is key in identifying important differences between you and your competitors. You can leverage these differences in your direct marketing communications to distinguish your company and product.

You should also examine company strengths that could be considered assets vis-à-vis the product, such as brand awareness, marketing muscle, distribution, and a skilled sales force. What can you leverage to succeed? Is your company or product well known? Do you have an extensive distribution channel?

Finally, how does the marketplace and competition perceive and react to your strengths? This is where you compare your internal company beliefs to external marketplace perceptions. Sales executives who see prospects and customers will have the most input on this question.

Understand Your Product's *Weaknesses*

In the second part of the SWOT session, you'll examine weaknesses. The goal is to determine the obstacles or problems that your product poses and that you will need to work around. Now you want to search for the hard answers. What are the product's three biggest weaknesses or negative features? What doesn't your product have? What weaknesses or missing features will the sales force need to sell around? Do not be afraid to continue probing for additional weaknesses. Again, this is a chance to squeeze more information from your participants.

On the other hand, you should also delve into what can be done to improve the product. Contrast your company with the competition. Are competitors already making improvements? Have competitors already addressed these issues?

Return to issues related to the company itself: What company weaknesses could be considered liabilities vis-à-vis the product, such as no brand awareness, limited marketing resources, no distribution channel?

Once again, a sanity check is needed to compare internal beliefs and perceptions to marketplace realities. How do the marketplace and competition perceive and react to these weaknesses?

Seek Marketing *Opportunities*

In the third part of the SWOT session, the moderator is looking for participants to provide ideas for the most effective marketing opportunities. The focus is on the best place to invest marketing dollars to generate the largest return in the shortest period of time. What targets, markets, segments, titles, companies, and industries show a deep need for the product or service? This question is designed to identify markets or groups of individuals that desire or need your product. It is far easier to generate leads from audiences that are in need than from those that require education about why they need your product.

You also want to investigate the size of the opportunity to find out where, in the long term, the large market opportunities are. Which opportunities can generate the most revenue for your company? What needs to be overcome to leverage these large market opportunities? Do you need a special sales force? Do you need to modify your product for the market? Do you need case studies showing that others are using your product in a given market?

Carefully consider any marketing edge you may have, such as marketing opportunities the competition doesn't know about. What do you know that your competitors do not? For example, have you identified a trade show or market segment they have not?

Opportunities also stem from the characteristics of the market: Is the market growing, dying, static, changing? Are people looking to buy, or is the market in a state of contraction? For example, the marketplace needs your product, but the number of companies you can sell to is shrinking. These questions are required to gauge your future opportunity.

Deal with *Threats*

Finally, the moderator should get participants to identify what the marketing team needs to watch out for—ripples in the market or in competitive response that could impact the marketing program. What changes in the market could influence the success of the lead generation campaign? This question is designed to identify anything on the horizon that could have a long-term impact on results, such as changes in interest rates, a softening of the stock market, import-tax increases, or new government regulations.

Short-term changeability can also have major effects on marketing: Will seasonality impact program success? Will time of year impact response rates and selling patterns? Are you going to be marketing during a favorable or unfavorable time of year?

Look for peculiarities of the market too, since these may afford opportunities or have negative impacts. What trade shows, competitive events, or promotions could hurt the program? What are important trade show dates? Are you affected by year-end holiday closings? Are your prospects focused on taking care of their business and not interested in looking at your product at certain times of the year?

Analyze Your Competition

Now you need to repeat the procedure by going through the SWOT question process for the top three to five competitive products or companies. In this part of the process you will discover how much or how little you know about your competitors. Questions include:

- What are their strengths?
- What are their weaknesses?
- What are their opportunities?
- What are their threats?
- What are their marketing and sales tactics?
- What are their prices?
- What are their distribution methods?

Further Analysis

Since you seldom have all key marketing, sales, and executive personnel in a room at the same time, it is valuable to ask some additional questions during the SWOT session. The following questions can provoke useful marketing insights.

Tips for SWOT Implementation

- Distribute the SWOT questions to all participants a few days before the meeting.
- At the start of the meeting, the moderator should restate the goals of the meeting and the purpose of conducting a SWOT analysis. The moderator also should explain the SWOT process.
- Draw a four-by-four SWOT grid on a large pad or board to help you categorize information for your product and competitors. Write SWOT vertically and then place your product and the names of each competitor in each column horizontally.
- Begin asking the entire group the SWOT questions, in order.
- Write down all relevant points the attendees give the moderator.
- The moderator must draw no conclusions about information the group provides, instead simply posting it for review and summation at the end of the meeting.
- Keep the meeting moving. Don't allow the discussion to snag on any one point.
- To enable the group to gain focus and momentum, always start by asking the strengths of the product or service to be promoted. Then go through the questions about weaknesses, opportunities, and threats.
- Ask the exact same questions in the same order for the top three to five competitive products.
- It is important for the moderator to probe and to be flexible during questioning and to allow the group to digress on tangential marketing or sales issues as they arise. A SWOT analysis brings out all marketing issues relevant to the lead generation process, and the moderator must conduct the meeting in a way that encourages the discussion of valuable ideas that arise unexpectedly.
- Ask participants about two types of strengths and weaknesses during a SWOT session. First, ask about factors that can impact lead generation, such as unique features that grab a prospect's attention and cause him or her to want to find out more about the product or service. Second, ask about factors that impact the sales process and help win a sale, such as a unique cost-value ratio.
- After all the information is collected, perform a sanity check. Ask, "Does the marketplace perceive the strengths and weaknesses expressed today in the same way as the people in this room?" Remember that the perceptions of external prospects are your marketplace realities.

Identifying the Target Market

Your first question should focus on what markets or industries should be targeted. Is there a consensus? Can you identify the industries by SIC (standard industry classification) code? Conversely, you should also determine which industries to exclude. What do you want to avoid? Don't waste money contacting people who cannot become your customers. The goal of direct marketing is to target your message. For example, do you want to exclude certain industries, geographic areas, and/or companies that have just purchased your product category in the past year?

Your goal is to produce the highest return on your marketing investment. Do not waste money mailing to companies that are probably too small to purchase your product. What is the employee or revenue size you should target? Where is your best revenue opportunity? Should you spend time on small companies or big companies?

Search for all the ways to focus your effort on your target, and determine what other criteria should govern target selection. Criteria include geography, the age of the business, the company's growth rate, companies just going public, and dot-com companies. The better picture you can paint of your target audience, the better targeted your marketing will be.

Does your customer base match the targeting criteria you have identified? If not, make sure that there are valid reasons—are you being overly optimistic regarding the segments that would be interested in your product? These questions are designed to determine if the past is reflective of the future. Have past marketing efforts skipped these market opportunities, or have new market segments arisen from changes in the marketplace? Consider, for example, the birth of dot-com companies. A follow-up to this question is: Why have you been unable to sell to all your market segments in the past? Is it because of a lack of resources or a lack of focus?

Targeting the Right Titles

As a continuation of painting a picture of your target market, look at functional titles. Identify the departments (such as operations, finance, or information systems) and the levels (such as VP, manager, or staff) of the people who might initiate consideration of your product or service. Try to determine what titles will start the sales process and what titles have the authority to purchase. Asking your salespeople is one of the best ways to get this information. Have them look over their contact databases so they do not rely on their memories.

You also want to seek out the target market's sources of industry information. What publications and books does the target read? How do they stay current? Where do they turn for education? What conferences or trade association meetings does the target attend? This is a follow-up to the questions above about the competition's use of seasonal selling or trade shows. All of this information will help you with your list or media selection process.

Solving the Target Market's Problems

This group of questions is designed to help you collect information on the belief systems and perceptions of the target audience. First, try to determine what customers worry about: What problems do they struggle with daily? What keeps them up at night? What magic solution are they looking for? Once you ascertain what problems your customers face daily, focus on how your product addresses these pains. Compare the product features and benefits to the problems faced by customers. How many problems does your product solve? Understanding this is critical for developing effective lead generation campaigns.

What are members of your target market doing now to deal with these problems? This question will help you to figure out what your target audience is doing without you. People are rather innovative. They can find many different solutions to their problems. Is their current solution inadequate? Do you need to address this in your marketing? Next, determine why members of the target audience would switch to your product from what they are currently using. After all, people are reluctant to change. What will move them to action? Some economic force, like E-commerce, may already be forcing a change in your target market. What is this driving force, and how can you capitalize on it?

Establishing Sales Process and Goals

During your SWOT, you need to understand fully the sales situation and the resources available to achieve the desired financial objective. This set of questions can help establish the objectives for a given program as well as for all lead generation campaigns. This information will be used in more formal mathematical calculations in Chapter 2.

Among your first tasks are determining the sales goals and how much revenue management is looking to generate over a certain period of time. Do you need to generate $5 million in six months or $50 million in one year? Estimate how many products or units will have to be sold to meet these goals. This is calculated by dividing the financial goal by the average selling price (ASP) of the product.

The number of salespeople or distribution outlets in place to meet these goals is an important factor. Do you have five or five hundred salespeople? A salesperson can only generate so much revenue; there are only so many hours in a day.

You also need to ask whether your sales goals are consistent with the number of companies that can realistically buy the product. In other words, are there enough prospects to meet the sales goals? Are there a thousand prospects or one hundred thousand prospects? Are the goals realistic given these numbers?

Thoroughly review the lead-capture, qualification, and distribution process. If this is the first meeting, you need to gain a detailed view of the current state of this process. How are leads captured? What happens when a lead is captured? How is a lead qualified? When does it go to the field and by what criteria? What attention do responders receive? How fast do they receive the information? What happens after the lead is sent to the field and information is sent to the responder? How do you report on the disposition of a lead?

Focusing on a Message

When you turn to this line of questioning, let the participants pretend that they are the advertising agency. What you want to do is open up their creative minds. Encourage your participants to generate ideas. I have found that everyone is creative, and gemlike ideas can come from asking questions about messaging. Remember that all the information collected will be validated in the next phase of the S.U.R.E.-Fire planning process.

Start with an open-ended question that will free up participants' thinking. For example: "If you had a magic wand, what three messages would you include in the promotion?" You are asking them to take the limits off their thinking. The phrase "magic wand" gives them permission to imagine that anything is possible. So give them the freedom to think daringly, and listen to what they say. And remember that sometimes the best ideas are not the first ideas. Keep asking. Squeeze a little more out of your participants.

After your participants imagine what they want to say, it is time to ask if there are any facts or proof points that can lend credibility to the promises. What support, claim, endorsement, or testimonial can be used as proof for these messages? Specifics add credibility to your message.

Tracking Your Marketing Programs

To discuss these questions, it is useful to have participants bring trade magazines, company and competitors' literature, direct mail packages, print advertisements, and sales letters to the SWOT session. Your goal in this part of the session is to assess what worked and what did not work. Studying the history of your campaigns or programs is valuable. It can keep you from repeating mistakes. It also can generate ideas for new programs based on refinements to past programs. The following questions speak for themselves.

- What marketing programs have worked or failed in the past?

- What offers have you used? What worked, and what failed?
- What existing offers may be used in future lead generation campaigns?
- What source provides the highest-quality sales leads?
- Why is a marketing program needed? Why can't the sales organization just pick up the phone and be successful?
- When do customers buy? What are the best months and the worst months?
- Where do customers buy? What distribution channels do they prefer?
- What is your share of the total market? What are the trends in your sales, profit, and market share?

Summarize the Answers

After the moderator has asked all the questions and displayed the answers around the room, it is time to summarize. Starting with the product or service to be promoted, the moderator needs to review the information provided and see if there are any more ideas to capture. The moderator should note key opportunities for exploration and validation. After the session, the meeting notes should be typed and distributed to all participants for review and approval. The moderator and participants need time to digest the information before reaching any conclusions.

When drafting the SWOT conclusions, distinguish the difference between internal beliefs and marketplace perceptions about strengths and weaknesses. Use the information from the SWOT session to find a direction, but don't draw final conclusions. The central concept of the S.U.R.E.-Fire planning process is to use external conversations and market research to validate or contradict information generated during the SWOT session.

Look at both aspects of the sales process—how people are brought into the sales pipeline, and how they are converted into customers. Try to determine whether the target identified during the SWOT analysis is a "hoped-for" market. In other words, is it a market in which salespeople or executives wish the product would sell, or is it a market in which the product is currently being sold? Asking what percentage of current customers matching the profile outlined in the SWOT session can validate this.

Competitive Advertising Review

To succeed in business, you must not try to fight competitors using brawn. Only the biggest organizations have the money to slug it out with their competition. The rise of the Internet, database marketing, data-mining techniques, and other new research methodologies are leveling the playing field. Instead of out-muscling competitors, I encourage you to out-think them. The simple truth remains: you can't beat competitors if you do not know them, yourself, and your customers. Gaining these levels of knowledge requires patience. As British statesman and novelist Benjamin Disraeli said, "Patience is the necessary ingredient for genius."

The SWOT analysis is just the first step in identifying market opportunities and crafting a unique strategy for the promotion. After you look at the competition during the SWOT, it is useful to look at how the competition positions itself through the most visible marketing communications. These include trade press ads, Web advertising, and direct mail. Physically looking at competitive advertising provides perspective as to how a particular competitor's product promotion compares to yours. It also will help you develop a lead generation program that contains unique messages for your promotion, product, or service. It enables you to answer key strategic questions, such as:

- What is the positioning of competitors, and what promises do they make to the marketplace?
- How will your future set of promotional messages stack up against the competition?
- What messages, offers, and creative strategies do competitors use?
- How much marketing investment is the competition making, and will your company survive or become buried by those investments?
- What types of advertising, Web-based marketing, and direct mail promotions do competitors use?
- What types of messages, offers, and creative implementations must be avoided so future promotions do not look like competitors' promotions?

Conducting a competitive advertising review is not difficult, but it does require time and careful record keeping. Here is a practical approach.

Collect six months' worth of the publications in which your company and its competitors frequently advertise. Then, remove all the competitors' ads from the publications and pin the ads to the wall. Note the date and name of the magazine from which the advertisement was removed. Pinning the ads on a wall makes it possible to scan the entire range of competitive messages at once.

Carefully study the advertising messages. What are the competitors communicating to prospects? What visuals are they using? Is their advertising building brand awareness? Is it geared to generating leads, or does it have multiple objectives? If lead generation is the goal, what is the offer? Does the competitor use a magazine bind-in reply card? How large are the ads: full page or fractions? Are the competitors using four-color, two-color, or black-and-white graphics? In a table, summarize the tag lines, key selling messages, offers, and size and frequency of placement for each competitor. This enables the marketing team to compare various competitive positioning approaches, creative executions, key benefit messages, tone, offers, and tag lines.

Also visit each competitor's website. Print out the home page and the pages containing key messages and methodologies. Pin these up too. Repeat the same review and analysis process for each competitive website. Later on, you can place all the ads and the website material in a notebook for future reference.

To further test your competitors' systems, you can respond to their advertising and collect fulfillment information. See how long it takes to receive the fulfillment information, and study what is delivered. Competitive fulfillment packages play a crucial role as you construct or refine your own follow-up materials. Is the information sent extensive or brief? Does it drive the recipient to buy? Does it connect the recipient with a salesperson or sales channel? Is there a next step in the buying process? Does the fulfillment information convince the recipient to take that next step?

By reviewing all competitive information, either pinned up on a wall or in a handy binder, you can gain an overall impression of what competitors are saying to the marketplace, the images and graphics they use, and the messages and positioning statements they convey. Review and analysis position you to provide specific direction to creative resources (or to give the creative resources the chance to review competitive advertising themselves) and to craft a unique look and message. This process obviates the problem of advertising messages or styles that "accidentally" copy or imitate those of competitors.

Determine Competitive Ad Spending

As part of the S.U.R.E.-Fire planning process, you must evaluate how your company's marketing voice compares to that of the competition. Is your company in a screaming match? Is your company's voice the loudest, or is a larger competitor drowning out your company? It is important to know advertising spending levels, because business-to-business lead generation programs generally are more successful for companies with higher and more positive brand recognition. Collecting competitive spending levels for advertising and direct mail lets you and your management team know what you are up against.

The first way to collect competitive advertising spending information is through "Leading National Advertisers" reports published by *Advertising Age*. If you are marketing a high-technology product, you can also use information from *Adscope, Inc.* Both sources provide data on competitive advertising spending by company and industry. Smaller business-to-business companies that may be interested in ad spending data that *Advertising Age* or *Adscope* do not track can follow this step-by-step method:

1. Gather six months' worth of all industry publications.
2. Count the number of advertisements the competitor placed in each publication.
3. Using the publisher's rate card, determine the cost per ad placement based on size and color.
4. Multiply the number of placements by the cost per placement in each publication to calculate advertising spending per publication. Bear in mind that most advertisers negotiate lower rates, so your calculations may be on the high side.
5. Add up total spending in each publication to estimate the competitor's budget.
6. Repeat the above for each competitor.
7. Arrange the competitors' spending levels in order, from highest to lowest; then calculate total spending in the category and the percentage each competitor contributed to the total, as in Figure 1.1. This calculation enables you to compare your company's share of voice in the marketplace to that of the competition. The analysis reveals whether your company spends as much as its competitors. If there is a spending differential, it shows how much.

Remember that advertising investments help build awareness in the marketplace and make prospects receptive to lead generation promotions. It is harder for an unknown company to produce a hugely successful lead generation program than for a market leader.

Imagine that two direct mail pieces arrive in your in-basket on the same day. The only identification on the outside of the each envelope is the company name.

FIGURE 1.1 Calculating Competitive Advertising and Share of Voice

	Magazine 1		Magazine 2		Magazine 3			
	# of Pages	Rate per	# of Pages	Rate per	# of Pages	Rate per	Total $	Share of Voice
Competitor A	10	$6,000	5	$50,000	5	$20,000	$410,000	61%
Competitor B	5	$6,000	2	$50,000	0	$20,000	$130,000	19%
Competitor C	3	$6,000	0	$50,000	5	$20,000	$118,000	18%
Competitor D	2	$6,000	0	$50,000	0	$20,000	$12,000	2%

The first direct mail piece carries the name ACME Software Company, and the second direct mail piece carries the name IBM Corporation. Which one would you pick up and open first? It is human nature to believe that the company you know and trust has something more important for you than an unknown company. This is the power of brand awareness and its impact on direct mail lead generation promotions.

Collecting Competitive Direct Mail and E-Mail

When time permits, it is advisable to conduct a competitive analysis of competitors' direct mail and E-mail in addition to their print advertising. Gathering direct mail and E-mail pieces is much harder than collecting competitive print ads because direct mail and E-mail are "out of public view." However, I have found some effective ways to collect competitive samples.

Ask all your sales personnel and internal staff to collect and save all the competitive direct mail, E-mail, and electronic newsletters they receive. Those who subscribe to major industry trade publications receive competitors' messages by virtue of being on the publication's list, which it sells to advertisers. Be sure everyone is on the lookout for these promotions.

A more active collection method is to send a research-request letter to a group of fifty to one hundred key customers. Ask them to collect and save all direct mail and third-party promotional E-mail for two to three weeks and return the entire lot to you at your expense. Provide a large FedEx envelope with the shipping label filled out and attached. Tell the customers that when they return their pile of direct mail and E-mail to you by a certain date, they will receive a valuable thank-you gift for their trouble.

You'll be amazed by how much direct mail and E-mail your customers receive weekly from competitors—and from anyone else who believes these customers are good prospects (it is also enlightening to see the wide range of direct mail and E-mail promotions).

After you receive the samples from your customers, sort it by competitor and by product promotion. Then repeat the competitive advertising review process conducted for print advertising and websites. When looking at competitive direct mail or E-mail, ask the following questions:

- What size direct mail package do competitors send?
- What is the outer message? Is there a teaser headline, or is it blank?
- What is the subject line?

- What is the objective of the direct mail package? Is it lead generation? Sales channel support? Direct selling?
- How did the E-mail begin? Where did it direct the reader?
- What is the offer? How is it merchandised?
- What are the package's tone, color, graphics, and key benefit messages?
- What percentage of the package sells the product or service instead of selling the reason to respond?

Given that direct mail and E-mail advertising changes quickly, this kind of information gathering should be conducted at least twice a year to stay current with competitive advertising strategies and messages.

Summing Up

Strategic planning does not mean cloning a competitive strategy. Craft a distinctive strategy suited to your company and product. This can be accomplished only by thoroughly understanding your own product, its relationship to the competition, and its position in the marketplace.

You must understand the marketing challenges and obstacles you face, and a SWOT analysis focused on lead generation is one analytical tool you can use to collect information. During the SWOT analysis, focus on uncovering your company's strengths, weaknesses, opportunities, and threats. Begin by examining the target market's characteristics. Look at your sales process and goals, your messaging, and previous marketing programs that have worked well—or failed miserably. Besides serving as an assessment of your own product and organization, a SWOT analysis generates information about competitors. You can investigate your competition further by gathering their direct mail pieces and analyzing their reach and effectiveness.

KNOW THE MARKET AND
KNOW YOUR NUMBERS

*Where there is no knowledge there can be no insight, and
where there is no insight there can be no knowledge.*

—THE MISHNAH
Sayings of the Fathers

Knowledge about the marketplace can only improve your lead generation campaign plans. You need to know the size of the market, how difficult or easy it will be to reach the market, and the financial investment that will be required to reach your sales goals. The next step in the strategic planning phase of the S.U.R.E.-Fire direct response marketing planning process is to collect quantitative marketing data. Specifically, you will collect marketing data to perform a media- and market-opportunity analysis, and a financial analysis and projections.

A media- and market-opportunity analysis can help you answer the following questions: How big or small is the market for your product or service? How difficult or easy is it to target this market? How many media options do you have at your disposal? The more you know about the market and the media that reach that market, the better positioned you are to manage a lead generation campaign. This information gives you an idea of the challenges and obstacles that could influence the implementation of your campaign. For example, if you are targeting technology professionals, it is important to know that the market opportunity is approximately 750,000 individuals in North America and that you can choose from more than 250 print advertising, direct mail, and electronic media options to reach them. If you are targeting credit union executives and only about 15,000 targets can be identified from just five sources, you might be more cautious in developing your campaigns.

This type of media intelligence, when collected early in the planning process, helps you establish realistic tactics, sales goals, and budgets.

The need for financial projections is equally profound. *Marketing is an investment.* Company management teams expect to generate a profitable return on this investment. Therefore, measurement is a must, and direct marketing is *the* measurable marketing method. Direct marketing strategies give business-to-business marketers the ability to capture responses for each media type and to track response by offer, creative execution, or media source. Thus, you can measure what media, message, or offer is generating results. You can also identify what is not working for you.

When you are in charge of lead generation campaigns, you should perform a series of financial projections and calculations before making marketing investments. In making your financial projections, do the following:

- Determine the sales unit goal based upon corporate financial objectives.
- Establish the sales inquiry flow needed to achieve this sales goal, based upon a set of assumptions about close rates, appointment rates, and qualified lead rates.
- Balance sales lead volumes with sales resources to ensure there are neither too many nor too few leads in the sales pipeline.
- Determine the number of contacts necessary for a direct response marketing program that will produce the ideal lead flow, given the established goals.
- Compare customer lifetime value (LTV) to customer acquisition cost projections to establish realistic acquisition program budgets.

Media- and Market-Opportunity Analysis

The second step in the strategic planning phase of the S.U.R.E.-Fire process is researching the size of your market and the various media options available to reach the target audience. During this step, it is your goal to conduct a complete media review, but not to select media. The final selection of media is part of the execution phase of the S.U.R.E.-Fire planning process, described in Chapter 9. The media review and analysis are designed to answer specific questions about the market and its needs.

How big or small is the target market for your product, service, or particular promotion? It is important to know the size of your target audience before you begin your campaign planning. For example, assume you want to generate leads from the university market. Specifically, you want to reach administrators and deans at major colleges. You will be in a much better position to make investment decisions about the type, size, and scope of a lead generation campaign if you know in advance that this market has 7,000 contacts instead of guessing at 50,000 contacts. Say you want to target all businesses in the United States that have ten to fifty employees. About 1.7 million businesses meet that criterion. With a market this large, you can conduct many different creative or offer tests. If you find a profitable marketing formula during your testing, you can roll out your final campaign to a much larger universe.

How easy or difficult is it to identify members of the market? This question is important to answer because, again, it influences your investment decisions. If a market is hard to reach—as when target titles or industries are not tracked by list owners or are buried within other list selection options—you will need to spend more money to cover a larger population if you are to reach your target audience. If a market is easily identifiable (e.g., physicians), your investment can be accurately targeted, minimizing marketing waste.

Does the prospective customer read trade magazines or visit websites? Which ones? You want to know with 100 percent certainty where your target audience turns for information. If you can send an E-mail message, rent the mailing list of this publication, place an advertisement, or run banner advertising on the content provider's website, you can pinpoint the delivery of your message.

A magazine's Business Publishers Audit (BPA; an audited report of a magazine's subscriber base) statement gives you valuable information about the readership including the circulation distribution percentage by region, the percentage of subscribers by title, and the percentage of subscribers by industry.

Determine whether key publications for your market rent their subscriber mailing and E-mail lists. If they do rent their lists, confirm the number of names on the lists. Again, you want to ascertain your market opportunity. Knowing the facts (whether the market is big or small, good or bad) is much better than guessing. Also determine what selection criteria are available for each list: What options can you use to select these lists? Can you select by title, industry, company size, number of employees, products specified, or departmental budget? Will these selection criteria help you to better focus the delivery of your message?

Business lead generation requires an organized contact plan. It is important to think ahead if you plan to implement a telemarketing program to increase response rates or generate additional leads. For example, if you rent names for mailings, can you also select and rent names with phone numbers for telemarketing follow-up? How many names are available for telemarketing? You should always find out the size of a file, publication, or E-mail list that offers telemarketing names. To make accurate plans, you need to know what you have to work with.

As part of your media-opportunity analysis, explore all contact options. Online marketing is now a standard practice of business-lead generation. Are there websites, E-mail lists, or electronic newsletters that reach the target audience?

Before Campaign Implementation

Having answered the questions in the previous section, you can compare the size of the target market (market opportunity) with the campaign size. For example, you have a small market—10,000 potential customers. But your financial projections (discussed later in this chapter) indicate that you need 250,000 pieces of direct mail and 50,000 E-mail messages to meet your revenue goals. Clearly, you have a problem to resolve. If, on the other hand, you have a large market opportunity—say 500,000 suspects—and your projections show you only need 50,000 contacts to meet your sales goals, you have a positive indication to proceed.

It is also worthwhile knowing how hard it will be to accurately deliver a promotional lead generation message directly to your target audience. A media- and market-opportunity analysis should reveal whether key job titles are bundled with other list selection criteria that cannot be teased out. In addition, the analysis will help you identify websites, E-mail lists, and specialized publications that focus on your target audience.

Consider this example: You are the marketing manager for Human Resource Management Software Company. Your ideal target audience is human resource (HR) managers at companies with more than a thousand employees. During your media- and market-opportunity research, you discover that you can only rent mailing lists from publications that lump together the titles for HR executives, payroll staff, HR staff, and HR trainers. Worse, selecting by company size is not an option. No websites or E-mail lists are available to you with a company size selection option. If you know this information before campaign development, you can confidently recommend investing more money than anticipated on a relatively large population who *are not* interested—to make sure you reach the prospects who *are* interested.

Media facts influence the assumptions you make when projecting response rates for lead generation direct mail, E-mail, or banner advertising programs. In the previous example, the marketing manager has the information needed to accurately budget marketing funds, given the limitations of market targeting.

Conducting the Analysis

Like all the analyses that are part of the S.U.R.E.-Fire planning process, a media analysis is not difficult. It simply requires time. The following steps will help you manage your time and resources.

Step 1: Using Key Directories or On-Line Data Card Research

The two comprehensive sources of media information for business-to-business marketers are Standard Rate and Data Services (SRDS) and Marketing Information Network. SRDS publishes several directories: *SRDS Business Publications Advertising Source®*, *SRDS Direct Marketing List Source®*, and *SRDS Interactive Advertising Source*™. These directories contain every major magazine, direct mail list, website, and E-mail supplier available for advertising or list use. Marketing Information Network (www.minokc.com) is an on-line research service for 30,000 active mail lists, E-mail lists, and alternative and interactive media.

Step 2: Business Publication Analysis

Start by turning to the index in the front of the *SRDS Business Publications Advertising Source* and looking up your industry. You will find all the magazines published for a particular product category. For example, look at the Domestic Classifications Grouping Index under Plant Engineering, Maintenance, Repair, and Operations. You will see that this section of the directory (section 113B) lists eleven audited magazines and two nonaudited magazines that reach this particular marketplace. As another example, in Figure 2.1 look at section 111, Petroleum and Oil, under which you will find fifteen audited publications and twenty-six nonaudited publications. This will give you a quick indication of the media choices you have for your market. While you are in the index, search for other sections that would list publications your target audience reads. For example, plant maintenance professionals may be concerned with pollution control and you should check section 115B, Pollution Control.

Step 3: Obtain Media Kits, Back Issues, Audit Statements

Now, turn to the specific section of the *SRDS Business Publications Advertising Source* that lists the publications. If you do not have an intimate knowledge of your marketplace, you will need to read the editorial description for each appropriate

FIGURE 2.1 SRDS Domestic Class Groupings: Indicates Number of Media Choices

111. PETROLEUM & OIL
AUDITED
The American Oil & Gas Reporter
Hart's Oil and Gas Investor
Hydrocarbon Processing
The Journal of Petroleum Marketing
Journal of Petroleum Technology
National Petroleum News
Offshore
Oil & Gas Journal
Oil & Gas Product News
Oil, Gas & Petrochem Equipment
Petroleum Equipment & Technology
Pipe Line & Gas Industry
Pipeline & Gas Journal
Today's Refinery
World Oil
NON-AUDITED
AAPG Explorer
Africa-Middle East Petroleum Directory
Composite Catalog of Oilfield Equipment & Services
Drilling Contractor
The Geophysical Directory
Geophysics
Gulf Coast Oil Directory
Hart Gulf States Petroleum Directory
Hart's E&P
Hart's Midcontinent Petroleum Directory
Hart's Rocky Mountain Petroleum Directory
Houston/Texas Oil Directory
Independent Gasoline Marketing
The Leading Edge
Michigan's Oil & Gas News
NLGI Spokesman
NPN International
O & A Marketing News
Oilizer World
SPE Drilling & Completion
SPE Production & Facilities
SPE Reservoir Evaluation Engineering
The Tipro Target
Tradequip International
Well Servicing
World Refining

113B. PLANT/ENGINEERING, MAINTENANCE, REPAIR & OPERATIONS
AUDITED
AFE Facilities Engineering Journal
Engineer's Digest
Industrial Maintenance and Plant Operation
Maintenance Technology
Materials Performance
MRO Today
PEM Plant Engineering & Maintenance
Plant, Canada's Industrial Newspaper
Plant Engineering
Plant Services
Pumps and Systems
NON-AUDITED
MRO Marketplace
Pumping Technology

115B. POLLUTION CONTROL (AIR & WATER)
AUDITED
Canadian Environmental Protection
Environmental Protection
Environmental Technology
Environmental Testing & Analysis
Hazardous Materials Management
Industrial Wastewater
Pollution Engineering
Pollution Equipment News
Pollution Equipment News Buyer's Guide
Soil & Groundwater
NON-AUDITED
Archives of Environmental Contamination and Toxicology
Bulletin of Environmental Contamination and Toxicology
EM
Environment
Environmental Management
Environmental Science & Technology
Environmental Science and Technology
EnviroSafety Directory
Georgia and Southeast Environmental News
Journal of Environmental Health
Microbial Ecology
Ozone Science and Engineering
Pollution Engineering International
Strategic Environmental Management
Wastewater Technology Showcase

magazine. For each magazine you select, note the circulation size and the name of the local sales representative. Then contact each sales representative and ask him or her to send you a copy of the magazine's media kit, three back issues of the magazine, and a BPA statement. Explain that you are conducting a media analysis of the market in preparation for lead generation campaigns that might or might not include print advertising. Magazine sales representatives can be a tremendous help in understanding the marketplace and providing third-party research. Remember that they make their living selling advertising space, so it is important not to mislead them or waste their time.

Step 4: Individual Publication Analysis

After you receive the media kits, compare each BPA statement. Your goal in reviewing the statements is to develop a picture of the circulation for each publication. This will give you insight into the value of placing print advertising in each publication, as well as the value of its mailing list. Each BPA statement is slightly different, but you should look for these specifics:

- Total circulation of the publication. This will tell you its total reach.
- The total number of subscribers, by *title*, who represent your target. Most BPA statements include a table that breaks out the subscribers by industry and title.
- The total number of subscribers, by *industry*, who represent your target. Perform the same kind of analysis you performed for titles. See how many industries your target audience resides in.
- The total number of subscribers, by title or industry, who do *not* represent your target. Calculate the percentage. This will tell you the percentage "waste" within the circulation.
- The percentage of circulation by region. How does this compare to your sales territory or distribution pattern? Most BPA statements have a break-out of circulation by region of the country.
- The percentage of the circulation that renewed its subscription in the last twelve months. A very high renewal rate means readers have a high interest in the publication. It also suggests that if you rent the mail list, the names will be deliverable.

Step 5: Direct Marketing List Analysis

Conduct the same type of analysis for the direct mail lists that are available in your category, using the *SRDS Direct Marketing List Source* directory. Search each section for lists that reach your marketplace. A simple way to begin is to look for the subscribers of the magazines you found in the *SRDS Business Publications Advertising Source*. SRDS keeps section categories consistent between directories. So section 111, Petroleum and Oil, is the same in both directories. During your list research, don't limit the scope of your search to subscriber files from trade magazines. Look for any type of list available for rent, including mail-order buyer files, noncompetitive but complementary inquiry files, lists of trade show attendees, book buyers or newsletter subscribers, or compiled files.

Another approach is to identify the industry directories typically found on the desks of people within that industry. For example, in the aerospace and medical industries, the publishers of key directories sell databases of companies and contacts within the industry.

Step 6: Obtain Data Cards

For each mail list, carefully read the description and note the source of the names, the size of the file, and the selection criteria. Call the list broker or manager and request a data card. The data card will give you all the detail available for that list. Alternatively, Acxiom Corporation's Marketing Information Network (mIn), an on-line service, gives you access to data cards for more than thirty thousand mailing lists (www.minokc.com).

Step 7: Analyzing and Ranking Your Lists

After you obtain all the data cards, repeat your examination of each direct mail list's data card as you did in the BPA statement review. Your goal in this analysis is to gain a confidence level about the quantity and quality of names you will receive when you rent the file. Will the file help you pinpoint your message? What trade-off will you need to make if some selection criteria are not as narrow as you would like? For example, assume you want to target the university market, but the data card shows that the industry select for a given publication only offers "education." You can conclude that this select includes all educational institutions ranging from elementary schools through universities. If you rent the file with this select, you will be forced to accept the bad with the good.

Look at each data card and determine the selection criteria available. For example, can you rent names by exact job title? Can you select by job function? You should also determine how narrowly you can select names, whether by individual title or as several titles lumped together. For example, can you select chief information officer (CIO) only, or are you forced to select information technology/manager information systems/chief information officer (IT/MIS/CIO) titles as a group?

Another important criterion is how many names are in each selection. You want to determine the relative number of names available. This information will play into your tactical planning.

Determine how focused you can make your mailing. Can you select by company size, product purchase influence, and current product type installed? Can you pinpoint the exact type of company or the product category purchased? For example, you are targeting the banking industry and want to rent a file from American Bank Institute. If you look at Figure 2.2, you will see that you can focus on the type of bank, but you cannot rent by institution size.

FIGURE 2.2 SRDS List Source for American Bank Institute

AMERICAN BANK INSTITUTE–CENTER FOR BANKING INFORMATION
Data Verified: Aug 16, 1999.
Location ID: 13 ICLS 23 · Mid 616445-000

1. **PERSONNEL**
   List Manager
   NRL Direct
      50 Piermont Road, Cresskill, NJ 07626. Phone 201-568-0707.
      Fax 201-568-0994.
      E-mail: bkimmel@nrldirect.com
      Key Contact: Monique Braban

2. **SUMMARY DESCRIPTION**
   Respondents to a resource and information center serving the banking and financial services industry.
   74% male.

3. **LIST SOURCE**
   Direct response.

4. **SELECTIONS WITH COUNTS**

   Updated: Mar. 29, 1999.

	Total Number	Price per/M
Banking professionals	.49,701	90.00
Internet respondents	.24,026	100.00
Executives:		
Banks	.19,701	+11.00
Foreign banks in the U.S.	.2,064	"
Credit unions	.3,907	"
Fund management	.5,971	"
Mortgage banking	.5,036	"
Security brokerage co.	.5,884	"
Insurance companies	.8,992	"
Real estate corporations	.7,402	"
Venture capital	.13,774	"

   Minimum order 5,000

4A. **OTHER SELECTIONS**
   Key coding. 3.50/M extra; state, SCF, Zip, gender, SIC. 6.00/M extra; executives by specialty. 11.00/M extra; telephone numbers. 16.00/M extra.

6. **METHOD OF ADDRESSING**
   Cheshire labels, 4-up; pressure sensitive labels, 4-up, 10.00/M extra; mag tape. 30.00 fee; diskette, 25.00 fee; E-mail, 25.00 fee.

8. **RESTRICTIONS**
   Sample mailing piece required.

11. **MAINTENANCE**
   Updated semi-annually.

Currency and deliverability of names are crucial to a program's success. You should know how often the file is updated and the policy on address deliverability. Generally, list managers guarantee 95 to 97 percent deliverability.

Knowing the original source of names is valuable, because it indicates interest and mail responsiveness. If a name comes from a magazine on food processing, you can deduce that the person has an interest in products or offers concerning food processing. Likewise, if a person subscribes to a newsletter on the subject, his or her willingness to invest in the newsletter points to a high propensity to read and respond to direct mail on anything related to food processing. The more a person subscribes, responds, or buys through the mail (such as from a mail-order catalog), the higher the individual's propensity to respond to offers sent through the mail. The same psychological dynamic is true for Internet buyers and responders.

If the list is a circulation file, is the publication free, or do the subscribers pay for subscriptions? If readers pay for subscriptions, the publisher has a responsibility to make sure the list is current and the magazine deliverable. Further, if people have paid for something, they have a high interest in the subject.

As you review the specifics of each data card, rank each file by letter grade (A, B, C). An "A" file gives you the exact selection criteria to reach your target. The source is relevant to the product you are marketing and the names are highly deliverable, meaning they come from a source such as a controlled subscriber file or database. You can select the exact title, job function, industry, or company size you desire.

A "B" file offers some of the selection criteria you desire to reach your target, but you need to forfeit something. A title selection may have five titles lumped together instead of just the one you want, or you can select by title but not by company size. Yet the source of a "B" file gives you high confidence in the quality of names and the deliverability. For example, the names are updated and current because they come from a controlled circulation file, a mail-order list, or a paid-newsletter circulation file.

A "C" file gives you only one of your criteria. The contact name is questionable because of the source. Compiled files from Dun & Bradstreet or one from American Business Index are examples of "C" files. These files are good at delivering a business address and one or two key contacts, such as owner, principal, president, or chief executive. If you are trying to target deep within an organization to titles such as design engineer or controller, though, they are not ideal. This is not to say that you will never use "C" files.

After ranking your files, sort and subtotal them by category. Finally, determine how many different list sources to use based on your program objectives.

Step 8: Interactive and Electronic Source Analysis

Now you need to repeat, for interactive media, the research and analysis steps you used to select and evaluate business publications and direct marketing list sources. The *SRDS Interactive Advertising Source* provides information on websites that accept banner ads, advertising networks and portals, search engines, and E-mail lists. I strongly advise you to hire an electronic media broker to help conduct your media research, however, because the interactive electronic marketplace is changing so rapidly.

The *SRDS Interactive Advertising Source* directory is organized the same way as the other SRDS directories. Continuing with the petroleum and oil industry example, if you turn to section 111 in *SRDS Interactive Advertising Source*, you will find websites such as Hydrocarbon Online (www.hydrocarbononline.com) and Oil and Gas Online (www.oilandgasonline.com). The same concepts we've applied to traditional print and direct mail lists—including source, selection criteria, quantity, and quality—are applicable to electronic media. Instead of renting names, though, you are buying impressions on a per thousand basis.

Step 9: Summarizing Your Findings

Summarize the results of your BPA review, data card review, and electronic media review on one spreadsheet. Placing all your options on a spreadsheet will give you an overview of the size of your market space and the number of media options. This spreadsheet will tell you at a glance how easy or how difficult a time you will have targeting your lead generation campaign. Most importantly, this spreadsheet will tell you if the market size is consistent with the campaign size dictated by your financial goals.

Financial Analysis and Projections

Knowing your sales goals and establishing the ideal lead flow to meet those goals are critical to the management of a business-to-business lead generation program. The challenge you face as a campaign manager is to provide just the right quantity and quality of sales leads to your sales channel. Too few sales leads will leave the sales department screaming for more, too many will waste the company's money because the sales organization does not have enough time to follow up on all of them. Many opportunities will fall through the cracks and be permanently lost.

The next step in the S.U.R.E.-Fire planning process is a series of financial calculations designed to help you determine optimum lead flow requirements and campaign size. Specifically, you will learn the following:

- How to determine the exact number of sales required based on a sales volume goal and the average unit of sale.
- How to determine the sales inquiry flow based on assumptions about close ratios, appointment rates, qualified lead rates, and response rates.
- How to compare desired sales lead volumes with current sales capacity to ensure that a campaign does not produce too many or too few sales leads.
- How to determine the number of contacts needed to produce enough sales inquiries for a direct response marketing program.
- How to use customer lifetime value to help set realistic budgets.

Lead campaigns fail when budgets and campaign sizes have been "plucked from air" (PFA) instead of developed through methodical financial calculations. Before you can decide how much to invest in a lead generation direct marketing program, you need to set specific financial goals for the program and provide a realistic assessment of the sales resources available to achieve the sales goal.

The most effective way to determine the size, scope, and budget for a lead generation program is to work backward from the sales goals of the organization. Backward calculation allows you to see the exact number of sales required to meet corporate sales goals. Then, by using your product or service average sales price (ASP)—combined with well-founded assumptions about your sales close rates, appointment rates, qualified lead rates, and media response rates—you can estimate campaign size, campaign budgets, and quantity of sales inquiries required to meet sales goals.

Calculating Required Sales Volume

To determine the sales volume you need, divide the incremental sales volume to be generated by the average sale per customer or per transaction. The result is the number of sales required to meet the goal.

The following equation shows the number of sales required if your sales goal is $3 million and each sale averages $30,000.

Sales goal		$3,000,000
Average sales price of product or service	÷	$30,000
Number of sales transactions required	=	100

This calculation is important because it tells you the specific number of transactions required to meet the financial objectives established by your management.

Determining Sales Inquiry Requirements

The next set of calculations requires assumptions or knowledge about three parts of the sales process: close rate, appointment rate, and qualified lead percentage. One way to collect these data is to analyze past campaigns. Another is to interview members of the sales force. The information you gather will help you calculate lead flow requirements and understand the sales inquiry pipeline.

The closing rate is the number of times customers buy your product or service after your sales staff has presented all its features and benefits. Do your salespeople close one out of three of these customers? One out of four? While it depends on the price and complexity of the product you are selling, the industry average close rate is 25 percent. Good salespeople close on a minimum one of every four proposals they present to qualified prospects.

The appointment rate is the percentage of leads the sales force receives from marketing that result in a sales call, an appointment, or a demonstration. Using the inquiries the sales force receives from marketing, which are presumed to be qualified, you can calculate the appointment rate. Is it one out of four? One out of five? The rule of thumb is about 30 percent of qualified leads should result in an appointment.

The qualified lead rate is the percentage of all raw sales inquiries generated from all sources (direct mail, print, trade shows, telemarketing, electronic marketing) that can be screened and determined ready for your sales force. An inquirer is someone who might be interested or researching but not ready to buy. An unqualified inquirer is often simply collecting information. They do not have a budget, and they are not decision makers. Conversely, a qualified lead is someone in-market and ready to buy who can make or influence the decision. The offer you use (to be discussed in Chapter 6) will influence your qualified lead rate, but for projections, you should use an average. The industry average is that 20 to 30 percent of all raw inquiries turn into qualified sales leads.

Determining Campaign Size by Medium

Once you know the number of inquiries your company must generate to meet your sales goals, the challenge is to determine the best media mix to generate the leads. Begin this process by understanding that each lead generation method

Calculating the Number of Inquiries Required to Meet Sales Goals

Calculating Sales Inquiry Volume

Number of sales transactions required	100 (A)
% of sales that result from presentation of a proposal to buy	÷ 50% (B)
# of presentation appointments required	= 200 (C)
% of presentation appointments set from qualified leads	÷ 15% (D)
# of qualified leads required	= 1,333 (E)
% of all sales inquiries that become qualified to turn over to the sales force	÷ 30% (F)
# of gross sales inquiries required	= 4,444

Determine the number of sales appointments or demonstration calls

1. Determine your sales goal.
2. Determine the close percentage.
3. Divide the number of sales units (A) by the close percentage (B). The quotient is the number of sales calls/demonstrations your sales force must make to meet the sales goal (C).

Determine the number of qualified leads required

4. Determine the percentage of qualified leads given to the sales force that generate a sales call. What percentage of all leads that a salesperson calls on the telephone result in a presentation or demonstration appointment?
5. Divide the number of appointments (C) by the appointment percentage (D). The quotient is the number of qualified leads that must be generated to meet the sales goal (E).

Determine the number of inquiries required

6. Determine the percentage of sales inquiries generated from all sources that are qualified. What percentage of inquiries do you pass to the field for them to call?
7. Divide the number of qualified leads (E) by the qualified lead percentage (F).
8. The quotient is the total number of gross sales inquiries your marketing campaign(s) must generate to meet your sales goals.

(e.g., trade shows, telemarketing, direct mail, print advertising, E-mail blasts, seminars/road shows) has a different response rate and lead quality. I find that I have to conduct a series of back-and-forth calculations to determine the right mixture of investments given marketing objectives that may include branding, awareness, lead generation, and field sales support.

For example, if your goal from the example in the box above is 4,444 total sales inquiries, you may decide the fastest way to achieve this goal is solely through trade show participation. Trade shows are expensive, however, and take the majority of your sales staff out of the office. You might decide the cheapest way to do it is solely through telemarketing—not a good medium for building industry awareness and product credibility. Maybe you believe it would be better for the company to invest 25 percent in brand advertising, 25 percent in direct mail, 25 percent in electronic advertising, and 25 percent in trade shows. There is no magic formula for developing the proper media mix, but conducting a series of "what if" scenarios can be extremely helpful.

To determine campaign size, simply divide the total number of sales inquiries required by the estimated response rate for a given medium. Figure 2.3 gives you a sense of the range of response rates by medium. Response rates are influenced by many factors, including the market's awareness of your company, the interest in the product category, the offer, the list, the creative, the time of year, and the competition. Only when you begin to implement your own lead campaigns will you be able to establish benchmark response rates for your company. Figure 2.4 shows how to take a sales goal (in this case 4,444) and determine the campaign size based on a chosen medium and its response rates. This figure shows how different assumptions (a .5 percent as opposed to a 3 percent response) can have great impacts on the size of the campaign.

Figure 2.3 Typical Response Rates Based on Medium

Media	Cost/ Thousand	Response	Time Frame for Lead Generation	Primary Objective
Targeted Print	$50–$100	.03%–.05%	4–6 months	Awareness
Trade Shows	$500–$2,000	2%–4%	1–3 months	Leads, Awareness
Telemarketing	$1,000–$2,000	10%–20%	1–4 months	Leads
Direct Mail	$750–$2,000	.5%–3%	2–3 months	Leads, Awareness
E-mail	$250–$650 (includes transmission cost)	.5%–3%	1 day–2 weeks	Leads
Banner Ads				
Search engine site	$30–$40	.1%–1%	1–2 weeks	Leads, Awareness
Trade site	$40–$100	.1%–1%	1–2 weeks	Leads, Awareness

Figure 2.4 Determining Campaign Size Based upon Sales Inquiry Levels

# of gross sales inquiries required to meet sales goal	4,444			
% response from a given medium (direct mail)	4,444	÷	0.5%	3%
# of direct mail contacts required		=	888,800	148,133
% response from a given medium (print)	4,444	÷	0.03%	0.05%
# of print ad exposures required		=	14,813,333	8,888,000
% response from a given medium (E-mail)	4,444	÷	0.5%	3%
# of E-mail contacts required		=	888,800	148,133
% response from a given medium (telemarketing)	4,444	÷	10%	20%
# of telemarketing contacts required		=	44,440	22,220

Budgeting Your Lead Generation Campaigns

Using the campaign size requirements and the cost per thousand by medium, you are now in a position to create a budget for the lead generation program. Equipped with the information you collected about the target market in your media analysis, the number of media options available to reach the target, and the objectives of the program, you can invest your marketing budget to achieve your goals cost-effectively.

If you are marketing a new company or a new product, you may need to invest more heavily in awareness strategies to establish company credibility. If you have established market share and a strong sales organization, you may choose to invest more in strong lead generation strategies, such as telemarketing, E-mail, banner advertising, direct mail, and trade shows, to keep your sales pipeline filled. Again, there is no simple answer, but careful tracking and review of past campaigns can provide valuable insight for future decision making.

Consider the following example. A call-center software company has a $3 million sales goal for the upcoming quarter. The average price of its product is $40,000. The lead flow calculations show that the marketing manager needs to generate 4,500 inquiries to meet the sales goal. The total universe of potential buyers (call-center professionals) is about 262,500 names. Historical review shows that direct mail advertising has been effective in lead generation as well as building brand awareness. In addition, media research indicates that three websites reach the target audience. Trade advertising is helpful in generating company awareness but will not generate sales leads quickly. For this reason, the company decides not to use trade advertising. Figure 2.5 shows the solution. A budget of $284,375 is allocated. It is 88 percent direct mail and 12 percent interactive advertising.

Figure 2.5 Call-Center Software Program Budget

Media	Quantity	Estimated Response	Sales Inquiries	Cost/M	Budget	Cost/ Inquiry
Direct mail	200,000	2.0%	4,000	$1,250	$250,000	$63
Interactive	62,500	0.8%	500	$550	$34,375	$69
Total	262,500		4,500		$284,375	

Reality Check

After lead flow calculations are complete, I suggest you compare the lead goals to your sales resources to ensure that your programs will not be wasting money by generating more sales inquiries than can be handled by your sales and marketing organizations. This also obviates the problem of too few leads, which leaves valuable resources idle. The projected lead flow rate must be manageable when added to current sales activity.

Every sales organization has a baseline of business activity. This baseline is the amount of business that would be generated if marketing never contributed to the lead generation effort. The marketer should determine the incremental lead flow the sales organization can manage. The marketer can begin with the number of sales leads currently in the sales pipeline. What are the salespeople doing when they have no leads from marketing activities? Are they cold calling? If so, how many calls per day?

A second important issue is the base sales volume your salespeople require to make a living. Salespeople are motivated by money. Do your salespeople have high financial goals, and are they hungry for leads to help them make their goals? Find out how many sales they need to be financially successful. When you know this number, you can determine the incremental number of sales per month each individual requires to achieve his or her personal financial objectives.

Other numbers that will bring reality home involve the size of the universe of buyers and the budget. Is the universe large enough—and the budget large enough—to meet the campaign size requirement projections? Are there enough prospects in the marketplace? Do you have enough opportunity to find fresh prospects, or do you need to remarket and continue to market to the same population pool?

Examine whether close rates, appointment rates, and qualified lead rates are reasonable and realistic. Check the source of your information. Would your sales vice president and field sales managers agree? If not, modify your calculations accordingly.

Because it takes time to start up marketing programs, get appointments, and close sales, you should determine whether revenue objectives are realistic given the time frame. Do you have sales momentum, or are you starting from scratch? Have you given yourself enough time to build sales momentum and meet your sales goals, or do you need to modify your projections? In general it takes three to six months to build sales momentum.

You need to balance the number of direct response pieces or contacts that will be made within a target organization against the number of different organizations to be contacted. Your calculations determine the number of contacts a campaign must reach to meet sales goals. But when a quantity of one is the most of your product you can ever sell to an organization, you need to focus your calculations based on the number of organizations rather than on the number of contacts. Be sure you know which is right for you.

As part of your reality check, determine how much projected business will affect each salesperson. The following calculation determines the number of sales presentations each salesperson must make per month to meet sales goals. Is this realistic?

Determining if the Number of Presentations per Salesperson Is Realistic

Number of qualified leads		1,333
% of presentation appointments set from qualified leads	×	15%
Number of presentations	=	200
Number of salespeople in the organization	÷	10
Number of presentations per person to meet goal	=	20
Number of presentations per person per month to meet goal		1.7

Once you have gathered information and completed these calculations, you will need to ask the following:

- Do we have enough financial resources to make this happen?
- Do we have enough resources to handle this inquiry volume?
- Do we have enough salespeople to follow up on all the qualified leads, make the appointments, and present sales proposals in the time frame allotted?

The benefit of asking these questions in advance is that you can change course *before* making a marketing investment. In addition, you can try out some alternatives to determine how changes to media options will impact financial and resource requirements. Can you generate 25 percent of your leads through electronic media? What about trade shows? Can telemarketing fill in for you? What about banner advertising? Will print advertising generate leads? Asking the right questions before you implement is the crux of the S.U.R.E.-Fire planning process.

ABC Software Company Sets Its Sights on $50 Million

It is essential to compare sales goals with direct response goals before the campaign begins. Financial analysis enables the marketer to conduct a reality check of a company's sales goals and a campaign's lead flow projections. This example shows how to use financial analysis to ensure that sales goals and lead flow goals are realistic. The calculations take into account the company's existing financial and human resources, manufacturing operations, and distribution channels.

ABC Software Company has a sales goal of $50 million in new revenue with a product that has an average sales price of $100,000. You, as the company's direct marketing manager, need to generate five hundred sales to meet the sales goal. Sales staff say the average closing rate is 20 percent, that is, one-fifth of the people who make a sales appointment actually buy. The average appointment rate is 25 percent of qualified leads. ABC will need staff and finances to follow up on 2,500 appointments and 10,000 qualified leads.

Marketing history shows that 27 percent of all sales inquiries generated by direct response marketing are sufficiently qualified to give to the sales staff. ABC will need a lead generation system that can process and handle 37,037 inquiries.

If your campaign plan will use only direct mail, then given a 2 percent response rate, ABC will need a direct mail campaign of 1,851,851 pieces. If you assume an average cost per contact of $1.25, ABC will need a budget of $2,314,814.

Sales goal		$50,000,000
ASP	÷	$100,000
Units to be sold	=	500
Close	÷	20%
Appointments	=	2,500
Appointment percentage from qualified leads	÷	25%
Qualified leads	=	10,000
Qualified lead percentage	÷	27%
Total sales inquiries	=	37,037
Response	÷	2%
Contacts	=	1,851,851
Budget/contact	×	$1.25
Total cost of campaign	=	$2,314,814
Profit margin		50%
Net income on sales of $50 million		$25,000,000
Return on investment		11:1

Assessing Cost-Effectiveness

After determining the number of sales inquiries and qualified sales leads a program requires and ensuring that there are adequate sales resources to handle this lead flow, check the financial effectiveness of your lead generation campaign before making the marketing investment. Specifically:

- Is the investment justified, given the revenue projections?
- Does the program generate sales inquiries at an acceptable cost per inquiry?
- What is cost per qualified lead and cost per sale?
- Are these acceptable?

Calculating Costs

As part of the reality check, marketers should determine how much it costs them to generate inquiries, to turn an inquiry into a qualified lead, and to make a sale. Each of these three calculations includes other costs besides the cost of generating an inquiry. Capture costs, fulfillment costs, travel costs, and other costs generated to support a sale have to be considered. The following recaps these three tests:

- Cost per inquiry = (cost to generate inquiry + capture costs + fulfillment costs)/number of inquiries
- Cost per qualified lead = (cost to generate inquiry + capture costs + fulfillment costs)/number of qualified leads
- Cost per sale = (cost to generate inquiry + capture costs + fulfillment costs + sales-related travel, proposal cost, presentation cost)/number of sales

The acceptable price for a sales inquiry, qualified lead, or sale is established based on the sales price of the product, the profit margin, and the marketing investment required to fill the sales pipeline.

The Importance of Customer Lifetime Value

Marketing is about leverage: making an investment today to acquire a customer and generate a future revenue stream. By definition, the purpose of direct marketing is to create customers and foster relationships that generate repeat sales. Repeat selling—maximizing customer lifetime value—is how companies maximize their return on marketing investments. A customer's lifetime value is an important calculation to consider when establishing customer acquisition budgets.

Budgeting for a two-step business-to-business direct marketing lead generation campaign must take into account that the return on the initial marketing investment is not limited to revenue derived solely from the first sale to a customer. Instead, the return is measured with the understanding that a valuable asset is being created: the customer relationship and the revenue stream it will produce for months or even years to come. Customer lifetime value analysis plays a key role in determining an acceptable cost to acquire new customers. Knowledge of customer value is the one way to determine how much to spend on a direct marketing program. Without this knowledge, budget development is one-sided.

To calculate the approximate customer lifetime value, a rule of thumb is that LTV equals the total revenue a customer will generate over a two- to four-year period. Some companies keep customers for only six months, others for six years. You will need to determine what time period is right for your company, industry, and customer set. Knowing how much a customer will ultimately spend on your products and services can help you make intelligent budget decisions for direct marketing campaigns. You should, however, exercise caution when using lifetime value to establish a program budget. Just because a customer will spend $10,000 with you over a two-year period does not give you carte blanche to invest $9,750 to acquire that customer. There must be balance between customer value and acceptable acquisition cost. Shareholders, the CFO, and your president need the cost of customer acquisition to remain as close to zero as possible, regardless of customer lifetime value. Yet you, as the direct marketer, must determine a reasonable and acceptable acquisition cost given the LTV and the realities of the marketplace. Figure 2.6 gives a simple way to calculate lifetime value.

Customer lifetime value analysis is crucial in setting a business-to-business lead generation budget. Consider the case of a major money center bank that wants to expand its customer base of business accounts. The campaign manager has determined the bank needs to generate leads for small-business checking accounts. Cross-sell reports indicate that for each new business customer who opens a checking account, the bank generates four additional banking relationships within twenty-four months. A business checking customer goes on to get a credit card, start a savings account, and open a payroll account and a business line of credit.

Each of these accounts has revenue value to the bank. Rather than thinking about the value of the customer over the life of the relationship, bank management has historically forced the marketing team to build program budgets based on the value of the checking relationship alone. Instead of considering the value of a customer at $500 per year for the full relationship, a new customer was only valued at $50 per year. Therefore, the marketing team's budget for acquisition was severely limited. The team was unable to budget for an effective offer, and the lead generation mail packages did not reflect the high quality of the financial organization. Response rates were low, and program success was marginal.

Summing Up

A fundamental part of S.U.R.E.-Fire strategic planning is gaining knowledge of the marketplace and the media landscape. The first part of this chapter focused on gathering information about the market, including the size of the market, how to

Figure 2.6 Estimating Customer Lifetime Value

Step 1. Value of Initial Transaction

A. Determine the average total sale value for a new customer on the first transaction.

Step 2. Value of Subsequent Transactions

B. Determine the average total value each time a customer buys from you again.

C. Determine the number of times (frequency) a customer will buy more goods or services from your company.

D. Multiply the average value of subsequent transactions (B) by the frequency of repeat purchases (C).

Step 3. Value of Additional Revenue from the Customer

E. Determine the average sale amount for any additional sales opportunity that results from having this customer. This includes cross-marketing with other companies, list-rental income, warranty income, and so on.

Step 4. Total Lifetime Value of the Customer

F. Add the results from steps 1, 2, and 3 to produce a total lifetime value estimation for the customer.

Sample Calculation:

Step 1	**Gross Sales Value of Initial Purchase**	=	**$40,000**
Step 2	Gross sales value of each repeat purchase	$10,000	
	Frequency of repurchase over a reasonable time frame	× 6	
	Gross revenue from repeat purchases	+	**$60,000**
Step 3	All additional revenue from customer relationship sales opportunities		
	Cross-sell of additional products	$15,000	
	Revenue from third-party marketing	+$5,000	
	Gross revenue from additional revenue opportunities	+	**$20,000**
Step 4	**Total Customer Lifetime Value Revenue**	=	**$120,000**

target the market, and what media are available. Financial calculations also play a key role in guiding program development. The second half of the chapter dealt with various financial measures. Finances are a central issue in deciding on the scope of a campaign, and financial measures indicate how many contacts must be made to generate the right number of leads to meet the goals of a sales campaign. Customer lifetime value, another financial measure, factors into the thinking of marketers because the value of the customer over the long term justifies initial expenses in approaching and acquiring that customer through direct response marketing.

BRIDGING THE GAP BETWEEN MARKETING AND SALES

We have something in this industry called the 10-3-1 ratio. This means that for every ten calls a salesperson makes, he will only get to make a presentation to three, and if he's got a good success rate, he'll make one sale. We need people who won't shrink from that kind of rejection.

—Dennis Tamcsin, Senior Vice President
Northwestern Mutual Life Insurance

Generating sales leads is only the initial step in the sales cycle. Your responsibility as a direct marketing campaign manager goes well beyond lead generation. You must also be concerned with creating and implementing marketing and sales support strategies that will convert the maximum number of sales leads into customers. By paying attention to the sales conversion process up front, you can avoid complaints from the sales department about lead quality later on. Tracking sales conversion will help you prove the program's return on investment and help you get approval for additional marketing dollars in the future. The best way to devise sales conversion programs is to study your company's current sales process before launching your lead generation campaigns.

Studying your sales process will help you understand what criteria are required by sales staff to consider a sales inquiry a qualified sales lead. You will know how customers buy from you (their purchase process) and why they buy from you (their rationale). You will understand how your product's Unique Sales Proposition (USP) impacts sales effectiveness. You will see where your product needs to be positioned on the product life cycle positioning curve and how to use this positioning to direct creative message development.

All the work you have done in the prior two strategic planning sessions needs to be summarized, and the framework of your marketing plan needs to be constructed. Thus, the last step in the strategic planning phase is the development of your S.U.R.E.-Fire marketing plan. This document will serve as your template for establishing marketing goals, strategy, and tactics for future implementation.

Focusing on Your Sales Process

Understanding how your company's sales organization moves prospects through the sales process will help bridge the gap between marketing and sales. When you know intimately how your company sells and the problems your salespeople face, you are in a position to partner with your sales managers on campaign development. Understanding the differences between how potential customers actually make a buying decision and how your sales force sells your product is one of the best ways to gain insight into the entire sales process.

This next step in the strategic planning phase of the S.U.R.E.-Fire planning process uses two analyses to uncover the facts about your sales process: buy cycle versus sales cycle analysis, and win/loss analysis. The knowledge gained from these analyses will help you:

- Select an offer that brings prospects into the sales cycle.
- Design a sales lead qualification process that separates tire-kickers from serious buyers.
- Determine investment levels and sales pipeline volumes by quarter, based on the actual length of time it takes to close sales.
- Justify and establish a relationship marketing (lead cultivation) strategy that maximizes the conversion of sales leads to revenue.

Customers Buy at Their Own Speed in Their Own Time

Buy cycle/sales cycle analysis sheds light on the fact that your customers do not buy at the same rate that your company and your salespeople want to sell. Marketing people tend to think the sales process goes something like this: Create awareness through advertising and public relations. Generate sales inquiries from direct response marketing activities and trade show participation. Qualify the sales inquiries. Forward qualified sales leads to the sales force. Voilà! The sales force closes a sale.

The reality is that buyers of business products, especially high-ticket products, make their purchase decisions methodically and cautiously. Commonly, for a high-ticket business-to-business product or service, the steps the salesperson takes in the course of the sales cycle go something like this:

1. Receive a lead from the marketing organization.
2. Make a series of follow-up phone calls to a prospect.
3. After a prospect is on the phone, conduct a needs-assessment interview to determine interest and opportunity.
4. Assuming there is a need, make an appointment for a product presentation or demonstration.
5. Go to the appointment and conduct a more in-depth needs analysis. Do a product demonstration presentation.
6. Perform a series of follow-up sales steps to overcome fear, uncertainty, and doubt. For example, prepare a quote or proposal and provide testimonials, recommendations, or case studies.
7. Negotiate on price.
8. Close the sale.

This series of steps can take sixty days to two years, depending on the complexity and price of the product. For lower-priced, less-complex products, the sales cycle typically is faster and simpler. For complex products, there may be a series of presentations to various management levels as the sale moves through the organization. In many corporations, the purchase process mandated by senior management requires buyers to research competitive vendors' products or services. Many business buyers are afraid of making a wrong decision. To minimize the risk of error, they look at competitive products and solutions, collect reference information, ask for demos, visit installations, and finally negotiate on price and terms.

The process a business buyer goes through to purchase a product is called the *buy cycle*. The process your company uses to sell its product to potential customers is called the *sales cycle*. Marketing organizations that match their sales cycle to their prospect's buy cycle are successful. To accomplish this, you must first assess the current state of your sales process by collecting information and studying the history on both sides of the sales transaction. Let's start with some important background.

The Eight Phases of the Buy Cycle

The purchase of every product moves through the eight phases of the buy cycle, summarized in Figure 3.1. Each phase is characterized by a particular customer mind-set toward the company and its products. Purchases of low-priced consumer products such as cereal, soap, or soft drinks move through the buy cycle very quickly.

Figure 3.1 The Buy Cycle

Phase	Stage	Customer Mind-Set
Phase 1	No awareness	I don't know who you are. I've never heard of your product. I'm not even sure I have a need for your product.
Phase 2	Awareness	I think I've heard of you. I am aware of the product category. I have an opinion about your product that is either negative, neutral, or positive.
Phase 3	Interest	I have a problem. I want to know if you can help me.
Phase 4	Research	Who besides you can help me solve my problem? I'm afraid of making a mistake. I want to get the best deal. What do other people say about you?
Phase 5	Trial	Okay, I am willing to give you a try. I want to see if I like what you sell and how it works for me.
Phase 6	First purchase	I'll buy your product and see if it lives up to all the promises and claims you've made to me. What sort of guarantee, price, and terms are you offering?
Phase 7	Second purchase	Hey, I really like your product. I want to buy some more. What else do you sell? Maybe I need something else from you.
Phase 8	Loyal customer	I am going to tell my friends and neighbors about your product. I am going to buy your product only. As a matter of fact, I will go out of my way to buy your product only. Thanks for making me feel like a special customer.

Consider what happens when you walk into a grocery store to buy a box of breakfast cereal. You stand in front of three shelves packed full of cereal brands. You scan the packages. You might even remember a commercial you saw on TV last night. In a matter of seconds, you pick up a product that is right for you and place it in your cart. You've just gone through the entire buy cycle in about ten seconds.

In contrast, consider the purchase of high-ticket, complex business products such as software systems, manufacturing equipment, and other office machines. When a company acquires these types of products, it moves through the same steps of the buy cycle, but generally over a much longer period of time. Purchasing high-ticket products takes more time than buying inexpensive consumer products because of the risk involved in making the investment, and the number of people and departments involved in the decision-making process.

Another way in which the buy cycle is different for consumer goods as opposed to business-to-business products relates to the frequency of purchase. A company might be in the market to buy a high-ticket business product only once every two to ten years. Because it is hard to know who is in the market to buy your product or service, generating sales leads from direct response advertising must be an ongoing process. You should consider promoting lead generation offers that cast a wide net into the sea of potential prospects. The goal is to pull in a mix of sales inquiries. Some sales inquiries will be ready to buy, and some will need more time to decide.

Consider the case of a financial software product used companywide. Most companies only upgrade or replace a high-end software system every five to seven years. Marketers are faced with the challenge of constantly creating awareness for their product and constantly generating sales leads—knowing it may be three to four years before the lead is ready to move into the research phase of the buying process.

After the potential customer moves into the research phase, the process of product selection can go on for weeks, months, or even years. Committee meetings, plant visits, customer references, and trial periods all need to be part of the research phase for business-to-business customers.

Finally, the time between the first purchase and the second purchase can vary dramatically, depending on the category. The marketer needs to understand the trade-off between investing future marketing dollars in generating repeat business and generating new business.

The buy cycle for every business and product category is unique. Knowing how fast or how slowly a prospective customer travels through the buy cycle is helpful in setting marketing investment levels, given sales pipeline requirements. For example, if you have a very slow buy cycle, you might need to invest heavily to fill your sales pipeline and to keep working the pipeline over time until prospects are ready to buy. If you have a fast buy cycle, you might only need to invest in filling the sales pipeline because the rest of the sales transaction happens quickly.

Conducting Buy Cycle Analysis

Although every buy cycle includes the eight phases described, the buy cycle is somewhat different for every product and service. Variables include the average time to complete the buy cycle, the specific steps customers take during the purchase decision, and the number of people involved in the purchase decision. A buy cycle analysis provides this detailed information.

To conduct this analysis, you must interview a representative sample of the parties involved in recently closed sales transactions. A review of past transactions reveals how your customers buy and how your salespeople sell. Depending on the industry and the average size of a sale, a representative sampling may be as few as ten or as many as fifty transactions.

Buy Cycle Interview Questions

The following questions will help you uncover the details of the buy cycle for your product or service. The answers will provide insight into how your customers and potential customers buy. You will see how long it takes them to go through each phase of the buying process and learn what information they seek from you during the process. You will also have the facts to determine how you can do a better job in each phase of the purchase process. This is one key to improving sales lead conversion rates.

Note that you must tailor the exact wording of each question to your particular business and to the type of person you are interviewing. For example, if the interviewees are potential customers, your questions about the purchase process need to be asked about the future. On the other hand, if your interviewees are recent buyers, you need to ask your questions from a historical perspective.

- *Before you bought our product (or before you inquired for more information), how aware were you of our company and our product?* The answer reveals the buyers' awareness level of your company and product.
- *How did you gain this awareness, or why do you think you did not have a high awareness level?* The answer tells you if your advertising (how and where) is working. It is not a quantitative measure, just an indication.
- *What were the three most important reasons you responded for more information?* The answer to this question will tell you the pain or hot buttons that motivated your customers to seek information. This answer will be valuable in future concept development.
- *What were the three most important issues you considered when buying our product or service?* This question helps you identify the difference, if any, between requesting information and making a purchase decision. After the buyers saw your product and learned more about it, did other benefits influence their purchase decision? Again, this information will assist in the development of sales support materials.
- *How long were you thinking about collecting information on this product or finding out how to solve your problem before you acted?* This question tells you about purchase time frame. How long did the buyers live with the problem before deciding to investigate a solution? After they started collecting information, how long did it take to make a final purchase decision? Each answer gives you insight into the sales puzzle.

- *How many other companies or products did you investigate?* This reveals the degree and intensity of the research phase. If your buyers investigated ten competitive companies, was it because they were unsure of the market leaders, or because they wanted more education? If they investigated only two companies, did they know what they were looking for from the start?
- *How did you choose which competitive companies or products to consider?* This question identifies your buyers' sources of information. Are they asking peers? Are they looking at advertisements? Are they searching the Internet?
- *How did you compare products?* This answer reveals your buyers' comparison methods. Did they develop a matrix to conduct a head-to-head comparison on a given set of criteria, or did they conduct interviews or request bids then select on price?
- *What was your process? Was it formal or informal? Was there a committee or was there a single decision maker?* The answers to these questions reveal the structure of the research process. Was it well thought out? Did it involve many levels of people in the organization, or was it a relatively simple process?
- *How long did the comparison take?* This is a crucial question and will tell you how closely you need to stay in contact with prospects during the sales process.
- *What factors made you consider trying the product?* This question helps you determine what finally moved the prospects from the research phase of the buy cycle into the trial phase.
- *What were the biggest fears or concerns to overcome?* Purchase decisions are made both emotionally and logically. You want to find out what buyers were afraid of. Your company's size, your product price, or your product complexity may have been factors.
- *After you bought the product, how would you rate your satisfaction with the quality or intensity of follow-up?* With this question, you are trying to find out the quality of the sales relationship after the purchase. Buyers go through buyer's remorse, questioning if they really made the right decision. How your organization addresses this issue and communicates with new buyers will bring you valuable insights.
- *When might you buy this product or service again? Might you buy additional products or services from our company?* These related questions are designed to show you what other sales opportunities exist. Now that a company owns one of your products, you should try to elicit information on what else might it need. This answer can help you devise customer add-on or customer-penetration marketing programs.

- *What would it take to make you a loyal customer (one who would only consider buying this type of product from our company)?* With this question, you are aiming to find out if loyalty programs can be part of your marketing mix. You want to know if you can tip the scale of loyalty in your favor through some combination of recognition, education, and possible rewards.

Analyzing the Sales Cycle Effectively

To gain perspective about the other side of the transaction, the sales cycle, begin by interviewing your sales team members. Line up interviews with your sales managers, telemarketers, and field sales personnel. Ask them the following series of questions:

- *How do you move a customer through a sale?* You are seeking an understanding of their sales approaches and techniques. Look at each sales transaction and try to recap the exact sales steps.
- *How do you qualify a prospect? What information do you need to determine if a prospect is worth calling on?* These questions will give you insight into the information your sales reps need to consider a sales inquiry qualified. You need to collect this information at the outset to help them do their jobs more efficiently.
- *How do you differentiate between near-term, middle-term, and long-term sales leads?* With this question, you're trying to identify the criteria they use to sort sales opportunities. Criteria could include company size, purchase opportunity, and purchase time frame.
- *How do your sales follow-up activities change between lead categories (near-term, middle-term, and long-term)?* By finding out what sales steps or processes salespeople perform for different types of sales prospects, you will gain insight into the type of cultivation and relationship marketing already in place.
- *With whom do you generally need contact during the initial phases of the sales process?* This question will give you insight into the titles and levels of individuals your sales staff call on.
- *Who is generally involved as the process progresses?* This will give you contrasting information you can use to confirm or deny the level of people involved in the sales process.
- *How many times do you need to call on a prospective customer to get an appointment?* This question will reveal the degree of difficulty or ease with which your sales staff are able to set appointments. If it is easy to get in

the door and set appointments, you might want to use telemarketing to set appointments. If it is hard, you need a series of contact steps (such as phone, E-mail, mail, and phone) after a lead is generated to help the salesperson get in the door.

- *Of the leads that have been qualified, what percentage do you set an appointment to see?* This question will help you see the relationship between a lead being labeled "qualified" and its conversion to a sales appointment. This will give you feedback on the ratio of qualified leads to appointments.

- *During the sales appointment, what are the prospective customer's three biggest concerns and fears?* This question will help you contrast and compare the perspectives of the salespeople and the buyers. What do the salespeople see as the customers' biggest fears, and what do customers say are their biggest fears? They should be the same.

- *What information does the prospective customer ask for most often to help with the purchase decision, for example, case studies, references, or specifications?* This question will help you verify the type of sales materials customers are looking for from sales representatives during the research phase.

- *When a salesperson asks the customer about the decision-making process, what does the customer say?* Ask your salespeople what they believe the typical sales process to be, including how many people are involved and from what levels in the organization.

- *How many competitive products, services, or vendors do prospective customers typically evaluate?* This question will determine your sales representatives' perspective on the competitive analysis being conducted by prospective buyers.

- *What do customers say would be an ideal solution to their problem?* Once again, you want to compare and contrast what the buyers say is an ideal solution and what the sales representatives *believe* customers say is the ideal solution.

- *What tools do you use to close the sale?* This question will help you determine how a prospect is converted into a customer. Is a proposal prepared? Is a presentation, price quote, estimate, or contract prepared?

- *What is the most effective way to close the sale?* After these documents are prepared, how do salespeople get final approval? Is a discount required? Are there any bonuses or additional service offers?

- *What percentage of sales presentations goes on to close?* This last question is especially important because it influences the lead projections you developed in Chapter 2.

Summarizing Your Findings

After you have conducted your customer interviews and your sales representative interviews, summarize your findings. Compare and contrast the results from the two sets of interviews. You should investigate gaps, holes, and problems within your sales process whose improvement will increase conversion rates. Look for data that will give you a clear picture of the purchase-process time frame. You need to know what information is required to move the purchase decision forward and overcome fear of the buying decision. You also need to determine the difference between your customers' actual problems and what your salespeople report as their customers' problems.

These findings will give you insight into the steps required to make a sale—and the parts of the sales process the sales organization believes need additional support from marketing. For example, this analysis might uncover a place in the sales cycle where sales stall or are lost because of lack of sales materials. You may find that you should add further contacts with potential buyers in the middle of the sales process to help overcome their fear and resistance. For example, instead of conducting field demonstrations, you can formally invite all potential customers to your headquarters for a detailed technical demonstration.

Strategies to Advance Prospects Through the Buy Cycle

Advancing a prospect through the buy cycle is an art and a science. After you have concluded your buy cycle and sales cycle analyses, you should devise strategies to fill in the gaps between the two. This section describes marketing strategies that can be used to fill these gaps and move a prospective customer from one phase of the buy cycle to the next as quickly as possible. These strategies include improvements to your lead generation campaigns, fulfillment packages, and sales conversion programs.

Movement from phase 1 to phase 8 of the buy cycle is not always linear. Multiple phases may occur at the same time, particularly before the first purchase occurs in phase 6. The people in your target market are at various stages in the purchase process. Thus, you should design multiple programs to move people who are in different phases of the purchase process through the buy cycle, and that provide flexibility for a nonlinear purchase process. For example, a customer may have a pressing problem. This customer doesn't want to receive literature (phase 3), but wants a salesperson to call right away to discuss details (phase 4). In this case, your response device should enable prospects to indicate that they want a sales representative to call on them immediately.

Phase 1: No Awareness Exists among Potential Customers

Assume in this phase that no prospects have ever heard of your company or your brand. Potential customers may even be unaware that your product category exists; they do not know that they have a problem that can be solved by your company and its products. This situation is commonly faced by new software products, high-tech start-up companies, dot-com companies, or companies that have recently merged and taken on a new name.

Phase 2: Begin to Create Awareness

You want prospective buyers to be aware of the product category, your company, and your solution. To best accomplish this task, investments in brand and product advertising, public relations, and trade show participation should be your primary focus. Over time, these marketing methods and investments will move people from phase 1 ("I've never heard of you") to phase 2 ("I think I've heard of you before"). The more compelling your advertising, the more you advertise, the more placements of publicity, the more arresting your trade show booth, and the more trade shows you attend, the faster awareness builds.

Phase 3: Interest Sparks

After a potential customer becomes aware of your product category, your company, and your product, you need to find prospects who have a problem to solve. Suppose a piece of advertising mail crosses a prospect's desk. It catches the person's eye and triggers the need to see how your product can solve his or her problem. This is where the use of direct response advertising (which makes an offer and requests immediate action) such as direct mail, E-mail, banner advertising, or direct response print advertising is most effective. When executed properly, direct response advertising motivates prospective customers to raise their hands and say, "I have a problem. Your offer sounds interesting. I'll respond to find out more. Even if I'm not ready to buy right now, I'll collect information for future reference, because I'm thinking about this problem." This is where you, as the campaign manager, need to promote the "right" offer, using compelling creative to bring prospects into the interest phase of the buy cycle.

Phase 4: Encouraging Prospects to Research Your Product

Moving prospects through the research phase is the most challenging aspect of business-to-business programs. The shift from the interest phase to the research phase happens when a potential buyer wants to buy but needs to know more about your product's or service's features, benefits, and cost. To move potential buyers through the research phase, you need to provide a range of product information, such as specifications, customer testimonials, research reports, white papers, samples, and demonstrations.

How you assemble and deliver your sales follow-up fulfillment materials are crucial in this stage of the buying process. The speed with which you send out information, the amount of information you send, and the frequency with which you send information should be tailored to each prospective buyer. Prospects have varying levels of interest. Some want all the facts now because the problem is pressing. Others have longer-term interest levels.

The rate at which prospects move through the research phase varies greatly. This variation often causes friction and frustration to build between sales and marketing departments. Salespeople are looking for hot buyers—right now. They need to close business this quarter, this month. As we will discuss in Chapters 7 and 8, though, statistics show that only 26 percent of sales inquiries generated from a direct response marketing program convert to sales within six months; another 19 percent convert to sales in seven to twelve months. This is why marketers need a system to qualify leads as part of their lead generation program. A sales lead filter system separates near-term sales opportunities from long-term opportunities. To help move longer-term sales prospects through the research phase, consider the strategy of staying in contact with potential buyers through a relationship marketing program. Relationship marketing requires consistent communication, such as dynamic E-mails, electronic newsletters, telephone calls, postcards, personal letters, printed newsletters, and success stories. Also, including current prospects as mailing names in ongoing lead generation campaigns keeps your name in front of them.

Not staying in close contact with potential buyers causes sales conversion programs to often fail. A sales force will focus on near-term sales opportunities, but often lack the resources or incentives to cultivate long-term opportunities. Consider establishing a policy for your organization that is an explicit agreement between sales and marketing regarding who takes primary responsibility for nurturing long-term opportunities. I recommend that direct marketing managers take responsibility for long-term prospect development.

Phase 5: The Prospect Decides on a Trial

Prospective buyers want to offset risk by taking a small step. To move prospects through the research phase and into trial, it is effective to offer low- or no-risk product involvement opportunities, for example thirty-day no-obligation trials, pilot programs, or a double-your-money-back guarantee of satisfaction.

Phase 6: The Prospect Becomes a Customer

This is when sales staff are trying to close the sale—and when the sales lead converts into a customer. Your sales representative wants to make the first sale, but buyers are cautious. A potential buyer wants the best price, terms, and conditions. To move a prospect from the trial phase to the purchase phase, you can offer price incentives or free add-ons if the sale is consummated by a certain date. Plus, you can offer a guarantee of satisfaction to overcome their fears.

As soon as prospects buy from you, they want to feel elevated to the status of *customer*—they are no longer just prospects. Recognition of this new status can set the stage for repeat business. Sending a thank-you letter from the president right after a purchase can have a long-term positive impact on the relationship. Having the vice president of sales or customer service make a follow-up call thirty days after a purchase to make sure everything is going well is another effective way to open the door for future sales opportunities.

Phase 7: Seek Repeat Business

Now you begin to realize the full monetary value of the customer relationship. In business-to-business marketing, the initial cost to acquire a customer is generally high. It is in subsequent sales that companies realize the lifetime value of a customer and can generate a higher return on investment in lead generation activities. Marketing tools such as customer satisfaction surveys, new product announcements, product upgrades, exclusive price offers, or special discounts for current customers can generate repeat orders.

Phase 8: Develop a Loyal Customer

The goal is to convert your customer from one who merely uses your services again and again to one who would never buy your type of product or service from anyone else. Customer loyalty results when you let your customers know they are special, listen to their needs, offer even more help solving their problems, and consistently provide superior service and high product value. Reward and recognition programs can help keep a customer loyal. Frequent-flyer miles, hotel points, or car-rental upgrades are a few examples of loyalty programs. Also effective in business-to-business marketing are recognition programs such as customer councils, customer dinners, user-group meetings at premier locations, training sessions, and customer award presentations.

Win/Loss Analysis

For a full perspective of your sales process and how sales close, you will need a win/loss analysis. The goal is to identify why the sales team wins business, and why it loses it. Win/loss analysis compares a sample of recently closed sales to a sample of lost sales, revealing any patterns that may be influencing sales conversion rates.

Conducting Win/Loss Analysis

It is important to find out the key decisions influencing the closing of a sale and the common characteristics among them. Specifically, you should ask the following:

- What were your clients using before they purchased your product?
- What caused them to consider an alternative to what they were using?
- How did they go about locating products to consider?
- How did they hear about your company?
- Did they have any perceptions about your company before contacting you?
- How many vendors did they consider, and who were they?
- What were the steps in the decision process (was a request for proposal [RFP] issued, did they see a product demonstration or conduct a product trial)?
- Who was involved in the decision?
- What criteria were used to select the winning vendor?
- Why did they decide to purchase your product?
- How long was the decision process?
- What collateral materials from your company helped them make a decision? What additional materials would they suggest you make available to potential clients?

The answers to these questions reveal your organizational strengths. Suppose, for example, the decision makers at several of the companies that bought your product cited the importance of postsale service to their organizations. They chose your company as their supplier because they see service as one of your strengths.

Similarly, look at the key buying decisions underlying the sales you lost: Can you determine why you lost each sale? What competitor did you lose to and why? Was it price, experience, service, or support? Do the lost sales share certain characteristics? If so, these point to your company's weaknesses. By providing clues about your company's strengths and weaknesses, the win/loss analysis can help you flesh out the SWOT analysis and vice versa (see Chapter 1).

The Million-Dollar Question

Questions are the most powerful part of the strategic planning process. They are the best way to find problems and recommend effective marketing solutions. Here is an example of how asking the right questions about the sales process revealed information that changed the course of the business of one of my clients.

The client sold Y2K software. For several years, the company had used a classic long-form mail-order package that included a 6- by 9-inch envelope, eight-page letter, large broadside brochure, and reply card. The company was mailing hundreds of thousands of pieces. Over time, responses had diminished to less than 0.2 percent. As I conducted a sales-process analysis, I asked a simple question: "How do you close business?"

I wanted to know what happened when someone responded to the direct mail campaign used at the time. The sales manager's answer to this question gave me a key piece of data. Eighty percent of people who bought needed to speak to a sales representative before they would make a purchase. It became obvious that the company was using one-step mail-order selling techniques but actually required a two-step, lead generation plus sales call follow-up selling process.

The company's marketing strategy should not have been to generate revenue via a one-step mail-order selling approach, but to generate qualified sales leads. However, the company had not put together the infrastructure and systems needed to manage a flow of leads. With proper planning, the client created a lead management infrastructure and switched to a classic two-step lead generation strategy.

The new direct mail package highlighted the Y2K issue and included a free guide and CD-ROM to help the prospect understand how to use the client's software. The direct mail package featured an arresting outside envelope, a brochure with a strong presentation of the offer, and a letter that followed through on the theme. The mail quantity was cut in half. This dramatic change of strategy produced response rates 2,000 percent greater than those generated with earlier mailings.

Use Knowledge of the Sales Process to Prepare Your Unique Sales Proposition

Promoting your product's unique characteristics and the advantages that differentiate it from competitive products is the fundamental principle of sales and marketing. A good, unique sales proposition (USP) statement can communicate your product's distinctive characteristics and advantages in less time than it takes to ride ten floors in an elevator—and it can be summarized in thirty or fewer words.

Your USP statement is the rationale for doing business with your company rather than with your competitor. An effective USP is clear, believable, and easy to understand. It defines what makes doing business with your company unique, better, more profitable, or more satisfying than buying from the competition. Sometimes called a value proposition, it states the value your company or product provides to customers who do business with you. During your sales interviews, you may hear different interpretations of your company's USP from each of your sales representatives. A well-stated USP that is consistently used by all sales reps can improve sales effectiveness.

Here are some examples of business-to-business USP statements:

We guarantee we will respond to your service request in one hour
or less.

We are the only manufacturer that will not charge you a penny for our
software until you are fully satisfied.

Our product reduces your time-to-market by 25 percent.

We are the only company that lets you buy 24 hours a day, 7 days a
week.

No other company has a wider range of products.

I recommend that you develop or solidify your USP during strategic planning for two reasons. First, you need it to give your creative resources direction on what makes your product or service unique. Your USP is an integral part of the creative process. Second, if, during the strategic planning process, you develop a USP you have doubts about, you can test it in the S.U.R.E.-Fire planning research phase (Understanding for Empathy, Chapter 4). Based on your research findings, you can refine and polish your USP statement.

Why Is a USP Important to Business Marketers?

Qualified sales leads result from potential buyers seeing messages that make them perceive that you can solve their business problems. To generate a sales lead, you must send messages into the marketplace and quickly communicate to prospective buyers why responding to your offer and doing business with you is in their best interest. People are searching for reasons to do business with you. Your USP articulates these reasons—fast. Your USP is one of the reasons prospective buyers respond to your lead generation campaign. A compelling USP results from understanding the wants and needs of the marketplace and matching those desires to your company's strengths and product line.

Your USP is not meant to appeal to everyone. Instead, it is designed to set out a clear promise to a specific market niche. You want to attract customers best served by your product or service. It is better to have a narrow focus than to try to be all things to all people. People prefer to do business with a company that has a clear idea of what it stands for. For example, Rolls Royce stands for the highest quality hand-built automobiles in the world. Hammacher Schlemmer's mail-order catalog promises that the company offers "the best, the only, and the unexpected for 150 years."

How to Develop a USP Statement

The most common USPs fall into seven categories—speed, product quality, price, service quality, product selection, array of services, and best guarantee. To develop a USP for your company or product, you need to use the completed competitive review from Chapter 1. Write out or plot the USP statements of all your competitors. See how they cluster, based on these seven major USP categories. Then see where you can place yourself, in light of your SWOT analysis. Is there an opportunity for you to position yourself apart from your competition?

Be sure to choose a USP you can deliver on, one that is consistent within your company. Remember that it becomes a business promise to prospective and current customers. All your employees and corporate managers need to understand your USP, and their actions and decisions should be consistent with it.

Writing a USP Statement

A USP statement defines who you are, what business you are in, what customers you serve, the benefit of doing business with you, why your company is better than the competition, and how doing business with you benefits the buyer. The more specific your USP, the easier it is for buyers to understand the benefit of doing business with you and to compare you to others. Which of the following companies would you rather do business with?

General: At ABC chips, we have the broadest range of semiconductors in the industry.

Specific: At ACME chips, we offer 128 types of semiconductor in five sizes. All our products are always in stock. We guarantee same-day shipping if you place your order before 3:00 P.M. If we don't ship out on the day you order, you pay nothing. Your order is *free*.

For example, a call-center software company used these questions to develop its USP:

Who: XYZ Software Co.

What business: building customer loyalty and growth

For what customers: consumer-based companies

Benefit: personalizes every customer interaction over the telephone

How/product: call-center and Internet software

USP statement: XYZ Software Co. builds *customer loyalty and growth* for consumer-based companies through call-center and Internet software that personalizes every telephone interaction with customers.

Here is an alternative framework you can follow when writing a USP statement:

To: (name the target audience)

Who are looking for: (problem to be solved)

Our product is: (describe your product)

Which provides: (give product benefits)

Unlike the competitive product, which: (name weaknesses or problems with competition)

Our product: (describe the unique strengths or advantages of your product)

For example:

To: network managers

Who are looking for: network security

Our product is: the world's most sophisticated network software, based on leading-edge technology

Which provides: 100 percent confidence that network viruses will never get into your system

Unlike the competitive product, which: is based on older technology
Our product: is used by all *Fortune* 1,000 companies and guarantees
100 percent security or double your money back

Write many variations of your USP statement. Share them with your senior management team, then research the best two or three. Gather feedback from the market and refine the wording of the USP until you have developed a statement that makes your company stand out from the competition.

Strategic Planning Using a Product Life Cycle Positioning Curve

Another helpful strategic planning tool is the product life cycle positioning curve (Figure 3.2). This curve shows the typical product life cycle from inception through maturity to decline. Under the curve are the five basic ways a direct marketer can position a campaign based on the life cycle stage of the product.

Inception: Create a Need

When a new technology or a new product or service is created and brought to the marketplace, potential buyers need to be educated as to why they need it. What benefits does this product or service offer that no one has thought of before? E-mail

Figure 3.2 Kern Product Life Cycle Positioning Curve

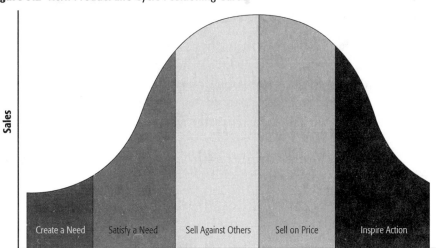

is a good example of an innovative new service for which a need had to be created. When E-mail first became available, there was confusion and a lack of understanding among potential users about the timesaving benefit of the technology. The industry created a need for the service by demonstrating E-mail's benefits to consumers.

Growth: Satisfy a Need

As products mature, sales increase and the marketplace understands the benefits of the product category. You no longer need to educate the market about why to consider your product. Instead, you have to demonstrate how your product or service solves existing problems in the marketplace. For example, all of us know we need Internet access. The challenge has shifted to what type and speed of access.

Maturity: Sell Competitively

In the third stage of the life cycle, the product category reaches maturity. All consumers know the product category and why they need the product. Cellular phones are an example of a category in this stage of the life cycle. In this stage, you begin to position yourself against your competitors. You generate sales by differentiating your products from those of your competitors. You promote the unique advantages of your product against competitive products or solutions. Automobile manufacturers are one of the most common users of competitive advertising techniques. Cars are constantly being compared to one another. One car is always bigger, roomier, quieter, faster, more powerful, or better built than its competitor.

Maturity/Margin Erosion: Sell on Price

Once the product has reached full maturity, its sales price becomes the key issue. Lower-priced competitors have flooded the market, creating a price war, and only those companies with the best economies of scale or the strongest competitive advantage survive. In this stage, it is assumed that the purchaser knows all about the product or only cares about prices because the product has become a commodity. You need to use price as the motivation to drive action. Common stationary products, usually sold strictly on price, exemplify this stage of the life cycle and the appropriate method of marketing.

Decline: Inspire Action

In the final stage of a product's life cycle, the marketer's goal is to squeeze out any remaining revenue or action. "Inspire action" is often used in consumer or nonprofit marketing. For example, nonprofit fundraisers typically use celebrities to ask potential donors for contributions of any amount. Consumers know the charity and why they need to give money. The issue is not competition or price but motivation to take action now.

Using the Product Life Cycle as Direction for Creative Development

Ask yourself where your product is in its life cycle. Is it a new category of product? Is it a new product in a well-established category? Do you have a mature product that needs to fight it out on competitive advantages or price? Because the marketplace is dynamic, it is often impossible to draw a hard boundary between two types of positioning. Therefore, pick the one or two positions most applicable to your marketing situation. Use this positioning in concert with your one-to-one interview research (see Chapter 4) as part of the input for creative development.

I use the product life cycle positioning curve to educate creative resources. I show my creative team where one of our client's products sits on the curve, and the need for a certain style of campaign becomes clear. For example, if I have a client with a new product in a new product category, I place the product to the far left on the curve. This shows the necessity for a "create a need" campaign, a campaign that is educational and appropriate for the client. It also shows why a "sell on price" strategy is not appropriate.

A secondary benefit of the product life cycle positioning curve is that it provides insight into potential response rates. New products, which have little awareness or are not well understood in the marketplace, demand consumer education. Consequently, response rates are low. Products on a fast growth curve—those that fill a strong need in the marketplace—enjoy high response rates. As product categories mature and many companies have one solution or another, response rates decline again because your solution is now an alternative or a replacement.

Creating a Plan of Attack

Now that you have completed the steps of the strategic planning process, it is time to summarize your top-level plan of attack. Although you have done a large amount of work, you are not ready to start tactical implementation just yet. Instead, you need to get an overview of the marketing landscape. Do this by placing all work and findings in a three-ring campaign notebook. I like to call this the S.U.R.E.-Fire direct response marketing planning notebook. This is the bible for present and future campaign development. It enables anyone working on the lead generation campaign to review information collected to date and to understand how the marketing team developed its marketing strategies. This notebook also lays the foundation for the second phase of the S.U.R.E.-Fire process, Understanding for Empathy.

After all your strategic planning information is compiled, you should develop an executive summary, which will be the overview of your strategic marketing plan. I view the executive summary as the outline for a game of chess. Before you begin, you should know what pieces you have to play with, how they move, and what pieces your competition has. You also have to define marketing checkmate. Next, you select an overall strategy. After the game begins, you can adjust your plan, accommodating developments that occur during the course of play. Use the following questions as the foundation for your executive summary:

- *What is your product or service, and what does it do? Why is it better than anything currently on the market?* This first set of questions helps you define who you are, what you are selling, and why someone should buy it. Look at your SWOT analysis, competitive advertising analysis (see Chapter 1), and USP statement for answers for this section of the summary.
- *Who is your customer?* Clearly identify the target market. Whom are you trying to sell to? The answer to this question comes partially from your SWOT analysis but mainly from the media- and market-opportunity analysis completed in Chapter 2. Spell out the exact titles of your target customers, their job function, what publications they read, and the type and size of company. This information will tell you the size of the market and how many media options you have to reach prospects.
- *What will the measure of success be?* A set of measurable objectives enables you and your management to track the campaign's progress. When establishing your goals, be sure they are quantifiable and include a time limit. For example, the goal is to generate $3 million in sales within six months. Use the financial calculations from Chapter 2 to spell out the small steps needed to reach that goal. These steps include the number of leads you need to generate in a certain period and the number of appointments and presentations required to reach the desired sales goal based on the conversion rate of sales leads to customers. Recall your calculation, in Chapter 2, of the cost to generate sales leads. What is an acceptable return on your marketing investment?

After you articulate your goals, you need to lay out your plan. What marketing approaches will help you reach your goal? By this point in the strategic planning process, you have probably begun to compare various marketing options. Depending on your marketing goals, your marketing strategy might include a mix of direct response print advertising, lead generation direct mail, E-mail and banner ads, and seminars. Don't be concerned if your plans are not fully formed. They will develop as you continue through the rest of the S.U.R.E.-Fire planning process.

At this point in your planning, you want to think beyond generating sales leads to how you will convert sales leads to revenue. Spell out how you will qualify leads, how you will follow up on leads, and how you will stay in contact with leads that do not buy right away.

Summing Up

Successful campaign strategic planning is a direct result of intensive background information collection. Equipped with knowledge of the sales process and the various strategic planning tools and concepts described in this chapter, you are in a position to effectively manage the entire sales lead generation process. You must also be concerned with creating and implementing marketing and sales-support strategies that will convert the maximum number of sales leads into customers. By paying attention to the sales conversion process up front, you can avoid complaints from the sales department about lead quality later on. In addition, tracking sales conversion is one of the best ways to get approval for additional marketing dollars in the future, because you can justify the program's return on investment. By managing the sales lead conversion processes, you reduce your headaches while expanding your opportunity to increase the direct marketing budget.

UNDERSTANDING
FOR EMPATHY

Seek first to understand, then to be understood.

—STEPHEN R. COVEY
The 7 Habits of Highly Effective People

The "U" phase of the S.U.R.E.-Fire planning process, Understanding for Empathy, focuses on listening—for the purpose of developing a deep empathy with your target market. This is empathy for who they are and the problems they face. After you have an understanding of your target customers and feel empathy for their problems, you can create campaigns that resonate within their hearts, heads, and souls.

Understanding and empathy for your customers comes from looking at their business issues. Ask yourself the following questions:

- What problems does your target market need to overcome each day?
- What keeps your target customers up at night? What do they worry about?
- How important is your product or service in the overall scheme of the problems they face?
- How are members of your target market currently solving these problems without your product or service?
- Why have people bought your product or service in the past? Does this reflect why others will buy it now and in the future?
- What benefits are your customers realizing from using your product, and how might that information be converted to marketing messages attractive to other buyers?

By answering these questions, you will gain insight into the lives of your buyers. You acquired some of the relevant information in the first phase of planning, but now it is time to gather the information directly from customers and prospects. This will help you manage direct response lead generation campaigns better because you will be able to influence and guide the flow of communications between buyer and seller. With knowledge of the buyer's needs, the direct marketer can honestly make the following statements:

I (the marketer) understand you (my potential customer).

I understand your problems. I care deeply about your problems.

I understand how difficult these problems are for you.

I truly want to help you solve your problems.

Given my understanding of your problems, would you trust me just a little?

Will you allow me to show you how I can help you?

You don't need to take a big risk, just a small step.

I have information that I know will be helpful to you.

All you need to do is ask for it. I'll rush it right to you.

This information is simple to get.

Just visit my website, call me, fax me, E-mail me, or return a card.

You see, I've done everything I can to make it easy and convenient.

You don't need to worry about a thing.

You're not obligated to do anything or buy anything.

After you get the information, I'll call to make sure you understand it.

If you have any questions, I'll be delighted to answer them.

When you want more proof, or want to see for yourself, just let me know.

I'll be right out.

I care about your problems.

I've helped many people just like you, people with similar problems.

They have all found relief.

You can too.

All you need to do is take the first step.

The second phase of the S.U.R.E.-Fire planning process includes three proven market research methodologies—one-to-one interviews, focus groups, and a mail study—and preliminary concept development. These primary market research techniques are used to develop a deep understanding of the market and to help narrow the creative choices. Primary market research connects you directly with your target market so you can hear what they have to say. Further primary market research is used to evaluate, refine, and select creative concepts. After twenty years in the business, I have found that no creative director, copywriter, account executive, marketing manager, or even company president can consistently identify a winning direct response campaign. By using primary market research, the direct marketer gains a tremendous advantage over traditional ad hoc selection methods.

The Understanding for Empathy methodology is designed to reduce your risk by eliminating the guesswork involved in campaign creation and development. In this phase of the S.U.R.E.-Fire planning process, qualitative and quantitative market research is combined to help you make creative decisions and evaluate the strengths of your concepts, offers, and messages before you wager large marketing investments.

For example, assume your creative resources develop several campaign concepts. A presentation is made to the marketing team. During the meeting, a senior marketing director or president makes comments such as, "I like this one. I hate that one." Then a decision is made based on his or her opinion, the equivalent to throwing marketing dice and gambling with your marketing budget. Personal preference and bias are not effective ways to select winning direct response concepts.

Historically, direct marketers have been trained to test, test, and test. Direct marketers use A/B split testing to identify one winning concept over another. But for business-to-business marketers, whose time frames are often longer and whose markets are typically smaller than those of consumer goods marketers, this kind of testing is not always possible or practical. Too often, small and midsize business-to-business marketers investing $250,000, $1 million, or even $5 million in lead generation efforts do not offset their marketing risk by using primary market research strategies.

Although these research steps do not guarantee success (there are no silver bullets in direct response advertising), they provide an important foundation for successful implementation. By asking your target audience pertinent marketing questions, using their answers as the input for the creative process, and using market research to evaluate creative concepts, you can identify winning concepts or campaigns. I have found that this method works better than the old "guess-and-check" and "test, test, test" approaches.

Why Market Research Is Effective

In his book *Ogilvy on Advertising*, David Ogilvy writes, "Advertising people who ignore research are as dangerous as generals who ignore decodes of enemy signals." Ogilvy knew from years of working in market research that if you ask the marketplace what it wants, it will tell you. However, listening to the market, interpreting what you hear, and then putting your market research findings into action are challenging tasks.

Effective communication stems from listening, understanding, and developing trust. For an advertising communication to be effective, it must appeal to the emotions of prospects as well as to their practicality and logic. It must be relevant and believable. If you look at your personal relationships, you will find that trust develops when you provide consistent support, understanding, and concern for another individual. The same is true in the world of marketing. Suspects, prospects, and customers develop trust in you when you demonstrate that you understand their problems and issues and that you care deeply about helping them solve their problems.

Thus, speaking the language of your prospective customer is a prerequisite to developing effective direct response advertising communication. Many of the prospects you solicit in a business-to-business marketplace are highly educated. They have spent five, ten, or even twenty years learning their profession. They know the nuances of their business. They live and breathe it daily. Unless you can speak to your potential customers in a way that shows you truly and honestly understand the problems they face, your messages risk falling into the large pile of thin, weak, uninspiring communications.

Learning the language of potential customers is not easy. Reading trade magazines helps, but this alone cannot teach you the relative importance of the business issues your target market faces. Interacting directly with your targets through one-to-one interviews is one of the most effective ways to learn to speak their language. Primary research can help you understand the problems and frustrations of your target audience, how they are solving these problems now, how they plan to solve them in the future, and what they think about your products and your competitors' products.

Building a Winning Marketing Case

The market research method of the S.U.R.E.-Fire process is designed to provide you with the information you need to build a marketing case. This marketing case will enable you to promote your product or service in the most advantageous manner. Like a prosecution attorney who pieces together evidence against a defendant to win a conviction, you, using the S.U.R.E.-Fire planning process, will collect layer upon layer of marketing evidence to win over your buyer. Once completed, this market research enables you to make, with a high degree of confidence, the necessary judgments and decisions to implement a lead generation campaign that produces high response rates and maximizes your return on investment.

Consider the traditional decision process for selecting creative concepts for a business-to-business campaign. Some creative resource, such as an ad agency or internal team, presents three to five creative concepts or ideas to a marketing team. The pros and cons of each idea are discussed until finally marketing management, using divine wisdom, selects what it feels is the most effective concept. This is purely subjective. Sometimes, creative concepts are then presented to a higher level of management, which makes an even more subjective choice.

The truth, especially from the direct marketing perspective, is that no one can consistently pick a winning idea, concept, or campaign. Any person evaluating creative ideas brings personal biases that influence his or her decision-making ability. Art directors like "artsy" ideas, copywriters like clever copy, managers prefer product-oriented ideas. None of that matters. What matters is what the marketplace wants, what it is receptive to, and what it will respond to. Having developed thousands of creative ideas and campaigns, I am constantly surprised to see the difference between what I think will be a winning campaign and what the marketplace actually responds to.

Further, direct marketers are traditionally taught that the guess-and-check method of testing is the best way to identify a winning campaign. Testing does work. I use it and support it. However, business-to-business marketers often have small marketplaces. After running a test, they may find there is no one left to send the campaign to. Developing multicell tests of various combinations of offers and creative (especially when a large rollout market does not exist) is expensive. The cost of creating and mailing these tests cannot be leveraged against a much larger universe.

In place of the guess-and-check testing method, the Understanding for Empathy phase of the S.U.R.E.-Fire planning process requires a methodical approach for primary market research. This market research method helps you listen to the marketplace, so you can reduce your risk before making large marketing investments. By using primary research to pretest creative, offers, and messages, I can increase campaign success by 100 to 300 percent over the guess-and-check method.

Six Steps to Understanding for Empathy

Below is a step-by-step account of the market research method used in the second phase of the S.U.R.E.-Fire planning process. This chapter will examine the first three steps. Chapter 5 will examine in depth the remaining steps.

1. Conduct one-to-one in-depth interviews with current customers, prospective customers, and the sales and telemarketing staffs.
2. Summarize and analyze data from one-to-one interviews, creating a visual reference (message map).
3. Use the findings from the one-to-one interviews to develop creative concepts based on the most prevalent themes.
4. Conduct multiple focus groups to gain further insight into the product category; test and probe deeper into conclusions you have drawn from one-to-one interviews regarding business problems, product benefits, and the buying process; and use sort test methodology to identify the most appealing and engaging creative concepts, messaging, and offers.
5. Based on comments from the one-to-one interviews and focus groups, develop and conduct a quantitative mail study to obtain projectable results about product interest, purchase intent, message importance, creative appeal, and offer interest.
6. Analyze all data from each research step.

Benefits of Combining Qualitative and Quantitative Research

The second phase of the S.U.R.E.-Fire planning process uses two qualitative and one quantitative research methods (see Figure 4.1). Although there are many research options and strategies, this combination will help you maximize your opportunity for success.

Qualitative research, when carefully conceived and executed, provides a descriptive map of consumers' opinions, beliefs, and attitudes. Qualitative research techniques such as individual in-depth interviewing (one-to-one interviews) and group in-depth interviewing (focus groups) are particularly useful because they can deliver rich, deep, and complex information.

For example, suppose you are going to produce a lead generation campaign, and to do so you need to learn how corporate health-care administrators recommend health insurance plans to their employees. You could devise a survey (quantitative research technique) to identify what factors they use to rank health plans. Your survey would show the rank order of decision factors, but you would not gain a great deal of insight into *why* these decision factors ranked in a given order. You would not know if the reasons relate to employee needs, employee census, or corporate financial goals. Without knowing the reasons for preferences, you do not have the information you need to create an enticing, impactive, and memorable

Figure 4.1 Three-Part Research Technique to Maximize Success

Research Technique	Purpose
One-to-One In-Depth Interviews	• Test assumptions identified during the SWOT analysis
	• Obtain qualitative information *from the prospect's viewpoint*
	• Form additional hypotheses regarding the marketplace
	• Gather enough information to develop messages, creative, and offers to test in focus groups and mail survey
	• Gather key phrases and quotes that could be used in future marketing materials
	• Identify broad range of possible responses that people have to key questions. This reduces bias in the mail survey caused by mistaken omission of an answer choice in a multiple-choice question. (To facilitate tabulation and analysis, most mail survey questions are multiple choice.)
Interactive Focus Groups	• Test marketplace assumptions identified during SWOT and one-to-one interviews
	• Obtain qualitative information *from the prospect's viewpoint*
	• Understand which creative concepts are most likely to be read (and opened)
	• Identify ways to improve each creative concept to increase the likelihood it will be read (and opened)
	• Test understanding and stopping power of key phrases and buzz words
	• Identify the creative concept and offer "finalists" to include in the mail survey
Mail Survey	• Gather quantitative information to choose the final creative concept and offer to use for the campaign rollout
	• Determine the top two or three business benefits and product features that should be emphasized in the text of the direct response advertisement or mail piece
	• Validate mailing list delivery rates and accuracy

message. Without a qualitative research technique to uncover information, you are merely guessing about the motivation for preference. Worse yet, you might completely miss a key preference.

Quantitative research makes it possible to collect and tabulate precise numerical measurements of prospects' and customers' attitudes. A well-constructed quantitative research study enables a direct marketer to obtain specific counts or tallies about information that will impact a marketing program. Because quantitative research is typically conducted among a large sample size, the results of such studies tend to be representative of the marketplace and more predictive of what will actually transpire in the market.

One-to-One Interviews

One-to-one interviews are a qualitative research technique. The information you gather during these interviews should trigger creative insights and help you develop a message map to guide creative development. The interviews help you understand your target market's key business problems and frustrations, as well as its lexicon, jargon, and buzzwords. An important goal of the interviews is to learn the business problems your product helps your clients solve and why your product initially grabbed their attention. You should also identify your product's benefits and liabilities from the user's perspective. In addition, your questioning should tease out such specifics as who within the buying organization drives the decision process and how people locate vendors when considering new products.

Focus Groups

Focus groups are an integral part of the research process. Although one-to-one interviews are useful in identifying significant business problems, important terminology, and key benefits of your product, they do not provide an effective forum for ranking the importance of each. Information collected during the one-to-one interviews can be used as a springboard for creative concept development; the concepts can then be presented in focus group studies. A focus group enables you to see and hear people's reactions to each of your concept ideas, then narrow that field of ideas and messages down to six finalist concepts for quantitative evaluation.

Focus groups are used to gain a better understanding of customers' and prospects' perceptions of your product and your product category. How interested are they in the product category? Do they believe it can have an impact on their business problems? What is the relative importance of the various business problems? Focus groups also help identify which messages, offers, and buzzwords have the most interest to a sample target population. For many marketers, focus groups are especially revealing because they show how potential customers react to creative concepts, which may cause marketing to make "stop," "modify," or "proceed" decisions about those concepts.

The Mail Study: A Quantitative Check

The S.U.R.E.-Fire planning process uses a quantitative study based on statistically valid sample sizes. Focus groups, comprising ten to twelve people per group, do not give you statistically valid data. They only give you indications or trends. When you combine your focus group findings with the results from a statistically valid quantitative study—the mail study—you can make your final creative decisions with a high degree of confidence.

The mail study enables the direct marketer to determine or validate the interest in a given product category, collect data about awareness levels and perceptions of competitive products or companies, and substantiate or refute the results of the focus groups regarding creative executions. The data collected can be used to determine the importance and ranking of various business problems, messages, creative concepts, offers, product features, and product benefits with a higher confidence level than that provided by one-to-one interviews or focus groups. A mail study will also provide direction on which combination of image and message to implement and which offers and offer titles to proceed with.

Managing Research: Begin with the End in Mind

The success of any market research study depends squarely on your ability to clearly state the goals or objectives of the research before starting it. You must know and precisely describe what learning needs to occur in the research process, or you run the risk of asking off-target questions and obtaining useless data. This can be disastrous, as the following example illustrates.

The marketing manager of a small photo lab was curious about what motivated customers' lab-patronizing habits. The lab created a telephone questionnaire that asked more than seventy questions of current and prospective customers. The questions included: Which is your favorite lab to obtain photo retouching? Where do you go when you must have pristine scanning work done? Have you used the latest slide-developing technology? These provided the lab with results that were interesting, yet the decisive question—why customers do or do not patronize this particular lab—was unanswered, because the questions were too vague.

In this case, the marketing manager's curiosity was good, but incomplete. The research results proved nearly useless because he failed to identify and verbalize the research goal before fielding the study. Specific questions—Why do you go to your favorite lab for retouching? How do you select a lab when you require pristine scanning? What results have you seen from the latest slide development technology?—would have yielded better findings.

You must also identify the most suitable research participants or respondents. Asking the right questions of the wrong individuals can produce misleading findings. So before embarking on a research project, answer the following questions thoroughly and carefully, preferably in writing. Doing so will help you avoid a research debacle.

- What do you need to know? The answer to this question will focus your research and set its goals.
- Why do you need to know it? You need to state the purpose, or the hypothesis, of the research. For example, "I want to know which creative concept is most appealing to my target audience, because I believe an appealing concept will generate better results than one that is not."
- Whom do you need to learn it from? This question determines the target. Here you want to use demographic, "firmographic" (business entity demographic), and job-function criteria to determine your target.
- How much detail and depth of information do you need from your research? How much accuracy do you require?
- What will you do with the information after you get it?

Research Participants

The individuals who will become participants in your market research are the same individuals who constitute the target market for your product or service. Your research will be conducted among current customers, prospective customers (prospects), sales personnel, and potential buyers (suspects). Current customers have made the purchase decision and understand your product. Prospects are those currently in the buying process, or "in-market." These people are thinking about buying your product, so you need to understand what motivated them to move into the purchase process. Sales personnel include managers, telephone salespeople, and field salespeople. These individuals talk to prospective buyers and customers daily. Potential buyers are members of your target audience. They are the ones to whom you are currently sending lead generation solicitation, but who have not indicated whether they are in-market. Typically, these individuals subscribe to your industry's trade magazines.

Conducting your studies among both current and future customers will help you understand market issues and evaluate future communication programs. For

Research Objectives: A Template

Overall Objective:
Identify the most impactful, meaningful way to communicate to prospective customers via direct response advertising, with the goal of motivating the largest number of qualified prospective customers to move into the purchase process.

Specific Objectives:
- Determine interest in the product category.
- Determine recognition of your product's brand name or company name.
- Assess perceptions of the product.
- Identify the key business problems, fears, concerns, and unique challenges the target market faces in relationship to the product category.
- Identify which solutions the target market is using instead of your product.
- Identify the key words, phrases, terminology, and jargon customers and prospective customers use to discuss their problems and the anticipated solutions (as they relate to your product category).
- Identify the key words, phrases, terminology, and jargon customers and prospective customers use to discuss the product and competitive product attributes, features, benefits, and liabilities.
- Understand what benefits current customers are realizing from a competitive product and learn how these benefits are similar or dissimilar to those claimed by the product's marketer.
- Identify which creative concept(s), message(s), word(s), and offer(s) are most likely to gain prospective customers' attention and response.

Outputs:
- Summary of one-to-one interviews, plus all backup information
- Executive summary of focus group findings, plus transcript
- Executive summary of quantitative study, plus full tabulation report

Decisions to Be Made:
- Creative concept most likely to be opened by target audience
- Messages ranked according to their interest to the target audience
- Offers ranked according to their appeal to the target audience

Target Audience:
- Demographic
- Firmographic (business entity demographic information)
- Functional responsibilities

one-to-one interviews, use customers, prospects, and salespeople. For focus groups and mail surveys, use suspects and prospects—they most closely match the people you will target for future lead generation marketing communications.

Orchestrating and Conducting One-to-One Interviews

The first research step in the Understanding for Empathy phase is one-to-one interviews. The goal of the interviews is to collect words, phrases, and ideas that together will serve as the springboard for creative and copy development.

I recommend that you conduct at least ten and up to twenty interviews if possible. Because this is a qualitative study, you want to conduct enough interviews to gain perspective and identify trends or patterns. Each interview will take fifteen to thirty minutes. About half should be conducted among current customers. It is beneficial to interview recent buyers (those who have purchased within the last year), because their purchase experience is fresh in their minds and they can recall the competitive products they considered. Another 25 percent of your interviews should be conducted among the sales personnel currently pitching your product, and the remaining 25 percent with individuals who have not bought your product or service but are considering buying it soon.

The interviews can be conducted in the field, so the researcher can sit eye to eye with the respondents, or they can be conducted over the telephone. One-to-one field interviews give you the unique opportunity to connect and observe the reactions of the subject. Nonverbal clues help the researcher fully understand a subject's answer. Field interviews can take over an hour and go into great depth and detailed questioning.

If field interviews are not possible, don't hesitate to use the telephone for your one-to-one interviews. Telephone interviews can give you almost as much detail as field interviews but they are shorter in length. They can be conducted nationally, and because they are kept between fifteen and twenty minutes, they are time-efficient for both the interviewer and interviewee. You are more likely to secure telephone interviews with top executives, because a telephone interview is considered less intrusive on their time.

Regardless of the interview method, you will find that, when time permits, people enjoy talking to others about their situations and problems. Thus, you have a golden opportunity to gather critical marketing information.

Before the interviews can begin, you must create a list of customers, prospects, and salespeople to call. This list should include a range of companies in terms of size, industry, and geography that match your target as defined in the SWOT analysis, and customers who are satisfied and customers who are not. Speaking with dissatisfied customers gives you a realistic view of your product's weaknesses.

Given the realities of voice mail, you will need twenty names for every interview you want to conduct. In other words, to set up ten interviews you will need to provide your interviewer with two hundred telephone numbers. In the case of your own company's sales and telemarketing staff, you will need only two names for each interview you would like to conduct.

Don't forget housekeeping details, which will pay off in the long run. Include contact names and phone numbers on the list. This is mandatory. Also include contact title, company size, and industry, if possible. This information increases the quality of the data because it allows the interviewer to sort through the list and focus on setting up the best interviews possible. Put the list in an electronic format that you can sort in zip code order. This lets you arrange the list by time zone and speeds up the interview process.

Questions for One-to-One Interviews

Interviewers should be knowledgeable—or at least thoroughly briefed—about the product and category so they can comfortably and efficiently ask relevant tangential questions as they arise. If necessary, provide the interviewer with a copy of the SWOT analysis, trade magazines, the product or a product manual, and any other helpful materials.

Each interview will consist of a set of predefined questions. These questions are commonly referred to as the discussion guide. The discussion guide should derive directly from the specific research objectives or goals.

For each objective, create three to five questions or subtopics. This helps ensure that enough detail about a topic is gathered. For critical pieces of information, such as product benefits, ask the salient question several times in slightly different contexts. This helps the interviewee recall information that may not come to mind following a single question. Interviewees tend to mention additional key points if they are asked about the same topic in a different manner later in the interview.

The discussion guide should be constructed so that the more sensitive questions fall toward the end of the interview. It is important to build rapport with the respondent by asking general questions first. Later, you can move to more specific (and sometimes sensitive) issues. Most important, you must ensure that earlier questions do not affect answers to later questions. For example, how they heard about your company before you ask whether they remember receiving a specific direct mail piece.

The following questions are from the discussion guide used in one-to-one interviews for a call-center workforce-scheduling software product. These questions are designed for a customer interview. If you were conducting interviews among prospects or sales personnel, the wording would need to be adjusted accordingly.

- What is your job title and function, and to whom do you report?
- What type of business or industry are you in?
- What is your company's approximate annual revenue (or number of employees)?
- What is the function of your call center?
- How many agents do you have?
- What are the three biggest problems you face in your job?
- What are the three biggest problems you face related to scheduling call-center agents?
- How long have you had the product installed?
- What were you using before you installed the product?
- What are the five most important benefits you have realized from installing the product?
- What was the "final straw" that made you change from your old method?
- How long did it take from the time you decided to make a change to the time you purchased a solution?
- What was the "short list" of other companies, products, or solutions you considered?
- What perception did you have about XYZ company before you started your decision-making process?
- Why did you finally decide to buy from XYZ company?
- Now that you are using the product, what do you like most about it?
- What do you like least about it?
- Who was involved in the purchase process? Who first identified the need? Who located solutions to consider? To whom would you suggest we target our marketing materials?
- How did you first hear about XYZ software?
- What was it about the product that first grabbed your attention and caused you to investigate further?
- Where do you turn first when looking for products or services for your call center? What are the actual names of the sources (magazines, web-sites, reports, trade associations, conferences)?
- If you have responded to business promotional mail in the past, what was it for and what was the offer?

Tips for Conducting an Effective One-to-One Interview

Dos:

- Prepare for the interview by learning as much about the product and its category as possible.
- Set up appointments in advance. It lends a professional tone to the telephone interview. People are more likely to agree to speak with you by telephone if they can choose the time that is most convenient for them.
- Assure respondents that what they say will be used for internal marketing purposes only and that your discussion will not be quoted in external marketing communications.
- Use a prepared discussion guide formulated from research objectives.
- Ask open-ended questions. By asking open-ended questions, you will have the advantage of hearing the customer/prospect speak freely.
- Follow a line of questioning until you are satisfied that it has been answered or until you understand what the respondent is trying to communicate.
- Ask probing questions whenever feasible. A probe can be a simple: "Why do you say that?" or "What do you mean by that?"
- Regularly summarize and "play back" what a respondent is saying. Reflecting back to the respondent what he or she has said ensures that the interviewer accurately grasps the problem. Reflecting back also builds rapport between the interviewer and respondent, which can lead to better depth and breadth of information.
- Record (with the subject's permission), and later transcribe, the interviews. It is nearly impossible to conduct the interview effectively and take notes at the same time. Interviews are a great source of headline ideas. Therefore, it is important to audio-tape or videotape your interviews for later review and/or transcription.
- Confirm your appointment the day before the interview.

Don'ts:

- Do not ask leading questions. Ask questions in the most neutral way possible. For example, ask "What strengths and weaknesses do you perceive this product to have?" instead of "You must like this product because you purchased it. Tell me how you have benefited from it."
- Do not suggest to the respondent through verbal or nonverbal cues (e.g., smiling or frowning) that there is a correct or preferred answer to any question.
- Do not be bashful about asking for clarification if you are confused or may have misunderstood a response. It wastes time and energy (and is quite difficult) to track down a respondent after an interview to clarify his or her comments.

Analyzing Data from One-to-One Interviews

The SWOT and the one-to-one interview processes will provide you with a long list of business problems and product benefits. You and your research team must make some tough choices to select the four or five major problems. Identifying these helps your creative team focus on developing concepts that address the important issues.

After your research team has completed and individually documented each of the interviews, I suggest you summarize the data in three different documents: a response summary, a message map, and a message map narrative.

A response summary is a consolidation of the responses into a single document. This document is formatted so that each question is followed by all interviewee responses to that question. It enables you to see the variety and frequency of answers provided for any given question.

A message map is a visual presentation of ideas and thoughts that shows their relationships to one another (see Figure 4.2). The purpose of creating a message map is to quickly see the major themes that resulted from the one-to-one interviews, plus any key phrases, words, or ideas associated with each theme. Unlike a linear summary, a message map enables the direct marketer and the creative team to get a snapshot of the marketplace.

The message map narrative discusses the four or five key problems and frustrations your customers face and the key benefits driving them to buy a particular product or service, thereby complementing the message map with detail that is helpful to the creative team. For example, an important benefit may be that your product helps companies handle more customer service calls. Letting the creative team know that the "problem" is "explosive growth" helps them put the creative in the right context. Without this information, the creative team might have assumed prospects needed to streamline customer service to reduce costs or to deal with a limited labor pool.

One-to-One Interviews as the Springboard to Creative Concept Development

The S.U.R.E.-Fire planning process is effective because creative campaign ideas come directly from and are validated by the marketplace. After you have completed all the strategic planning steps and the one-to-one interviews, you are in a position to engage in creative concept development. This is where the fun begins—in the conceptualization and development of lead generation campaigns.

Figure 4.2 Message Map: Snapshot of Marketplace Hot Buttons

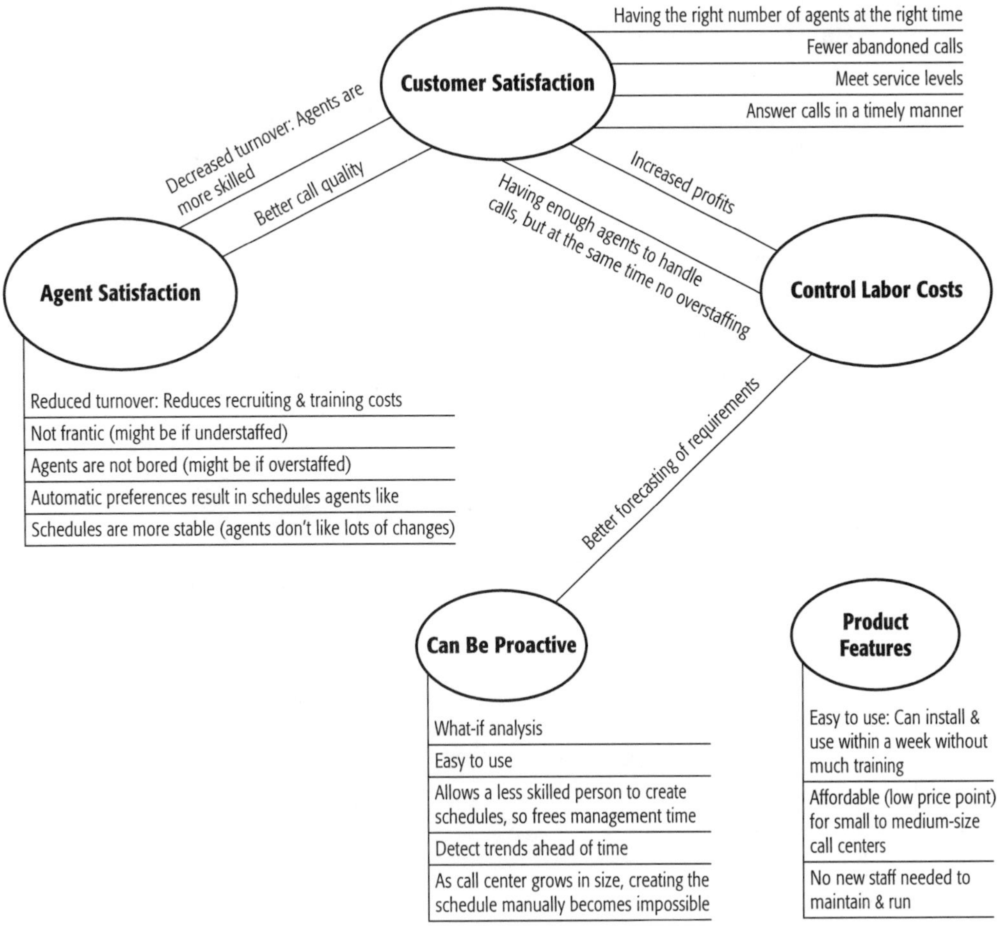

Customer Satisfaction

Having the right number of agents at the right time

Fewer abandoned calls

Meet service levels

Answer calls in a timely manner

Decreased turnover: Agents are more skilled

Better call quality

Increased profits

Having enough agents to handle calls, but at the same time no overstaffing

Agent Satisfaction

Control Labor Costs

Reduced turnover: Reduces recruiting & training costs

Not frantic (might be if understaffed)

Agents are not bored (might be if overstaffed)

Automatic preferences result in schedules agents like

Schedules are more stable (agents don't like lots of changes)

Better forecasting of requirements

Can Be Proactive

Product Features

What-if analysis

Easy to use

Allows a less skilled person to create schedules, so frees management time

Detect trends ahead of time

As call center grows in size, creating the schedule manually becomes impossible

Easy to use: Can install & use within a week without much training

Affordable (low price point) for small to medium-size call centers

No new staff needed to maintain & run

Blue Pumpkin Software: Reprinted with permission.

Because the initial goal was to listen to the market and respond accordingly, you need to thoroughly examine all the information gathered from the one-to-one in-depth interviews, the message map narrative, and the message map. Then develop a list of problem/solution situations and begin to develop creative concepts for each situation.

In contrast to the analytical portion of the S.U.R.E.-Fire planning process, which is time-consuming but not hard, the creative development process can be challenging. Concept development requires the combining of many different types of input and ideas into a single, totally new idea. The goal is to create something distinct, relevant, appealing, involving, engaging, and compelling. If you do not feel comfortable with creative conceptualizing or are not expert in the fundamental principles of direct response marketing, I suggest you seek a professional creative resource.

It is imperative to develop many ideas before evaluating them. If you are directing creative development, make sure you develop a creative concept for each major benefit statement on your message map. Also, don't begin editing or criticizing your creative concepts too soon. The purpose of a creative exploratory step is to give yourself, or your creative resources, the freedom to explore every possible idea that is relevant to the message map and to findings from the one-to-one interviews. There will be time to edit and refine concepts later, but at this stage of the process it is important to let the imagination run wild. Figure 4.3 contains the creative concepts that were developed from the interviews and message map.

Figure 4.3a
Creative Concepts: Be Imaginative, But Stay on Message

Blue Pumpkin Software: Reprinted with permission.

Figure 4.3b

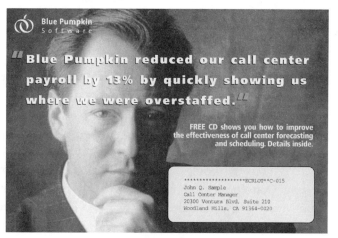

Blue Pumpkin Software: Reprinted with permission.

Figure 4.3c

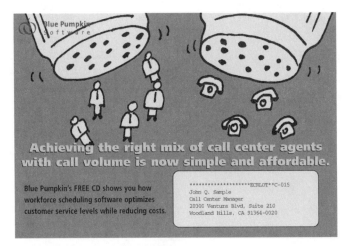

Blue Pumpkin Software: Reprinted with permission.

Figure 4.3d

Blue Pumpkin Software: Reprinted with permission.

Figure 4.3e

Blue Pumpkin Software: Reprinted with permission.

Figure 4.3f

Blue Pumpkin Software: Reprinted with permission.

Summing Up

Primary research enables you to get close to the market so you can gain insight into customers' and prospects' unique business issues. After you have spoken to representatives from your market and know their problems, it is much easier to develop appropriate creative concepts.

Understanding your marketplace allows you to direct future copy development, evaluate creative concepts, and fully understand the dynamics involved in the purchase of your product or service. Used properly, primary market research reduces your risk, helps you avoid costly marketing mistakes, increases response rates, and improves your return on investment. In this chapter, you examined three of the six steps to Understanding for Empathy: how to orchestrate and conduct one-to-one interviews, how to summarize and analyze data from one-to-one interviews, and how to use research for creative concept development. You also saw the benefits of combining qualitative and quantitative research and the importance of setting research goals. The next chapter examines the last three steps to Understanding for Empathy, in which you will learn how to use qualitative and quantitative market research and how to collect the evidence needed to create a winning marketing campaign.

LISTENING TO THE MARKET TO REDUCE YOUR RISK

It is the disease of not listening, the malady of not marking,
that I am troubled withal.

—WILLIAM SHAKESPEARE
King Henry IV, Part 2
Falstaff

For the past fifty years, general advertisers have relied on market research to help evaluate and refine messages, images, and offers. In my experience, business-to-business marketers often feel they do not have the time or funds to use market research. I have found, though, that when business-to-business direct marketers borrow and combine the methods of general advertising, they can avoid costly mistakes, reduce guesswork, and maximize their opportunity for success.

Interpreting Qualitative and Quantitative Research

This chapter details steps four through six of the Understand for Empathy phase. You will learn how to use qualitative focus group research to expand your understanding of purchase behavior and key market trends. You can also gauge awareness levels, and perceptions of your company and of your competitors. Most importantly, the focus groups will help you evaluate the effectiveness of and interest in your advertising concepts, messages, and offers. You will next learn how to use the quantitative research method of mail-based surveys to measure market interest in your product category, and the relative importance of the product- and company-selection criteria. You will also identify the advertising image, message, offer type, and the title most interesting to your target audience.

Used in tandem, qualitative and quantitative research reduce your marketing risk and increase the probability of implementing a winning lead generation program. Although some might argue that you do not need both methods, I have found that each has important and complementary benefits. If you rely solely on focus groups, you run the risk of basing decisions on a very small sample size. Also, your findings are subject to group bias. Doing two, three, or four focus groups does not eliminate the qualitative character of this research method. On the other hand, merely doing a quantitative study such as a survey leaves you only with hard numbers to interpret; you miss out on the rich insights you can gain from observing focus groups and on the insights available from brainstorming ideas. You can spot trends with your focus group studies and validate these trends during your quantitative survey. This one-two research combination allows you to make important marketing decisions with a high degree of confidence.

Using Focus Groups to Evaluate Concepts and Gain Insight into the Buying Process

Focus groups help you gain insight into your target customers' attitudes, beliefs, and buying habits. They also provide a forum for monitoring participants' reactions to your advertising messages, headlines, creative concepts, and offers. Focus groups typically include eight to twelve people with similar target-audience characteristics. Participants are asked to come into a research center, where they are observed while carrying on a one- to two-hour conversation with an experienced moderator.

Focus groups help you evaluate whether your intended advertising messages resonate with your target market. You and your creative resources can hear firsthand how your target market thinks and feels about your product category. You see and hear how people interact with your creative concepts. Do they understand them? Do the concepts grab their attention? Do they motivate the reader to find out more? You will gain a richer, deeper perspective about market trends, issues, and developments.

Focus groups can be held live, locally, or nationally using teleconference tools. Thus, you can speak to your target audience in a given city or gather representatives from across the country. Internet conferencing also allows you to hear viewpoints from across the country all in one meeting.

Focus groups also have downsides. They are not statistically valid because the sample size is so small. Making important marketing decisions based on the answers of just a few individuals is risky. Also, participants influence each other's opinions; you may not get a true reaction, because some participants are being swayed by others. This dynamic is known as "group think," and most groups suffer from it in one form or another.

Focus group observers, such as creative resources, tend to use comments and phrases heard during a group to justify preconceptions. For example, if one person in the focus group says, "Using green tomatoes is a great creative idea," and someone on the marketing team had a similar thought, there is a tendency to project this statement onto the entire marketplace as the truth. Focus groups are also time consuming. Depending on the product and the influence of regional factors on the buying process, you may need to run focus groups in several cities around the country. This translates into time and travel costs.

Preparing an Effective Focus Group

Conduct at least two focus groups to help balance any group bias and to determine whether trends are consistent between groups. I recommend that you schedule your focus groups at least one week apart, because it gives you time to absorb the information from the first group and make adjustments or improvements in your creative concepts before the next group meets. There are three major steps to prepare for a focus group study: selecting a facility and moderator, developing a recruitment screener, and developing a discussion guide.

Selecting an Appropriate Facility and Moderator

I suggest you use a professional research facility and moderator. These can be found in the Yellow Pages under Marketing Research. A professional facility provides you with a room that lets you observe participants easily. This is important during the creative evaluation portion of the process.

Facilities work with many different moderators, and they can refer you to a professional. Moderators know how to control a group, how to probe for answers, and how to get the most from participants during the session.

Professional facilities can also recruit participants for your study. Proper recruitment of participants is essential to high-quality results. If you talk to the wrong people, you will get the wrong answers.

The Recruitment Screener and Criteria for Participation

The recruitment screener is a document that specifies the kind of individuals you want as participants in your focus groups. The screener gives the recruiters criteria for participation, including desired job titles, job functions, company size, and industries. The criteria should mirror the characteristics of your target audience. Your recruitment screener also specifies the dollar amount you will pay participants as an incentive. Obviously, the higher the position of the person you need to recruit, the greater the incentive should be—senior executives are offered a greater incentive than office managers. After the screener is developed, it is given to recruiters at the research facility so they can find individuals who match the criteria.

The recruitment process must be monitored. Communicate frequently with the recruiters so you'll know if they are running into any trouble and to confirm that the people they are recruiting meet your criteria. For example, if the recruitment process is taking longer than anticipated because people do not want to participate, you might need to increase the incentive to make participation more attractive.

Compiling the Discussion Guide

When recruitment is under way, you will need to prepare a discussion guide. The moderator will use this guide to lead the group. It will be similar in certain ways to the guide developed for your one-to-one interviews, and should be updated to integrate any important findings from the one-to-one interviews. Remember, the research process continues to evolve as new information or questions arise. At a minimum, your discussion guide should strive to understand perceptions of your product, motivations and barriers to purchasing the product, and the communication effectiveness of potential advertising messages and concepts.

Your discussion guide should contain sections dedicated to the "sort testing" of messages, creative executions, and offers (described later in this chapter). As part of the focus group process— but before you begin the sort testing—I suggest giving participants ranking sheets for recording their answers prior to open-ended discussion. Writing down rankings before open discussion helps limit bias generated by other people's opinions. It also helps approximate people's quick and immediate reaction to direct mail creative—as if they were sorting through their mail. Figure 5.1 shows the discussion guide used in focus groups for Blue Pumpkin workforce forecasting and scheduling software.

Who Should Observe Your Focus Groups?

Every member of the marketing team can benefit from attending the focus group. It gives everyone an opportunity to hear from the marketplace and to discuss participants' reactions. Anyone involved in the decision-making process for a campaign —typically product managers, campaign managers, copywriters, art directors, account executives (if using an agency), and media directors—should attend.

Figure 5.1 Focus Group Discussion Guide: Call-Center Workforce Forecasting and Scheduling Software

Objectives

- Learn which direct mail envelopes, headlines, and offers have the most stopping power and why.
- Determine the key business problems faced by the target audience.
- Gain insight into the relative importance of customer satisfaction versus agent satisfaction versus cost reductions.
- Ascertain the target audience's perceptions regarding how workforce forecasting and scheduling software can solve their business problems.
- Understand whether the marketplace has a perception that workforce forecasting and scheduling software is too complex and costly to install and use.

Warm-up (10 min.)

- "I'd like to start off by going around the room and introducing ourselves. Please tell us your name, your title, size of your call center (how many agents), the type of call center (inbound, outbound, customer support, sales), and whether you are an 'internal' call center or an 'outsourcer'."

Copy Test

- Have participants rank **headlines**. (Have them fill out yellow ranking sheet.)
  "Which one of these headlines is most attention-getting to you? The one that grabs your attention the most would be ranked a 1, the second most, a 2, etcetera."
- Have participants rank **envelope images**. (Have them fill out orange ranking sheet.)
  "I want you to imagine that you're in your office, and that you're about to be handed your business mail for the day.
  "Please take one of these that I'm passing around (envelope containing six images).
  "Now open it up. Each of these envelope images represents a different piece of mail. I want you to sort through these images just as fast as you would if it were your business mail. And I want to know which envelope would you be most likely to open, and which you would be the second-most likely to open? Please record your responses on the ranking sheet."

Discussion

- "How do you currently schedule and forecast agent work hours?"
  Probe: "How well is this working for you? Are you satisfied? Why? Why not? How could it be improved?"
- "What impact do you think a workforce forecasting and scheduling system would have on your business?"
  If customer satisfaction, agent satisfaction, or reducing costs are mentioned, probe.
  "For those who do not see benefits, why not?

Figure 5.1 Continued

> "Which forecasting and scheduling systems (software) have you heard of and what have you heard?"
> - "What prevents your company from purchasing/using workforce forecasting and scheduling software?"
>   If cost or installation complexity is mentioned ask: "If you could have an affordable system fully operational in a week, what would be standing in your way?"
> - Discuss **headline and envelope image** rankings.
>   Why ranked high or low? Is it the wording or the image that they like or dislike?
> - Have participants rank **offers**. (Have them fill out blue ranking sheet.)
>   Why ranked high or low?
>   "Are there any other offers, not listed here, that would grab your attention?"

Close and thank!

Blue Pumpkin Software: Reprinted with permission.

How to Get the Best Results

To get the best results from your focus groups, meet with your moderator and review the discussion guide before the focus group session. I prefer to meet a few days before the group to allow plenty of time to make changes based on the moderator's suggestions. Show the moderator the creative concepts. Let him or her become familiar with the messages you are going to test. Provide a last-minute refresher about the product and the goals for the group. Review the discussion guide with the moderator to help him or her understand the nuances or key issues that should be probed during the session. Make sure the moderator knows to probe whether a benefit or product feature is "attention-grabbing" as opposed to "sale closing." You need to understand this so you can focus your lead generation campaign on the variables that are most important during the initial phase of the buying process.

After the group begins, set aside your biases. Don't go into the group expecting to validate ideas or opinions. A focus group is research, and it is important to observe the session neutrally. You might find support for your ideas, or you might not. Either way, remember that you are looking to build up evidence for implementation.

During the group, when your moderator is asking participants to evaluate your creative concepts, watch how each person in the group looks at each concept. See how they sort through your concepts, how fast they take in the idea. If you have never seen people sort through ads or direct mail packages, you will be surprised how little time you have to grab a reader's attention. After the discussion about the

---

Dos and Don'ts for Focus Group Implementation

Here are some things to do—and not do—when supervising a focus group study.

Dos:

- Take notes. Write down key ideas you had not thought of previously.
- Look for trends. See what the group members agree on, and what they disagree on. See what the major differences are and try to understand what is behind them.
- Listen intently. Observing a focus group requires you to listen through the words. Sometimes it takes a few sentences for a participant to articulate his or her key thoughts.
- Work closely with your moderator and facility management to make sure the right participants have been recruited and that your moderator understands the goal of your study.
- Record sort test rankings on paper prior to discussions.

Don'ts:

- Do not look for words, ideas, or thoughts from the group that substantiate your preconceived beliefs or point of view. This tendency is the main problem with focus groups. Collect all the evidence, then draw conclusions.
- Do not make a decision based on focus groups; the sample size is small, and results are always influenced by biases and group dynamics. Remember the great marketing lesson provided by the introduction of New Coke: During focus groups, people preferred the taste of New Coke. However, a strong loyalty to the Coke brand manifested as a zealous loyalty to Coke Classic after the launch of New Coke.

---

creative begins, listen for what grabs participants' attention or creates curiosity to read or see more.

If you believe an area has not been covered, or if you feel one individual is dominating the group, send a note to the moderator so he or she can adjust accordingly. While the group is in session, you can send notes to your moderator to help guide the discussion. Sometimes one person dominates the conversation, and you want to hear from others. Sometimes, important issues come up that you want to hear more about.

The Power of Sort Testing in Evaluating Creative Concepts

The primary objective of running focus groups within the S.U.R.E.-Fire planning process is to gain insight and evaluate the communication effectiveness of your creative before implementation. You want to reduce your risk and guesswork by listening to the market. In a focus group, this is accomplished with a research technique known as sort testing. Sort testing forces participants to rank various choices in response to a given question. Here is how you would test direct mail concepts during a focus group:

1. Label each creative concept with a simple alpha code for easy identification.
2. Place one of each creative concept in a large envelope (one envelope per participant). When you put the concepts in each envelope make sure they are in different orders to reduce order bias.
3. Pass out the large envelopes to the focus group participants.
4. Ask each participant to pull all the concepts out of the large envelope.
5. Direct the participants to look quickly at each creative concept as if it were a piece of direct mail that had arrived in their mailbox. Then instruct them to sort through the concepts and put them in order, ranging from "most likely to open first" to "least likely to open."
6. After the sort process is completed, ask participants to write down their sort order.
7. Finally, hold a discussion with the group about the rationale for their rankings of each concept. This is where the focus group can provide significant benefits, because you learn why a concept is liked or disliked. You will see how messages speak to or hit the hot buttons of your participants, and you will find out if your graphic images or ideas mean anything to your target market. As mentioned earlier, it is important to record the rankings before open-ended discussions to avoid bias. If you are testing direct response print advertising, E-mail messages, or banner ads, the same sort process is used.

During the discussion of each creative concept, the moderator's goal is to find out what made participants say they would open or read a particular creative concept as opposed to another concept. Therefore, you want to ask questions such as: What caught your eye? What stopped you or drew your attention to the ad or envelope? Why didn't you like a certain concept? It is especially important to determine whether the graphic image, the wording, or the combination attract participants' interest. Generally, a creative concept can be effective or ineffective for one of three reasons: wording, imagery, or benefit. If you don't understand the participants' reactions to each of these components, you may not be able to determine whether a concept can be improved or whether it should be eliminated altogether. Perhaps the wording or creative idea is good, but the overall benefit the concept conveys is not important. On the other hand, the benefit may be important, but the wording is ineffective or participants do not care for the graphic image. In other cases, participants may favor a concept, but on further discussion you discover they like the graphic for personal reasons, not because it is relevant to the product story or benefit.

Using Sort Testing for Message and Offer Evaluation

In addition to creative concept sort testing, ask focus group participants to fill out ranking sheets for messages and offers. On these sheets, participants will sort, in order of "most interesting" to "least interesting," the following: various headline approaches; titles for offers, such as guides or white papers; and offer categories, such as value-add websites, CDs, return on investment (ROI) calculators, books, and seminars. Note that, because of the small sample size, this type of sort testing is not statistically valid. It does, however, help you see if there are any trends that might influence final creative selection. Figure 5.2 is an example of a ranking sheet.

How Focus Groups Improve Direct Response Creative

Observing numerous research studies of direct mail envelopes can teach you a great deal about how people react. I have learned that an envelope gets only a half second of a reader's time. Further, I have learned from observing focus group studies that people react best to advertising concepts that are:

- **Clear.** They want a concept that makes sense. They do not want to work hard to figure it out.

Figure 5.2 Focus Group Message Ranking Sheet

Which of the following headlines grabs your interest most?

Please rank 1 = grabs interest most, 6 = grabs interest least. *Please use each number only once*.

_____Balancing call-center staff levels is now surprisingly simple and affordable.

_____Achieving the right mix of *call-center agents* and *call volume* is now simple and affordable.

_____Reduce your call-center payroll by 13 percent by quickly identifying where you are overstaffed.

_____Find out how to increase customer satisfaction, minimize abandoned calls, and reduce hold times.

_____Frustrated with call-center forecasting and scheduling? . . . announcing an easy and affordable solution.

_____Avoid the $10,000 coffee break . . . find out how correct scheduling of breaks can save 14 percent of your payroll budget.

Blue Pumpkin Software: Reprinted with permission.

- **Compelling.** They are willing to read a concept that calls to them and pulls them in.
- **Believable.** They are skeptical and therefore need specifics and facts that are believable or proven.
- **Readable.** People do not read ads for fun or entertainment, and they do not want to work at it. They want to be able to read messages quickly and easily.
- **Attention-getting.** Unless you grab people's attention, they will skip right over your marketing communication.
- **Relevant to their issues.** One of the best ways to get someone's attention is to call out to his or her specific pain, frustration, or problem.

I have also learned that people do not want to be reminded about their problems as a way to gain their attention. Instead, they want to see or hear about the positive outcome that they would gain from using your product or service. They want to see the benefits they will realize. For example, compare Figure 5.3 to Figure 5.4. Figure 5.3 says, "Put paper in its place," and shows a bored, overwhelmed woman. Readers did not like this. Conversely, they liked Figure 5.4, the "basketball" concept, with the headline "Think Strategy." It shows a positive image of people working as a team, because the product solution eliminates the need to handle details.

Whenever a creative concept strays too far from the original benefit or promise, becomes too cute or clever, or uses irrelevant images, the target audience misses the point. Clever for clever's sake, without being in context of the industry or category, does not communicate effectively. Again, compare Figure 5.5 to Figure 5.6. Here you see that "walk the dogs in the park" is a clever attempt to communicate an analogy, but readers found it irrelevant. In comparison, readers of "relaxed man on computer" said that they all wanted to be like the person shown in the illus-

Figure 5.3
Unsuccessful Creative
Concept: Dwells on
the Problem

The Ultimate Software Group, Inc.: Reprinted with permission.

tration. Although every advertiser wants to gain the attention of its target audience, doing so with outrageous, offbeat, irrelevant, weird, or wacky images, ideas, or concepts rarely delivers long-term value or profitable results.

Figure 5.4 Successful Creative Concept: Shows a Positive Outcome

Figure 5.5 Unsuccessful Creative Concept: Too Clever

Figure 5.6 Successful Creative Concept: Relevant and Easy to Understand

What to Do After Your First Session

Immediately after completing your first focus group session, you should summarize the key findings. Bring the moderator and all observers together. Write down the common agreements, disagreements, and trends. Write down the ranking of the messages, offers, and creative. Note what participants understood and did not understand. Then, in the week between the first and second focus group sessions, make any necessary changes to the discussion guide or creative. You might have found that some ideas are not communicating effectively, so you need to improve them. You also might have found some new areas you want to learn more about. You might have discovered that some of your messages were not on target or that some of your concepts were misunderstood or badly received. Be careful not to make too many changes between groups. You might find it necessary to eliminate the two worst-performing concepts before the next research study and add one or two concepts that cover an area of concern or interest that came up during the first group. Then, following the method described previously, conduct your second group.

What to Do Once Focus Group Studies Are Completed

After both groups are completed, identify where the groups as a whole agreed and disagreed. Try to understand what might have caused these similarities or differences. Perhaps the demographics (title, company size, or industry) of the two groups are slightly different. In some cases, the changes you made to the creative concepts might have changed your results.

Now, compile and summarize your findings. Your goals in sorting through the information are to identify the six creative concepts that communicate most effectively with the participants, confirm the key fears and motivators in the marketplace, and understand or confirm how your product is bought (specifically, who initiates the sales process). You should also identify any additional key words and phrases that should be integrated into the copy and fifteen to twenty key pieces of information you want to measure quantifiably during the survey step of the research process. Look for trends such as the common problems or frustrations mentioned most by participants, creative concepts most commonly liked by participants, message statements that they liked, and how the ranking of message statements differs from that of the creative corresponding concept.

Keep in mind that at this stage of the S.U.R.E.-Fire planning process, you only have two sources of *qualitative* data. The first is your one-to-one interviews, which provide a range of ideas and messages. The second is your focus group studies, which begin to identify winning—and losing—concepts and ideas. The sample sizes are simply too small to generate statistically valid information, however. Therefore, don't rush to judgment about any particular concept, message, or offer.

Using Quantitative Mail-Based Surveys

The final step in the research process is implementation of quantitative research in a mail-based survey. This step enables you to collect a large amount of marketing data, which will validate your findings and help you make crucial marketing decisions with confidence. The specific research goals of the survey are to identify which creative concepts have the highest readership or opening rates, which message statement or headline is of most interest, and which offer title and offer category have the most appeal. You also are seeking guidance from the target market about purchase interest for a given product category and awareness and perception of your product and the competition's product.

While there are many kinds of quantitative research methods, including Internet-based surveys and telephone surveys, the S.U.R.E.-Fire planning process relies on a mail-based survey. Mail-based surveys enable you to show creative work and get it ranked. I use them because many lead generation campaigns use direct mail advertising, and I want to gather results from people who have a bias toward opening direct mail packages. A mail-based survey collects marketing data and measures results from the same people you will be mailing to in the future. A typical survey asks fifteen to twenty research questions—you can collect a large amount of useful marketing information.

How to Construct an Effective Mail Survey Instrument

To be effective, a survey should look easy to fill out at first glance. It must get participants involved quickly by first asking simple demographic questions. It capitalizes on this momentum by posing more in-depth questions further into the survey.

The most important aspect of a survey is the wording of the questions. They must be neither leading nor biased. Most questions in my mail-based research surveys are multiple-choice, which makes it easy for people to respond and also simplifies tabulation. The danger of the multiple-choice format is that you might bias results by unintentionally leaving out a possible answer. But by the time you are ready to write your survey instrument, you have completed your SWOT analysis, one-to-one interviews, and focus group studies, so you should have a comprehensive understanding of marketing issues and be able to provide all reasonable answers to the questions.

When preparing your survey, write separate questions to help you evaluate each aspect of your creative concepts. For example, have one question that lets participants rank various headline statements, another that ranks various advertising concepts, and another that lets participants rank key copy points. The answers to these three questions will help you determine the best combination for a creative concept. Also, the responses will help you determine why concepts included in the survey worked or did not work for your target audience. For example, was it the headline or the graphic image that attracted the target?

Also, ask about the target audience's major business challenges. Write two questions, worded slightly differently. In one, confirm the importance of a given business problem; in the other, confirm whether the market perceives that your product or product category can help solve that problem. (See Appendix A, questions 7 and 15.)

As with your one-to-one interviews and focus groups, make sure your survey questions are relevant and important and can produce information that is a basis for action. Stay focused. Ask questions that will affect the decisions you need to make to implement your direct marketing programs.

Think through the order of your questions. You want to organize your survey so there is a logical flow and grouping of questions. The following is the order I use in S.U.R.E.-Fire mail surveys:

- **Demographic questions.** These confirm who the survey respondents are. What are their titles? What size company do they work for? What industry is their company in? This information prepares you to look at specific segments and their answers to other questions in the survey.
- **Product interest and purchase intent questions.** These identify the market interest in your product category as well as purchase plans for the product category. They help you determine if you have a high- or low-interest category. Response rates are generally higher for high-interest product categories.
- **Product awareness and perception questions.** These identify whether the market knows your product and your competitors and help you measure its perception (positive, neutral, or negative).
- **Business-issues questions.** These help you determine and confirm key business problems. The answers to these questions are useful in directing copy writing.

- **Message-ranking questions.** These help you determine what specific message or headline most appeals to your target audience. Because headlines affect readership, identifying the most-read headline will affect your campaign results.
- **Creative concept ranking question.** This one helps you determine what creative idea most interests your target market. The answer helps you confidently determine which campaign idea you should develop.
- **Offer category and title questions.** These questions help you verify the title and type of offer that most interests your target audience. The more the target wants your offer, the better your opportunity to generate sales inquiries.
- **Desire-to-be-contacted question.** Though generating leads is not the purpose of the survey, it makes good direct marketing sense to let people indicate they are interested in hearing more about your products, even at this stage of campaign development.

How to Use Mail Surveys to Pretest Creative Concepts

Because the primary goal of the S.U.R.E.-Fire planning process is to reduce creative guesswork and marketing risk through market research, all of my surveys include sort testing of creative concepts. Participants are shown six creative concepts and asked to rank them in order of most to least appealing.

The wording of this question varies, depending on whether you are testing advertising concepts or direct mail concepts. For direct mail packages, I use this wording: "Look at the six images below. Assuming these arrived in your mailbox today, which one would you be most likely to open first? Which one would you be most likely to open next, and so on." For print advertising, I use different wording: "Look at the six images below. If you saw these advertisements in a magazine, which one would grab your attention the most and would compel you to read the body copy?"

The answers to this question will help you determine which of your creative concepts or direct mail envelopes has the most draw for your target market. When testing a direct mail campaign, I study envelope surfaces because 95 percent of direct mail is delivered with the address surface facing up. If the surface graphics and copy grab readers' attention and motivate them to open the envelope, the package has a much greater chance of generating a strong response rate.

The same principle is true for print advertisements. If you show headlines and their corresponding visuals to target audience members and ask them to rank the concepts in order of readership, you will see which idea has the most appeal—before you invest in an expensive media campaign.

Some advertisers and most agency creative teams consider this research strategy heretical. They find it absurd to ask target audience members what creative concept they would read. This crucial decision about creative is supposed to be left to the creative genius. What does the target audience know about advertising? Ask, and your market will tell you what you need to hear. Appendix A (question 8) is an example of the format used to rank creative concepts. As a businessperson, which advertisement or direct mail campaign would you rather invest your money in? One that when shown to a thousand people caused 55 percent to say they would read it first, or another that your agency's creative director thinks is marvelous and potentially award-winning, but that you barely understand? Never forget the words of David Ogilvy: "Advertising people who ignore research are as dangerous as generals who ignore decodes of enemy signals."

Using Mail Surveys to Identify Compelling Offers

The mail survey also is used to identify compelling offers. One question in the survey asks the participant to rank, in order, which types of offers they find most appealing. See Appendix A (questions 12 and 13) for the format used to rank offers. This helps you answer a variety of marketing questions: Should you invest in an exclusive educational value-add website or a new product video? A new multimedia CD? Does the market want educational white papers? What is the value of giving away a book? Is the market interested in attending Internet conferences?

When writing your survey, include separate research questions on hard offers such as on-site consultation or free estimates and soft offers such as a free gift or free demo CD. These two offer categories have drastically different appeals. You will not get an accurate result by combining them into one offer evaluation question. Offer selection will be discussed in more detail in Chapter 6.

As part of your offer research, I recommend testing the names or titles of potential offers. The title of your offer is like a headline. Research shows that headlines increase readership by 40 percent, so identifying the most compelling offer title will help you generate maximum response. Figure 5.7 is an example of an offer title question. Appendix A, at the end of the book, is an example of a four-page survey.

How to Select a Sample for Your Mail Survey

When conducting a mail survey, you need to measure the interest level from a sample population that is representative of the population that you will be marketing

Figure 5.7 Mail Survey: Testing Offer Titles to Generate Maximum Response

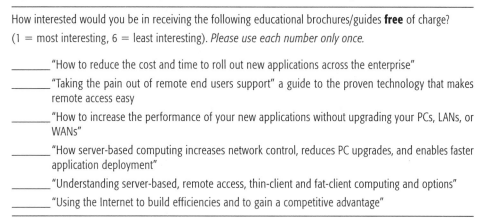

How interested would you be in receiving the following educational brochures/guides **free** of charge?

(1 = most interesting, 6 = least interesting). *Please use each number only once.*

_____ "How to reduce the cost and time to roll out new applications across the enterprise"

_____ "Taking the pain out of remote end users support" a guide to the proven technology that makes remote access easy

_____ "How to increase the performance of your new applications without upgrading your PCs, LANs, or WANs"

_____ "How server-based computing increases network control, reduces PC upgrades, and enables faster application deployment"

_____ "Understanding server-based, remote access, thin-client and fat-client computing and options"

_____ "Using the Internet to build efficiencies and to gain a competitive advantage"

to in the future. Therefore, you want to select your sample population from the mailing lists of the magazines that you plan to advertise in or from other mailing lists you plan to use. You need 500 to 1,000 names to conduct your study; you will probably need to pay a "minimum charge," but the investment is wise considering the value of the marketing information you will collect with these names.

Other populations to consider for your survey are past responders and current customers. Because these individuals represent the types of prospects you want to attract in the future, measuring their opinions about your campaigns can be valuable. I recommend you track responses from each sample population so you can compare results between populations.

Targeting of the mailing list is extremely important to the survey process. If your target market comprises companies with more than three hundred employees, send the survey only to people in companies that meet that criterion. I find the mailing list is often the weakest link in the survey process. A bad list will likely result in a large percentage of completed surveys from outside your target. This may render your survey results unusable.

Don't discount the importance of the list because the quantity is so small or because you have not yet reached campaign implementation. There are entire books on sample size selection and statistical validation of research studies, but my rule of thumb is this: You need at least 50 responses from a sample set to have a 90 percent confidence level in the data you receive. Usually, my mail survey population sizes are between 500 and 1,000 individuals. Response rates range from 15 to 45 percent depending on the quality of the list, the length of the survey, and the incentive I use.

This provides 150 to 450 responses. If you want to do extensive subtabulation analysis, I suggest using a larger sample size so the subtabs end up with at least fifty responses in each.

How to Send Out Your Survey Packages

Research companies use everything from a closed-faced personal letter package to double postcards. The S.U.R.E.-Fire mail-based survey package was created to have high impact, high opening rates, high credibility, and high response rates. It is composed of a simulated express-pack outer envelope, a personalized one-page letter, a four- to six-page questionnaire, a postage-paid response envelope, and a cash incentive.

There is a wide variety of simulated overnight envelope designs. More information can be obtained from Response Mail Express. The amount of the cash incentive varies depending on the survey's degree of difficulty and the professional level of the target audience. The higher the target audience is on the corporate ladder, or the more professional their status (e.g., doctor or CEO), the greater the cash incentive. The minimum is $1, but cash incentives can go as high as $20.

Tabulating Your Results and Reading Your Findings

The fastest way to tabulate your survey results is to send them to a professional tabulation company that will enter all the responses from each question into a database and provide you with a set of statistical reports. Within these reports, you will find the quantitative information that becomes part of your final decision process.

It is advisable to have the tabulation company run significance tests against cross-tabulations. These reports show whether there are any statistically meaningful differences between the responses of your subgroups. For example, cross-tabulations can identify whether different job titles respond differently to your messages, or whether reactions to the creative concepts differ between those who plan to buy your category of product within twelve months and those who do not plan to buy.

Be sure to learn how to read your reports, so you know how to identify what answers have true statistical significance. Figure 5.8 is an example of a typical report from Data Specialists, Inc., a tabulation company. The report shows that 48.4 percent ranked image Q as their first or second choice, and 44.6 percent ranked image J as their first or second choice. Both were statistically significantly ranked higher than the other four images (correlate to columns A, B, E, and F).

Figure 5.8 Tabulated Survey Results: Images Q and J Are Significant Winners

Workstation Data Protection & Recovery

Q.8 Based on the wording and images on the front of the envelopes, which one would you be most likely to open?
200+ PC Workstations In Company/All Information Systems Titles

		Image N End Users (A)	Image L Old Jim (B)	Image Q Sit Back (C)	Image J Upgrade PCs (D)	Image G Flying Saucer (E)	Image H Mouse Click (F)
Total Responses		92*	91*	91*	92*	91*	92*
Top Two Box	#	25	16	44	41	28	27
	%	27.2	17.6	48.4ABEF	44.6ABEF	30.8B	29.3B
Rank 1		10	8	25	24	15	8
		10.9	8.8	27.5ABF	26.1ABF	16.5	8.7
Rank 2		15	8	19	17	13	19
		16.3	8.8	20.9B	18.5B	14.3	20.7B
Rank 3		16	7	12	15	20	21
		17.4B	7.7	13.2	16.3B	22.0B	22.8B
Rank 4		13	14	11	20	15	15
		14.1	15.4	12.1	21.7	16.5	16.3
Rank 5		21	19	12	6	18	16
		22.8D	20.9D	13.2	6.5	19.8D	17.4D
Rank 6		17	35	12	10	10	13
		18.5	38.5ACDEF	13.2	10.9	11.0	14.1
Bottom Two Box		38	54	24	16	28	29
		41.3CD	59.3ACDEF	26.4	17.4	30.8D	31.5D
Mean		3.23B	2.54	3.98ABF	4.03ABF	3.58B	3.45B
Std. Dev.		1.66	1.67	1.78	1.65	1.61	1.55
Std. Err.		0.17	0.17	0.19	0.17	0.17	0.16

Proportions/Means: All Columns Tested (10% risk level). Overlap formulae used. *small base
Source: Stac Software, Inc.: Reprinted with permission.

When looking at these reports, go back to the objectives of the mail study. See what percentage of respondents plan to buy, change, or upgrade to your product category. This will tell you their product interest. Look at the answers to your ranking of message or headline tests. What headline ranked the highest? How does this headline compare to the result found in your focus group? Look at the image rank test. What two images had the highest rankings? Again, are these findings consistent with your focus group study? Are they consistent with your headline tests? What offers had the highest rankings? What offer titles had the highest rankings? What business problems did the survey report as most important to solve? Are your best images and headlines consistent with this finding? Analyzing your research results is like looking at a jigsaw puzzle. You need to examine all the pieces separately, then put them together so you see the big picture they create. Interpret your results carefully. It takes experience to read research findings, which can be contradictory.

Summing Up

The combination of qualitative focus group studies and a quantitative mail study can help you avoid PFA (pluck from air) creative selection and give you confidence that you are investing your marketing budget in winning creative concepts. These two research methods help you listen to the market to gain deep understanding and empathy about its problems and business issues. They enable you to hear, see, and measure your target audiences' reactions to industry issues and advertising approaches before you make substantial marketing investments.

The S.U.R.E.-Fire planning process uses market research to identify the best offers for your lead generation campaigns. Offer testing is important because, regardless of the quality or impact of a creative concept, it will not generate response without a compelling offer. Being able to select a compelling title for your offer before you implement your campaign can improve your results by 20 to 50 percent.

These research methods, though not a silver bullet for business-to-business direct marketers, provide a high degree of insurance. Market research gives you the data you need to make your marketing case with confidence. When all the evidence points in one direction toward one concept, one message, and one headline, it is much easier to proceed. Time and again, I find research studies crucial to the development of effective lead generation campaigns. The results companies receive from S.U.R.E.-Fire planning and its research process justify the time and money invested.

RESPONSE GENERATION

The fastest way to improve your results is to change your offer.

—BOB HACKER
President, Hacker Group

In the "R" phase of the S.U.R.E.-Fire planning process, you concentrate on the sales process. The *R* stands for response generation, response management, and relationship marketing. The next three chapters focus on why offers generate sales inquiries, and how to select the best offer for your lead generation campaigns. You will also learn how to sort and qualify sales inquiries so your salespeople can focus their time on the highest and most productive opportunities. Nurturing sales inquiries using relationship marketing will then be discussed. This will maximize your campaign's long-term return on investment.

I equate the processes of response generation and response management to fishing in the ocean. Think of your target market as the universe of potential buyers, all swimming in an ocean called the marketplace. These potential buyers swim all over. Sometimes they are grouped in schools, as when you have many buyers at one large company location. Sometimes they are swimming on their own. Fish are hard to spot in the ocean, just as sales prospects are hard to spot in the marketplace. Even with sophisticated sonar, or sophisticated targeting methods, sales prospects are elusive. Nets, however, are extraordinarily effective.

The most productive way to capture sales leads is with the marketing net of your campaign. In studying response generation, you will learn that the type of offer and hardness or softness of the offer in your campaign are the weave of your marketing net. Your offer affects the quantity and quality of your catch. The additional concepts of response generation—why people respond to advertising messages and how to leverage these motivations—will also be reviewed in depth.

Like fishermen who sort the catch as it is hauled on board, the business-to-business direct marketer must sort sales inquiries by size, opportunity, and interest. This process, which I call response management, includes lead capture, qualification, distribution, and fulfillment. Response management will be covered in Chapter 7.

The final concept within the "R" of the S.U.R.E.-Fire process is relationship marketing. To describe relationship marketing, I expand the fishing analogy to include stocking a lake. This lake is your sales database. It is stocked with sales prospects of all sizes and in various stages of buying. Some prospects are newcomers, some are fingerlings, and some are almost ready to buy. All prospects in the lake need care, attention, feeding, and nurturing to stay alive. In Chapter 8, you will learn how to use the strategies of relationship marketing and electronic permission marketing to maximize conversion of sales inquiries to sales.

Why Generating Sales Leads Is Important

When you look at the cost of a field sales call, it quickly becomes clear why you need to generate sales leads. The latest reports indicate that field sales cost a company $500 to $650 per call. One of the reasons for this high expense is the time value of top sales executives, who earn $75,000 to $250,000 a year. Thus, their time is worth $40 to $130 an hour. Making your highly talented sales professionals perform low-level sale prospecting activities is a waste of their time and your financial resources. Given the high cost of a sales call, you want your salespeople putting their time and talent to best use—face-to-face with prospects.

One of the most effective methods for getting your sales force face-to-face with prospects is direct response advertising. Direct response advertising is any communication designed to motivate readers to take immediate action. There are three basic strategies of direct response advertising for sales lead generation:

- Make a compelling offer that provides an unwavering reason for a reader to take action immediately. This concept will be covered in this chapter.
- Capture the responses generated in a database for further qualification, follow-up, and long-term nurturing. These concepts will be covered in Chapters 7 and 8.

- Deliver your sales message or advertising to an audience of likely suspects. This concept of targeting will be discussed in Chapter 9.

One of the largest factors influencing the results of your direct response campaign is your offer. To generate response to your E-mail, direct mail, print advertising, or banner advertising, you need an offer. You must give a clear reason to respond now. Without this one element, your creative message might make an impression, but it will not make the phone ring.

One reason the S.U.R.E.-Fire planning process is effective is that it directs you to seek out and test offers. In the first two phases of the planning process, you are constantly searching for, testing, and measuring the types of offers that most appeal to your target. You are developing and testing offer titles, or offer concepts, that solve the problems of your target market. In this third phase, you take what you learned and combine it with knowledge about how to evaluate offers to make a final selection for your campaign.

The Physics and Psychology of Lead Generation

To generate sales leads, it is imperative to learn what motivates people to respond to solicitations. Why do people respond to the offers made in direct response ads? This education is extremely useful in the design and management of direct response marketing communications materials. To learn how to use advertising communications to motivate human behavior—to move a person to action—we turn to lessons from the fields of physics and psychology.

Heating Up the Offer

Two laws of physics can be used to illustrate the dynamics of lead generation. Sir Isaac Newton's first law of motion states that bodies of matter do not change their motion in any way except as the result of forces applied to them. A body at rest remains at rest unless an external force acts upon it. This is true in lead generation, too. Think of an audience of sales suspects as bodies at rest. People sitting at their desks, looking at their computers, answering phones, and working on important projects or tasks may be potential customers, but they are not moving in your direction. They have no reason to stop what they are doing and call you or visit your website.

To create motion in these sales suspects, you must provide some sort of force that will propel them into action. The force is your offer, and the motion occurs when a suspect contacts you, calls you, faxes you, E-mails you, or returns your reply device. Your offer and the promotion of your offer are how you create the desired response—the suspect's motion.

The other illustrative physics principle is the first law of thermodynamics, which states that energy can neither be created nor destroyed. Further, the more heat you put into a system, the more internal energy the system has. In the realm of lead generation, you could consider your offer to be the heat source. Your offer is how you transfer energy (heat) from your creative team to the sales suspects (the system). The greater the offer—the more powerful, the larger, the more compelling—the greater the energy transfer and the more suspects will respond to your advertising communication.

These concepts illustrate a fundamental truth of direct marketing: The offer used in a direct response advertisement is the single most important factor affecting response rates and, consequently, the volume of sales leads. I have met too many direct marketers who fail to understand or believe in the power of the offer to generate sales leads. Instead, they believe that if they just talk about their products and their company it will be so persuasive that prospects will come rushing. Unfortunately, prospects do not care about you or your product. They only care about themselves. They are looking for solutions to the problems they face daily. They want to know first if you can help solve their problem. Then they will determine if you or your product can be of service to them.

All readers or viewers of advertising communications approach advertising from the perspective of "what's in it for me." They say to themselves, "You interrupted me. Are you bringing me anything of value—anything I need to know?" This is a further rationale for why it is imperative, throughout your direct response advertising message, to sell the reason to respond rather than your product or company.

Before you can sell someone your product or service, they must identify themselves. The offer motivates them to raise their hands and indicate interest in your product category. All too often, marketers are unwilling to invest time, money, or energy into finding, creating, or promoting a motivating offer. Then they wonder why their campaigns fail. They are in a hurry to implement a program and so enamored of their product that they do not want to be bothered with the details of fulfillment. As a result, they fail to take care of that which is most fundamental to success: the motivator of action, or the offer.

So when you are responsible for generating sales leads, focus on promoting your offer as the solution to your target audience's pains before you start selling them your company and product. This is why the S.U.R.E.-Fire planning process requires that you invest time and energy in Understanding for Empathy (Chapters

4 and 5) to uncover the problems your sales prospects face. Using this information, you can identify or create compelling offers, which, in turn, will increase your success ratio.

Motivating Response Behavior

Advertising created by the greatest direct response marketers of our time, Bob Stone, Jim Caples, and David Ogilvy, shows three great psychologists at work. The ads they created reveal a solid understanding of what motivates human behavior. They leveraged this knowledge to create compelling advertising messages.

One core motivator of human behavior is that people do not want to be left out. They do not want to miss out on an opportunity, be left behind, or be deprived of something someone else has. As children, we wanted what all the other kids had. We wanted to be included. We as marketers can capitalize on this aspect of human nature by making our offer exclusive and limited. For example, the offer might state, "If you are among the first 500 to respond, you will receive a free book." The idea is to act now or miss out. This is called a *limited time offer*.

Another aspect of human nature is that people are always striving to satisfy their basic human desires. People want to save money, time, and energy. People want to solve their problems, avoid hassles, and gain the admiration of others. For example, businesspeople are constantly in search of new software solutions that can increase their company's profit or improve efficiency. Andi Emerson identified "8 Basic Human Needs to Increase Mailing Response" for *DMA Manual* (January 1978). All people want to make money, save money, win praise of others, help children and/or family, save time and effort, impress others, have fun, and improve themselves. These basic values hold true for every person throughout every stage of life.

Effective direct response offers tap one or more of these basic desires as lures to motivate behavior. For example: "Act now! Request a free guide that will show you how to gain the praise of your president by saving your company 20 percent on all office supply purchases—while improving the productivity of your fellow employees."

The third psychological aspect of offers is to position your offer as the reward a prospect receives in return for taking action or responding. People want to be appreciated and thanked for their time and consideration. Your offer is the thank-you gift you provide to a suspect for investing time in learning more about your company. For example, you could write in your letter, "This special gift is yours, because I know your time is valuable. Please accept it as my thank-you gift for investing your time to learn more about XYZ Company." I have heard in focus groups conducted among technology professionals that this audience likes to collect free T-shirts. They see these T-shirts as a thank-you gift for looking at a company's marketing materials.

A fourth aspect of psychology that direct marketers can leverage is people's tendency to be motivated by their emotions. Tony Robbins, motivational speaker and author, says, "People move away from pain and toward pleasure." Pleasure and pain are two of the biggest emotional motivators in humans. The more you can position your offer as able to make a reader's pain disappear, solve important problems, or transform his or her pain into pleasure, the greater the desire of the suspect to obtain your offer—and the greater the response. For example, the offer may exhort suspects to respond for a free demo CD that will reveal seven strategies for managing work stress and making their jobs more enjoyable. This offer not only helps them on the job but suggests a personal benefit.

Finally, psychologists know that people make decisions both logically and emotionally. People use both the right and left sides of the brain when they decide to act. Consider the following example. You walk into a high-end department store. As you walk down the aisle, you suddenly see a handsome wool suit or a beautiful silk blouse. You pull the garment from the hanger. You examine the garment, noticing the color, the cut, the fabric, and the maker. "Fantastic," you say. You hold it up to yourself and imagine how handsome or beautiful you will look wearing it. You try it on and look in the mirror again. "Wow," you say to yourself, "I feel great. I look attractive." You wonder how much the garment costs. Your hand finds the price tag. You gulp when you read the three-digit sales price. But after you catch your breath, you realize that you can wear the garment for several years. You tell yourself, "It's from the finest maker. It will last a long time, and I'll get a lot of use out of it. How wonderful I feel having it on." Next thing you know, you have bought the garment. It is in the bag you hold in your hand as you leave the store. "This was a great purchase," you say.

This same sort of emotional and logical reasoning occurs in business marketing. People are people. When businesspeople are at their offices, struggling with purchase decisions, they are thinking not only about themselves and how your product will benefit them but about their job situation and what is good for the company. Ideally, you as the business direct marketer want to promote both logical and emotional arguments and the personal and organizational benefits readers can derive from your offer. Here is an example of this kind of offer: "Respond for this free white paper to learn ten ways to cut manufacturing costs and demonstrate to management your leadership abilities." The offer provides the respondent with specific workplace benefits and goes on to promise an emotional benefit—that of being a recognized leader.

The Three Types of Offers for Business-to-Business Marketers

There are three general categories of offers for business marketing: hard offers, soft offers, and "super-soft" offers. In general, harder offers will result in fewer responses, lower cost of fulfilling the responses, and higher response quality. Conversely, the softer the offer, the more responses and the more information you can collect on responders to populate your database for future sales efforts. Therefore, the softer the offer, the more important it is to have a response qualification system and resources in place to capture and qualify responses.

The Hard Offer

A hard offer is one that allows prospects to indicate that they have a high interest in being contacted or speaking to a sales representative immediately. Hard offers identify people who are ready to move through the sales cycle.

Hard offers must overcome human hesitation to meet with salespeople. People are afraid of salespeople. They fear they will be sold, strong-armed, or persuaded to buy something they do not want. People do not like to say no to a salesperson. When you use a hard offer in business-to-business direct response advertising, the people who do respond generally have a high interest in solving their problem right away. Responders to hard offers are commonly classified as hot sales leads. They have an immediate need and want to speak to a salesperson right away. Examples of hard offers used by business-to-business marketers include the following:

- Please have a salesperson contact me.
- Please call, because I would like a price quotation.
- Call me to set up a time for a free needs assessment consultation.
- Contact me for a product demonstration.
- I'd like a free thirty-day on-site trial.

Hard offers in business-to-business marketing are used when the strategic planning process indicates that it is not economical to develop a large prospect pond. Hard offers are useful when the sales force needs qualified sales leads quickly. Although research shows 45 percent of all sales inquiries from any source convert to a sale within twelve months (see Chapter 7), some marketing organizations simply do not have the ability or resources to handle longer-term prospects. They must generate sales leads from prospects who want to buy right now. The direct marketer must be willing to accept the trade-off that hard offers have a lower response rate but a higher lead quality than soft offers. The downside of hard offers is that they reduce the number of long-term additional sales opportunities that are the natural result of alternative lead generation strategies.

The Soft Offer

A soft offer is an offer once removed from the actual sales situation. It helps you identify prospects with various levels of buying interest and bring them into your sales process. To continue with the fishing metaphor, a soft offer is the shiny lure that, by design, appeals to a prospect's personal desires. By its nature, content, title, or structure, it attracts prospects that have an interest in the product category you are selling. The reason to use a soft offer is to capture a large quantity of sales prospects in your marketing net so you can sort and nurture them and then convert the inquiries into revenue.

There is a wide range of soft offers for business-to-business marketing. I use white papers, case studies, article reprints, demo CDs, education (including live or Internet-based seminars), books, book-chapter reprints, educational guides, data sheets, technical specifications, videotapes, product configurators, slide guides, self-assessment guides, and kits (compilations of several of the elements above). An offer that is growing in importance is an invitation to information-rich or value-add websites. These websites contain educational information, interactive sections, and help the visitor know about your product or category.

The three keys to making a soft offer desirable are its credibility, its title, and its content. Regarding credibility, people do not want offers that are just sales hype. The source of your offer—the writer or publisher—lends it credibility and value. The more unbiased it is, the more relevant and useful, the more desirable the offer. The title of your offer is as important as the title of a book or an advertising headline. Titles create curiosity and interest to pick up the book and read it. In the context of lead generation, you are trying to create an offer title that motivates readers to pick up the phone or go to the Web to receive the offer you are promoting. For a soft offer to be effective, its content must be unique and valuable. Ideally, it will leverage the basic human motivators discussed previously.

The Super-Soft Offer

The third category of offer is what I call the super-soft offer. A super-soft offer might or might not be related to the product being promoted, but it always appeals to the basic emotion of human greed. It consists of a gift, bonus, premium, or sweepstakes. Examples include free T-shirts, clocks, calendars, pocket knives, multitools, trips, personal electronics, and cash giveaways.

Business-to-business direct marketers use super-soft offers to lift overall response to a campaign, to add excitement to a campaign, or to create a sense of urgency within a direct response advertisement. I find super-soft offers effective when promoted in limited quantities or for a limited time, because they leverage the motivator of not wanting to miss out. For example, "The first five hundred people to go to www.xyzcompany.com will receive a free clock."

The benefit of a super-soft offer is that it generates a larger response than a hard offer or a soft offer. Surprisingly, a super-soft offer does not always decrease lead quality. A human resource client reported that when it used a free Human Resources Franklin Planner as a bonus offer, the response rate doubled with no decrease in lead quality. The company's conclusion was that the super-soft offer, the Franklin Planner, was the motivation needed to make prospects respond. I have discussed the topic of a super-soft offer and its impact on lead quality with several other clients, and they report similar results. I strongly suggest you measure for yourself the impact of a super-soft offer on your response rates and lead quality.

Super-soft offers are effective because people are greedy. The super-soft offer acts like a large fishing net—one that sweeps up a great many short-term qualified sales prospects and many long-term sales opportunities, as well as responders who simply want your giveaway and are not interested in your product. On the other hand, the high volume of prospects and the revenue received from these leads more than pays for the super-soft offer and the cost of discarding the poor-quality responses. Before you use a super-soft offer, you must create a cost-effective qualification process to separate qualified prospects from those who just wanted the free gift.

Super-soft offers are exceptionally effective when you want to build or enhance a prospect database. Promoting a super-soft offer in a campaign that also includes a well-structured reply device or Web form can help you collect valuable marketing information. Super-soft offers can also help you collect names for relationship-based, one-to-one, or permission marketing campaigns.

One type of super-soft offer that I have found effective for business-to-business marketing is a sweepstakes. Here are some tips for promoting a successful sweepstakes offer:

- Try to make the sweepstakes relate to the product or product story. However, cash is always a draw.
- Plan to collect qualification data on all sweepstakes entries.
- Pretest your sweepstakes prizes to make sure they appeal to the target audience. You can do this during your focus groups or in your mail surveys, as discussed in Chapter 5.

- Rely on a sweepstakes administrator who knows the laws, regulations, and restrictions for sweepstakes implementation in your geographic area.

Figure 6.1 is an example of a six-part sweepstakes program for Mitsubishi Monitors. The grand prize was a $50,000 diamond, which tied back to the company's product, Diamondtron monitors. The use of a sweepstakes helped generate a 14 percent response per mailing.

Choosing a Hard, Soft, or Super-Soft Offer

The challenge you face as a campaign manager is determining when to use what type of offer. This question compels you to balance lead quantity (volume) with lead quality. Figure 6.2 shows that, in general, the softer the offer, the greater the response to the offer—but also the greater the decline in lead quality.

Figure 6.1 Diamond Sweepstakes Generated 14% Response

Mitsubishi Electronics America, Inc.

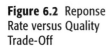

Figure 6.2 Reponse Rate versus Quality Trade-Off

To determine whether to use a hard or soft offer, you must know how many leads your system can handle based on your sales resources and lead capture capabilities. This is why you do the number crunching in the strategic planning phase of the S.U.R.E.-Fire planning process. Here is where the results become valuable. If you have a large sales organization and need to generate thousands of sales leads per month, you need to use a soft offer strategy and test it in combination with super-soft offers to see which strategy optimizes results. If you have very few salespeople and do not want to waste time or money following up and working long-term leads, a hard offer strategy is preferable.

Your offer is the weave of a fishing net. The softer your offer and the more you give away, the tighter the weave of your offer net and the more "fish" (prospects) of all sizes you haul in. If you use hard offers, your offer net has a very loose weave— the only prospects you will capture are those who are large and ready to be caught.

The closer your offer brings the prospect to a salesperson, or the more effort prospects must put out to receive your offer (e.g., write in their name, answer ten qualification questions, mail back a card), the higher the quality of sales leads. The more effort prospects expend to receive your information, the more interested they are in learning about your product or solution. Businesspeople do not complete time-consuming steps unless they are interested. For example, when I wanted to find out about a software technology for my company, I visited the software company's website, filled out the inquiry form's seven qualification questions and completed a registration form for the company's Internet conference. Then I called the sales representative. I invested about thirty minutes in filling out forms because I wanted information right away and was highly interested in learning about how this vendor's product could benefit my company.

In contrast, the easier you make it for a prospect to respond and the more distance you put between responders and salespeople, the higher your response rate and the lower your lead quality. In addition, the more valuable your offer is to the prospect, the higher the response. An example would be to offer a free guide explaining how to save $50,000 in long-distance phone charges; prospects simply need to drop a prefilled reply card in the mail or go to a website where all their information is prefilled. These options are so easy that even though prospects may not be highly interested in your product, they will request your offer. Because there are no obstacles to response, you will generate a larger response than if it were time consuming or difficult.

Surprisingly, hard and soft offers are not necessarily mutually exclusive. You can present both a hard and a soft offer in a direct response mail package and let prospects decide for themselves (see Figure 6.3). This combination offer strategy makes it possible to cast a wide net with the soft offer while using the hard offer to identify qualified prospects quickly.

Only experience and calculations can help you determine the right type of offer for your business. Figure 6.4 is a general comparison of the impact of the three

Figure 6.3 Combining Soft and Hard Offers: Increase Response and Identify Qualified Prospects

The Ultimate Software Group, Inc.: Reprinted with permission.

offer categories on a lead funnel. Lead quality is defined as percentage of total responses that are qualified leads. In this example, the lead quality with a hard offer is twice (60 percent versus 30 percent) the lead quality with a soft offer. In addition, the overall cost of a hard offer promotion is less ($150,000 versus $170,000). However, the soft offer cost per qualified lead is 43 percent less than the cost with a hard offer, because the added cost of fulfillment ($20,000) is more than offset by a higher quantity (600 versus 300) of qualified leads. In addition, because of the rule of long-term sales lead follow-up, the ultimate number of soft offer closed sales tends to be greater (180 versus 90). Soft offers yield greater response and greater revenue, but soft offers are not for every company. If you do not have the budget or infrastructure to handle all the sales leads, if the cost of fulfillment outweighs the return on investment, or if your situation does not permit you to invest in long-term lead development, soft offers are not for you.

Before you launch a lead generation campaign using your chosen offer, it is valuable to set internal expectations about lead quality. If you choose a super-soft

Figure 6.4 Cost-Effectiveness Comparison Between Hard and Soft Offers

	Hard Offer	Educational Soft Offer	$10,000 Sweepstakes Offer
Number of contacts	100,000	100,000	100,000
Response range	0.25%–1%	1%–3%	2%–10%
Average response	0.5%	2%	6%
Responses	500	2,000	6,000
Qualified lead %	60%	30%	15%
Number of qualified leads	300	600	900
Program investment	$150,000	$150,000	$150,000
Cost per qualified lead	$500	$250	$167
Fulfillment for offer	$ –	$20,000	$30,000
Cost per qualified lead/with offer burden	$500	$283	$200
Percentage less than hard offer	–	43%	60%
Close rate on qualified leads	30%	30%	30%
Number of sales from promotion	90	180	270
Average sales price of product	$15,000	$15,000	$15,000
Total revenue generated	$1,350,000	$2,700,000	$4,050,000
Total promotion cost	$150,000	$170,000	$180,000
Approximate return on promotion investment	9%	16%	23%

offer, you should let everyone know lead *quantity* will be high, but there also will be a wide range in lead *quality*. In the next chapter, you will learn to use a filtering system to avoid sending poor-quality leads to the field.

How to Select Your Response Generation Offer

When selecting an offer, consider your sales process and the product to be sold. The goal of any response offer is to reel in the maximum number of responders interested in buying your product. Therefore, your direct response advertising communication (E-mail, print, direct mail, banner ad) should demonstrate how your offer is going to be *of service* and *of value* to prospects. When selecting a lead generation offer, find one that ingratiates you with prospects and helps prospects understand the benefits of your product or service. You want offers that by their nature, title, content, or structure either educate, inform, or demonstrate how your product can get rid of a prospect's business problem—or how your product can help a prospect achieve business and personal goals.

Based on the physics and psychology of why people respond to offers, the following guidelines will help you evaluate offers for lead generation campaigns. The main guideline for selecting an offer is this: *Is the offer so compelling that people will stop whatever they are doing, go to the Web, pick up the phone, walk to the fax machine, or drop a card in the mail to request it right now?* If you cannot say yes to this question with conviction, you need to find a different offer.

The offer should be unique and exclusive. A strong offer sets in motion the psychological dynamic of exclusiveness. An effective offer is one that is only available from your company. It is human nature to want something that is one of a kind or in short supply, so making your offer both exclusive and time limited, or quantity limited, encourages fast response. For example: "Respond today for this exclusive report on health care benefits. Only 250 copies are available. First come, first served."

Is your offer related to the product being promoted? Does your offer bring prospects into the top of the sales funnel? The purpose of promoting a response offer is to start the sales cycle; it is too costly to generate response otherwise. Does the offer provide information that will help prospects solve their problems? Does it educate them on a category of business related to the service you sell? Does it tell the salesperson which prospects want immediate attention? And, when someone requests your offer, what will qualify the respondent to speak to a salesperson? For example: "Order this free demo CD. See how automatic personnel scheduling can reduce the time you spend scheduling staff by 50 percent over manual methods."

People want offers that appeal to them. They want something novel, something that is interactive, something they can use, try out, play with, experiment with, get answers from. People want offers that are of interest to them. You want your offer to provide new insight or information that can help prospects solve their problems. Remember, everyone has too much to read and too much to do. Select an offer that is so desirable and motivating that people will stop what they are doing to request it. A good offer would be a thirty-second self-assessment survey that enables prospects to see for themselves the top three alternatives to a given problem. A bad offer would be twenty pages of text that contain no new information or insights.

Does the offer recognize the relationship between you and your sales prospects? When you are fishing for new sales prospects among people who do not know you, your offers need to lure them by offering enticing education or by appealing to their self-interest. For example, you could use an educational white paper with a bonus gift to attract new prospects. When you are trying to generate leads from a group of prospects who have responded to you before, prospects who are in various stages of the buy cycle, your offer needs to be tailored to their place in the buy cycle. Are they still in the research phase and need more comparative information? In this case, you could use Internet conferencing as an offer because you can tailor the content to meet the audience's needs. Are your prospects ready to buy but afraid to purchase? In this instance, you might need to offer a price discount or some sort of no-risk guarantee.

Your offer must be relevant to your suspect's job and daily business problems. A compelling offer helps remove the suspect's problem. It helps suspects do their jobs better, gives them useful information, and provides guidance or a reference they can use frequently. Does your offer contain information a suspect must have or would use daily?

The offer should also match the tone and image of your company and product, who you are, and what your product stands for. For example, if you are a Wall Street investment firm, offering free trips to the circus is incongruous with your product and company image. Selectica, an Internet-selling solution for complex products, achieved offer congruency by promoting a free guide, "The Seven Secrets to Selling Complex Products over the Internet."

A good offer can be understood at a glance. The benefits of its content are easy to describe and can be photographed or illustrated clearly. People make a decision to respond within one or two seconds of seeing the offer. If you are going to motivate them to stop what they are doing and request your offer, they must quickly see a reason to act. Effective offers are visually strong, and their benefits are easy to grasp.

The cost of fulfillment (sending your offer to prospects) can quickly add up to a large marketing expense. When selecting your offer, consider the cost and packaging required to ship it. These days, instead of shipping educational offers such as guides or white papers, business marketers are delivering them electronically over the Internet. This reduces the cost and time to send the offer to responders. However, in my research studies, I have found that although prospects like the ease and speed of accessing electronic documents, they still like to see glossy color brochures and sales materials. The paper stock, print quality, and design used in these hard-copy materials communicate the company's size and credibility. It is wise to have both hard-copy and electronic versions of your offer.

Response Generation Offers in Action

Educational Guide Approach

Citrix Systems provides an example of an educational guide developed for and targeted at information technology and networking professionals (Figure 6.5). A leading author in the industry was commissioned to write the guide, the title of which was tested before publication. The contents were designed to educate the reader about this valuable new technology. This offer is effective because the content is original, and the guide is exclusively from Citrix Systems. It is easy to ship, easy to show, and can be made available in electronic format.

Educational Free Video Approach

Welch Allyn provides an example of a promotion for a free video that was produced to educate pediatricians and optometrists about the value of vision screening for two-, three-, and four-year-old children (Figure 6.6). The video explains why this test is important and why

FIGURE 6.5 Educational Guide Offer: Relevant, Exclusive, and Easy to Promote

older methods and tools such as eye charts are not accurate. The approach to vision screening presented in the video uses a new technology from Welch Allyn, a world leader in medical products manufacturing. This offer is effective because the video is educational to physicians. It is easy to show and ship. Further, a videotape has value, which makes the offer appear special. Of course, this tape is available exclusively from Welch Allyn.

FIGURE 6.6 Free Video Offer: Educational and Innovative

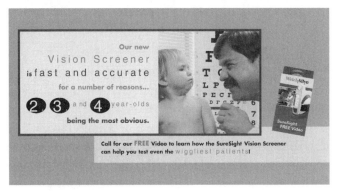

Welch Allyn: Reprinted with permission.

Educational Internet Conference Approach

Blue Pumpkin provides an example of a promotion for an Internet conference (Figure 6.7). Attendees hear educational information over the telephone and watch the presentation over the Internet. The offer's value is communicated through the title of the event, the quality of the speakers, and the take-away value of the information. To maximize attendance levels, a six-month subscription to *Call Center News Service* was offered, free, to anyone who signed up for the event. In this case, the offer is the event. It is exclusive. You need to be invited to attend. The information is unique and relevant. The information is valuable, because you are hearing from experts in the industry.

FIGURE 6.7 Internet Conference Offer: Relevant and Educational

Blue Pumpkin Software: Reprinted with persmission.

The Power of the Free Trial

It is human nature to be curious but fearful about new products or services. Businesspeople naturally want to learn more about new products and services that come to market. They also are skeptical. They are fearful about making a mistake, about being misled, and about buying the wrong product. Businesspeople approach new products with caution, and they want to try them before they make a commitment to buy. This is why sampling is an effective marketing strategy. If you can get people interested in your product by giving them a small taste or sample, they are more likely to buy your complete product at full price because they know what it can do. They have proven your advertised claims to themselves without you pressuring them. You have helped them set aside their fears.

The offer strategy of "letting people sample the goods" keeps the risk of the sales transaction where it belongs—in the hands of the seller. Consider this classic sales story: A man wants to buy a horse for his child. He is approached by two horse traders. Both sellers present their horses to the buyer as being gentle, well trained, and easy to handle. They each emphasize that the horse is so gentle it would be ideal for a child. The first horse trader makes the man this offer: "Buy my horse for $100. If, at the end of the week, you don't like the horse, just return him to me and I'll give you your money back in full." The second horse trader makes the buyer this offer: "Take the horse home with you for a week. I'll give you a bale of hay, his halter and bridle, plus a bucket for his water. Try the horse out. Be sure to have your children ride him. At the end of the week, if you like him, you can pay me. But if you don't like him, I'll take him back with no questions asked. No matter what happens, I want you to keep the halter, bridle, and bucket as my way of saying thank you for your consideration."

Which horse trader made the sale? Which would you buy from? Which type of marketer are you? This simple example illustrates the persuasiveness of spelling out all the details and benefits of your offer. It also shows how sampling keeps the risk with the seller until the buyer is 100 percent satisfied and ready to purchase.

The psychological principles of curiosity and fear create an opportunity for business-to-business direct marketers who can offer trials or samples of their product. For example, McAfee, which in 1998 became Network Associates, revolutionized the software industry by giving away its virus protection software. Management knew that if people installed the product and tried it, the company's sales reps could call thirty days later and convert trial users into customers.

There is a downside to free trials. Many people request a free trial and never actually try the product. You may spend money shipping and following up on free-trial requests but not generate high conversion. Free trials can also slow down the sales process. It takes time for people to try and evaluate a product. The longer they have to decide, the longer they can stall the buying decision. When using a free trial offer, you need a well-crafted follow-up process as well as a product that is easy to try without much explanation.

The Power of Personalized, Value-Add, Interactive Websites

One last aspect of human nature that business-to-business direct marketers can capitalize on when selecting an offer is people's desire to have something personal. Personalizing your offer or personalizing your response channel appeals to people's self-interest, and it increases response rates. People love things that have their names on them. People want things that have been reserved just for them. Claude Hopkins, advertising expert and author of the book *My Life in Advertising & Scientific Advertising*, tells the story of two booksellers. One bookseller sent out a letter promoting the quality of his leather-bound books. The other seller sent out a similar letter but promoted the fact that his books had the buyer's name imprinted in gold letters on the cover. The first bookseller went out of business, and the second sold hundreds of thousands of books.

The Internet has reintroduced personalization to business-to-business marketers. Now using E-relationship marketing software from companies such as MarketFirst and Responsys, direct marketers can set up a personalized website for each person who responds to a given promotional campaign. In your lead generation campaigns, you can direct readers to visit a website. When they enter their pin number, they are greeted personally. Once a prospect goes to this site, their profile information is populated for easy response, updating, and as a platform for all future correspondence. The contents of the site and how it educates become valuable to the responder. These sites use technology to help a prospect identify the right product given their needs using case studies, self-assessments, and return-on-investment (ROI) calculators. In addition, you can collect a prospect profile through click stream tracking. As a prospect interacts with the site, information is collected to serve as the foundation for future permission-based E-communication.

Summing Up

Response generation is the first and most important step in lead generation. Without response, you have no sales leads. Response generation means you, as a direct marketer, must be ready to go fishing. You need to determine where to fish and what bait to use to attract prospects. Do you cast a tightly woven net into an ocean of suspects, knowing you will haul in sales opportunities of all sizes? Or do you only go after the big fish, knowing you are making a quantity-for-quality trade-off? It is essential to stock your prospect pond (database) with sales leads for future sales development efforts.

This chapter also emphasized the particulars of making an offer; the key role of the offer and its positioning and merchandising in generating immediate action among sales suspects; and the difference between hard, soft, and super-soft offers and their impact on response rates. Marketers also need to be conscious of how to pick the best offer for a program and how to match the offer to the buying process to advance a sale.

The next two chapters will focus on the other half of response management, working the sales inquiries. Any smart fisherman knows that after you hook a fish, it does not start swimming toward the boat on its own. It must be worked and reeled in before it can be brought on board.

RESPONSE MANAGEMENT

Lead generation programs are a method devised to bring leads to the sales force and classify those leads so that the sales force knows which lead is "hot," "warm," or "cool." Thus, they can prioritize their efforts and focus on closing more sales, more often.

—BETTE ANNE HUTCHINGS
Partner and Managing Supervisor
Ogilvy-Mather Direct

The second aspect of "R" in the S.U.R.E.-Fire planning process is response management. Response management is central to business-to-business campaigns. You never get a second chance to make a first impression. Proper response management can significantly impact program payoff. Poor response management will quickly cause your program to fail. Too often, I have seen companies spend hundreds of thousands of dollars to develop lead generation campaigns and then neglect the crucial step of response management. Response management is not glamorous, but careful up-front planning, attention to the details, and meticulous thinking-through of the strategy of advancing a prospect toward a sale can reap the rewards that you and your company seek from your direct marketing investments.

In this chapter are some simple and relatively inexpensive steps that make a significant difference in a program's profitability. I am often surprised to see professional direct marketers completely abandon these steps in their haste to generate responses. Consider this real-life example from a manufacturing company: "We get a five percent response, and it's growing," the vice president of marketing said. "The inquiries are coming in by E-mail, toll-free number, and business reply cards. Two people even showed up on our doorstep. It has been five weeks, and we're reaching the peak in the response curve. But sales aren't where we think they should be. What's wrong with these leads?" Although tempted to give the knee-jerk response that she was simply impatient in expecting sales to be in lockstep with the response curve, I probed. "Let's review your response management system before we pass judgment on the inquiries," I stressed. Even when you fish in the right place and use the right bait, it still takes a plan and talent to reel the prospect in, land it, dress it, and prepare it for the table. All the company's effort had gone into targeting the mail to the right group of people and using a "must open" envelope concept. Few improvements were made in the basic structure and operation of this company's response management system. No one thought about the steps needed to convert the prospects into revenue. They just wanted to know why the dollars were not in the bank yet.

Common Response Management Weaknesses

In reviewing this company's response management system, I found weaknesses that are common in other companies' follow-up processes. How many of these problems do you face daily?

- **Poorly conceived response package or web pages.** In the example above, the content was not thought out. No message or image on the fulfillment envelope tied back to the campaign. Nor was there personalization on the letter to show a potential buyer that he or she was important to the company. There was no information included on where to buy the product locally through a sales representative or channel partner. Literature that was not requested was included in the package—the company threw in literature on the entire product line. Photocopied literature was added at the last minute. There was no reply card in the literature package. These same flaws apply equally to your web-based response information.
- **No planning or preparation to handle lead flow.** The inquiries came in so fast and in such high volume that the company fell behind in sending out the response packages. It hired temporary employees to stuff the packages, but fulfillment was taking three to four weeks from receipt of the responder's name.
- **Slow handoff to the sales force.** Responders' names were slow in being transferred to the sales force (either inside or outside people) through the sales force automation software.
- **Sales follow-up activities were not assigned.** Follow-up was not mandatory for either the inside or the outside sales channel, so salespeople took their time following up on the inquiries. Inside salespeople started calling the responders and had a hard time getting through. As a group, the sales-

people decided the leads were poor quality and stopped calling. No one reported this to management, and management did not follow up. Leads stopped going to the outside salespeople, and it was six weeks before anyone noticed the breakdown in the process.

- **Poor communication with sales in the field.** The outside salespeople had not been informed of the lead generation campaign before the launch. They did not have copies of the mailers, and thus the inquiries came as a surprise.
- **Too many leads for too few salespeople.** The amount of response was so great—more than eleven thousand responses in four weeks—that the sales channel was flooded with inquiries. The salespeople eventually stopped calling all but those who appeared to have the most immediate need.
- **Qualified lead systems not established.** Qualified responses (prospects) were not separated and flagged from nonqualified responses. "Immediate need" prospects—defined as having money, buying in less than three months, and wanting to hear from a salesperson—were not queued up for immediate callbacks.
- **Measurement of lead quality absent.** No means of capturing the quality of each sales lead was in place. Marketing focused on the huge response and neglected lead quality, follow-up sales calls, and conversion-to-revenue numbers.
- **Improper budgeting.** No one budgeted for the large response. Literature supplies were reduced, extra labor was needed to mail the response packages, and postage was a sizable expense. This shortcoming was not insurmountable, but it took management by surprise.
- **No long-term continuous relationship marketing campaign.** Because the company wanted sales now, it neither planned for nor implemented a long-term follow-up program. The executives forgot that only 26 percent of all sales inquiries are converted to sales within six months of the inquiry date.

In this example, management criticized the program because the rate of conversion to sales was low despite the high response. Management interpreted that as meaning the program had generated a large number of unqualified prospects. What really happened was that the company had focused solely on generating a large response because it needed immediate revenue. The response overwhelmed its sales systems. Even though there was high demand for its product and probably a large number of qualified inquiries, poor response management put the campaign's profitability at risk.

These are typical problems direct marketers encounter. From program creation to execution, the steps of sales conversion are skipped over too often. Direct marketing success cannot be measured by response rates or click-through rates alone. What is needed is a series of communication and sales processes for managing sales prospects until one of the following four decisions occurs: they buy your product, they buy a competitor's product, they buy something unrelated, or they do not buy anything.

For many products, the sales process can take as little as a few weeks or as long as several years. How the prospect is treated and nurtured during this buying period makes the difference between your success and the success of your competitor. The conversion ratios of sales inquiries over time have been well established in the book *Managing Sales Leads: How to Turn Every Prospect into a Customer* and in extensive "Did You Buy?" research reports quoted in the same book. In this work, Donath, Crocker, Dixon, and Obermayer establish the Rule of 45 as the benchmark projection for sales lead conversion: 45 percent of all business-to-business responders will make a purchasing decision for your product or your competitor's product within a year. Specifically, 26 percent buy within six months and another 19 percent buy within seven to twelve months (see Figure 7.1).

These statistics for business-to-business communications are predictable regardless of the communication strategy (direct response, print ads, trade shows, and even public relations). I have incorporated the numbers into my projections for clients (even with raw response rates of 1 to 10 percent).

Figure 7.1 Lead Conversion: 45% Convert to Sales Within 12 Months

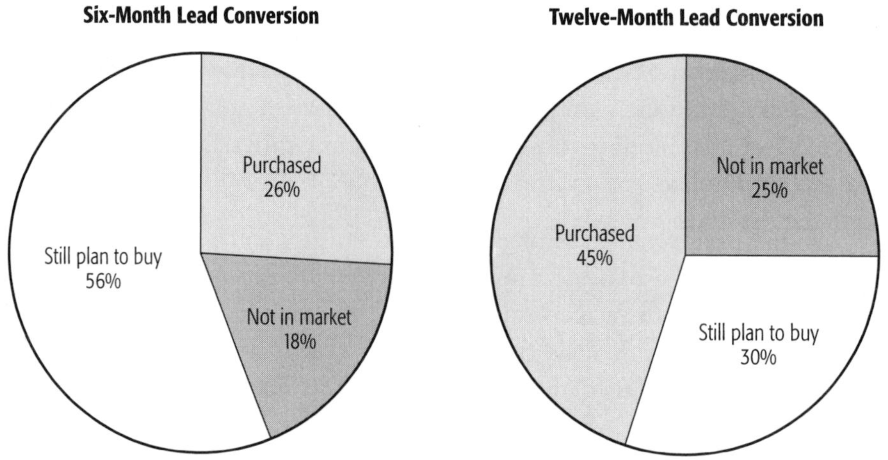

Six-Month Lead Conversion

Purchased 26%
Still plan to buy 56%
Not in market 18%

Twelve-Month Lead Conversion

Not in market 25%
Purchased 45%
Still plan to buy 30%

Source: Did-You-Buy? Study Database. Inquiry Handling Service, Inc.: Reprinted with permission.

Compare these findings to the 1996 study of 40,000 responders from print advertising and press releases conducted by Cahners Business Information. The study showed that within six months, 23 percent of the people or companies inquiring had purchased a product or service advertised from the advertiser or a competitor, 67 percent said they were still in the market planning to buy, and 10 percent said they were no longer considering a purchase. In addition, when they completed an analysis of older inquiries, they found that *of those who made a purchase,* 11 percent bought within three months of inquiring, 17 percent bought within four to six months, 25 percent bought within seven to twelve months, and 47 percent bought more than twelve months after inquiring.

Managing the Sales Inquiry

Let's begin with how to best manage the sales inquiry from lead capture through distribution to the sales organization. In Chapter 8, we will focus on lead conversion strategies. Research has consistently shown that when salespeople are left to their own judgment, they create a personal lead-filtering system that helps them decide who does or who does not receive a follow-up call. Sales lead management expert Jim Obermayer gives seven reasons why salespeople do not follow up on a sales lead:

1. Salespeople do not have a quota for the product.
2. The responder is geographically undesirable.
3. No phone number is on the lead (a big reason for channel partners).
4. No company name is on the lead (three-line addresses are considered home addresses or small businesses).
5. No profile information is included such as need, desire, buying authority, time frame for purchase, interested in lease or buy, or installed products.
6. The responder may have contacted the company before and not bought anything.
7. Sales management does not require its salespeople to follow up on 100 percent of the sales inquiries they receive.

Thus, sales representatives need a reason to overcome their prejudicial thinking regarding sales lead follow-up. If management says follow-up is a condition of employment, most salespeople will comply. For companies that use an indirect channel like resellers, it is a bigger struggle to motivate sales lead follow-up. The hard-to-accept but realistic answer is that motivation must come from the reseller's own desire for profit. Therefore, it is valuable to have an inside telesales or telemarketing department to push the sale and direct the responder to your channel partner.

In Chapter 14 of the book *Managing Sales Leads*, the authors describe how the percentage of people who recall some sales contact after the inquiry ranges from 36 to 43 percent. Roughly one-fifth of responders take the initiative and contact the company a second time rather than wait for a salesperson to follow up.

How to Capture Sales Inquiries

I once heard the president of a $30 million software company say, "I only want responses through our website. If they aren't on the Web, they don't fit the profile of the customer we're trying to sell." He did not want reply cards from mailers, toll-free calls, and other responses. Although he had a successful company, he did not know much about people. When given a choice, some people go to the Web. Some pick up the phone and call you or their own dealer or distributor. Some fill out a reply card. If they are going to a trade show where you will be exhibiting and they know it, some will stop by the booth. The reality is that limiting your response options restricts both response and sales opportunities.

Rules for Lead Capture
- Accept inquiries from all available sources to find all the available buyers. Emphasize a website URL, but be sure to offer toll-free numbers, business reply cards, and fax response.
- Regardless of the "source vehicle" used (business reply mail, toll-free number, Web) you must profile all respondents. Get more than a simple name and address. Find out each respondent's need, desire, time frame, current products used, company size, and industry.
- Don't be afraid to ask many qualification questions. In tests comparing a qualification form with six questions to one with fifteen questions, the response rates and compliance rates between the two cards were the same: 95 percent full compliance.

After you have decided *not* to limit your response options, make sure all portals of entry to your company are ready to receive sales inquiries. Review Figure 7.2 for a simple flow chart showing portals of entry.

Toll-Free Numbers

Make sure the person who answers your phone is qualified to profile the responder, and assure the caller that sales literature will be mailed and a salesperson will be in

Figure 7.2 Portals of Entry: Be Ready to Handle Inquiries

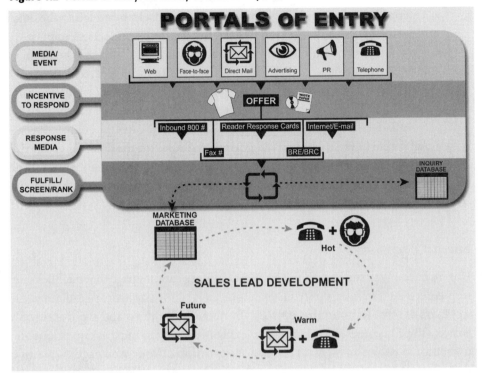

touch. If the person wants to buy, and you have set up the electronic process through the Web, you may direct callers to the Web or to the inside sales group. The most important aspect is to make sure someone is there to answer the phone. If you do not open in California until 9:00 A.M., and people on the East Coast have been trying to call you since 8:00 A.M. their time (5:00 A.M. your time), someone is going to be unhappy. If you have a telesales or telemarketing department, make sure its hours are convenient for your customers—not for the department. Cover the phones when your customers will be calling you. If you cannot do so, consider using an outside service bureau.

Rules for Toll-Free Numbers
- Print the toll-free number at least three times and in a prominent position in the direct marketing piece. Make it especially visible on the reply card. In print ads, place the toll-free number in a prominent position in a second color. Use large type with white space around it.
- Put the word *free* next to the number. Yes, everyone knows it is free, but placing the word *free* next to the number draws attention and prompts the reader to pick up the phone.

- Make sure someone is qualified to answer the phone and profile the caller.
- The profile form should gather information that can be added to the database, such as need, desire, time frame, budget, decision makers, application, buy-or-lease, and installed products. You should also use the profile form to capture source codes that can be used to track results related to lists, offers, and formats. In addition, ask, "Where did you originally hear about us?" This gives you the chance to verify the source of the inquiry (print advertisements, Web banner ads, direct mail, or trade shows).
- Act quickly. Get the phone caller's information into the channel of distribution that day—not the next day or whenever someone happens to think about it. Toll-free callers have urgency and buy at a higher rate than any other responder.

Internet Response

Do you have a Web site but fail to provide a response capture page that qualifies sales responders? An *Orange County Business Journal* (California) article spotlighted the weakness of most websites that only ask for name and address and avoid asking for answers to profile questions. The author explained that you must ask questions and use multiple-choice answers on the response portion of your Web page. A question that must be asked is where the person heard about you. Was it from a direct mail campaign? Was it a print or Web banner advertisement? At a trade show? Does he or she have personal buying preferences?

The Web has changed the way we do business. The majority of hits to your website are not coming from casual cruisers of the Web. The majority of visits are coming from people actively looking for a solution to their problem. They probably found your company through a Web search engine and then pursued you to get instant information. Make sure that when they arrive at your Web page you can credit the Web (or other sources) with finding them. Without this information, how can you possibly credit the right communications source when it comes time to prove the return on investment for your marketing programs? I suggest that you create a dedicated value-add website separate from your company's site.

Figure 7.3 shows the dramatic shift in inquiry method from toll-free numbers to the Web. Even with this shift, I still recommend you provide both phone and Web response options to meet the needs of your prospects.

Rules for Web Reply

- Ask the same profile questions on your "Contact Us" page on the Web that you use in other reply vehicles.

Figure 7.3 Toll-Free Number Versus Web Response Volumes

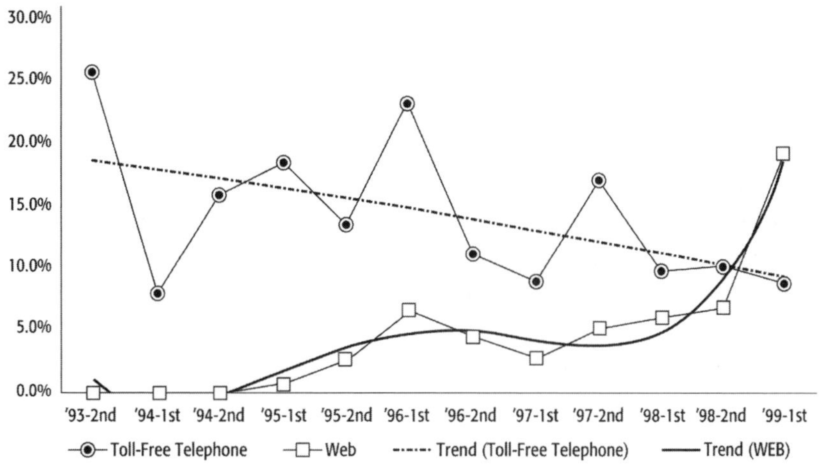

Protocol: Reprinted with permission.

- Make sure you add the question "Where did you originally hear about us?" Give them choices to check: print advertisements, Web banner ads, search engine, direct mail, trade shows, and so forth.
- Ask how they would like to be contacted in the future. Electronically? By fax? By mail?
- Explicitly ask for permission to stay in contact via E-mail in the future.
- Make it easy to inquire. Make your forms easy to use and fill out. Use drop-down menus and prepopulated response forms.
- When you drive responses to a URL, set up a landing page to capture responses. Tie in campaign visuals and copy into your landing page. Its design and copy must motivate prospects to continue to register. Reinforcing your offer is one way to motivate.
- When developing your registration form, use scripting that indicates which fields are mandatory. Also use scripting that tells prospects, after they click on "Submit," if they have missed a field. Indicate which field they did not enter or entered incorrectly. After a prospect has filled out the registration form, you will want to enable him or her to link to your home page.
- Be sure to say thank you after the form is properly submitted. Also, tell the prospect what will happen next.
- As part of your customer service, send an instant E-mail confirmation back to responders to let them know their request has been received. This E-mail should deliver the information they requested, as an attachment, and explain when they will be contacted.

Business Reply Mail

The business reply mail (BRM) means of response is not dead. Although it has rivals like the Web and toll-free numbers, business reply mail is still a viable response option. Remember, making it easy for people to respond boosts response rates. Because some responders believe that it is easier, simpler, and faster to fill out a reply card than to log onto the Web or call a toll-free number, you should give them the BRM option. Whether you use a reply card or a response vehicle that is returned in a postage-paid reply envelope, BRM is just as valuable as other inbound response options because it gives you the same opportunity to capture profile questions on sales responders.

Your goal for each sales inquiry is to find out as much about the person or company as possible. Profile questions on your reply form should seek to determine the responder's product need, desire level, time frame to purchase, budget level, application, purchase authority, and company size. Don't be timid. Ask the questions you need to know to make your database rich with knowledge. Response advertising is quid pro quo: if your sales prospects want information to help solve their problems, you have every right to know their situations so you can best help them. In my experience, if you ask, they will answer. As mentioned, our clients have received 95 percent compliance when asking up to fifteen questions.

Figure 7.4 compares response by all methods over a six-year period. The data show the rise in Web response, the decline in toll-free number response, and a relative stability in business reply mail. Clearly, it is important to provide all response methods to let your prospects reply in the most convenient manner.

Rules for Business Reply Mail

- Use the same profile questions on your BRM that you are using on inbound toll-free numbers, the Web, and for trade shows.
- Place a prominent toll-free number on the reply card. Show all response options on the reply card and let the prospect pick the appropriate one.
- If possible, preaddress the reply card with the addressee's name and other information. Preaddressing increases the number of returned cards and makes those you receive more legible. If there is a code associated with the name (showing the source of the list, program, offer, and format), make sure it is with the name so you can track the response.
- Prepay the postage. Let nothing stand in the way of getting the card back with the prospect's name on it.
- Summarize the entire reason to respond on the reply card. If suspects read only the reply card, will they know what they will receive and why it is attractive?

Figure 7.4 Inquiry Count by Year and Response Medium

Response Medium Count as % of Total Inquiries for Each Year

Year	Toll-Free Telephone	Reader Service #	BRM	Web	E-mail	Lead Card	Fax	Total Prospect-Initiated Inquiries
1993 - 1st	0.0%	0.0%	0.0%	0.0%	0.0%	0.0%	0.0%	
1993 - 2nd	26.0%	74.0%	0.0%	0.0%	0.0%	0.0%	0.0%	1,170
1994 - 1st	8.3%	38.5%	0.0%	0.0%	0.0%	0.0%	0.0%	
1994 - 2nd	16.1%	33.7%	0.0%	0.0%	0.0%	3.4%	0.0%	3,595
1995 - 1st	18.5%	30.5%	0.0%	0.9%	0.0%	4.4%	0.0%	
1995 - 2nd	13.5%	12.9%	14.0%	2.7%	0.0%	2.7%	0.0%	3,857
1996 - 1st	23.1%	25.7%	1.0%	6.4%	0.0%	3.8%	0.3%	
1996 - 2nd	10.9%	24.1%	0.1%	4.3%	0.0%	0.0%	0.2%	3,703
1997 - 1st	8.6%	15.4%	1.0%	2.5%	0.0%	2.0%	0.1%	
1997 - 2nd	16.7%	19.5%	2.5%	4.8%	0.0%	26.7%	0.0%	16,021
1998 - 1st	9.3%	8.2%	3.7%	5.6%	0.1%	25.7%	0.0%	
1998 - 2nd	9.6%	5.2%	11.1%	6.3%	0.1%	15.2%	0.1%	47,462
1999 - 1st	8.1%	2.5%	9.8%	18.7%	0.4%	5.8%	0.1%	24,618
1999 - 2nd (Project Total)				⟶				76,160

Protocol: Reprinted with permission.

- Design your reply card so that it can be faxed back to you. Put the pre-address prospect name on the same side as the qualification questions. When the reply card is faxed back, you capture both contact information and qualification information.*

Use Lead Qualification to Make Salespeople's Time Productive

In your role as a campaign manager, the most important rule is if you cannot find out more about a potential sales lead than a prospect's name, company, and address, don't waste your sales force's time. If you only give your sales people limited information, is it any wonder they do not follow up on inquiries?

Salespeople need hot sales opportunities now. They expect their marketing department to separate the ready-to-buy prospects from the tire-kickers. Fortunately, it is easy to qualify prospects. All you have to do is ask qualifying questions (see Figure 7.5), and 90 percent of the time prospects will tell you all you want to know. Qualifying questions are not an invasion of privacy. Prospects want to solve their problems through the purchase of your product. You need to know their exact situation so you can best serve their needs. Think of lead qualification as a customer service.

Figure 7.5 Typical Qualifying Profile Questions

- Do you need the product in:

  a. _____ 1–3 months   b. _____ 4–6 months   c. _____ 7–9 months   d. _____ 10–12 months

- Are you budgeted?

  a. _____ yes   b. _____ no

- What is your application for this product?

  a. _____   b. _____   c. _____

- Do you:

  a. _____ recommend   b. _____ specify   c. _____ have final approval

- Would you like to see a sales consultant?

  a. _____ yes   b. _____ no

- What is the best time of the day to contact you?

  a. _____ A.M.   b. _____ P.M.

- Do you have a similar product installed now?

  a. _____ yes   b. _____ no

- If you have a similar product, what do you like about it?

  _____

- If you have a similar product, what do you dislike about it?

  _____

- How many employees are in your company?

  _____

The best way to determine what qualification questions to ask is by talking to your salespeople. What do they need to know to qualify a responder? Gather this information in your sales process interviews, covered in Chapter 3. After you establish the core set of questions, be consistent. Ask everyone who inquires about your company or product the same questions, regardless of the inquiry method (trade show, Internet, direct mail, print). When the responses are placed in the database, you will be able to compare answers source to source or program to program. These comparisons will show you which programs, sources, or offers generate the highest-quality leads.

As a direct response manager, your goal should be to profile all responders. Realistically, if your qualification questions are asked on every trade show lead form, all inbound telephone calls, all reply cards, on coupons in advertisements, and on your website, you will only succeed in profiling 40 to 60 percent of those who inquire.

Outbound calling by the marketing department, before the leads are distributed to the sales force, is often a critical step in the process. This step brings in needed information the responder did not include when he or she responded. In the case of inquiries from reader service numbers in advertisements and press releases, all information must be obtained by this outbound call. Even if you budget the time and resources to make three to five outbound telephone calls to contact each inquiry, you still only profile 85 to 90 percent of the responders in your database. The names that you cannot qualify should not be distributed to the sales force. Instead, they should be kept in your marketing prospect database for long-term follow-up. If you stay in contact with them, they will be reachable when they are finally ready to buy.

The reason it is so important to profile sales inquiries is that the answers you collect are the foundation for qualifying, scoring, and sorting the prospects for your sales organization. Just because you have fully profiled a sales inquiry does not mean it is qualified or that you actually have a sales lead. A sales lead is an inquiry that has reached some level of qualification determined by marketing and the sales team.

Dick Evans, president of AdTrack Corporation of Cedar Rapids, Iowa, has consistently maintained that an inquiry is not a sales lead: "While an advertising inquiry is typically a request for more information and an invitation to a relationship, it should not be considered a 'sales lead' until it has been screened and qualified." I agree. This is where the evaluation of campaign success goes wrong. Marketing says it received a thousand leads—but it merely captured a thousand inquiries.

The answers to the profile questions are the basis for creating a qualification scheme that allows scoring or grade levels. The following shows a few examples.

Grade	Word	Score	Action
AA	Qualified	20+ points	Call within twenty-four hours
A	Hot	10–19 points	Call within three days
B	Warm	5–9 points	Call within ten days
C	Cold	Less than 4 points	No further action now

Your sales force is an excellent source to work with in developing scoring criteria. They can help you weigh the importance of each question. For example, if someone is a decision maker, you might give the lead a score five times as great as if the person were a specifier. A scoring system combines opportunity size with purchase intent and decision-maker status. This cannot be done using a traditional hot/warm/cold ranking system.

A high qualification score could indicate the person inquiring is hot, which often means he or she feels an immediate need, has the money, and can make the decision. However, immediate need time frame depends on your sales cycle. For example, if you sell a million-dollar product that takes eighteen months to close and install, and a prospect finds you six months into his or her acquisition cycle, you have found an "immediate need" prospect. However, you still have to work the lead twelve months before you close the deal. Unfortunately, until a sales inquiry is in the hands of the salesperson and the representative has spoken directly to the responder, you cannot be completely sure that the prospect is being truthful about the timetable for making a purchase—or about any other answers to the profiling questions. However, a scoring qualification process is a critical aspect of any lead generation program. It is not 100 percent accurate, but it is the best way to filter out the majority of lower-quality inquiries and help the sales force concentrate on speaking to the best possible prospects.

Distribute Leads Fast

A qualified sales lead is like a tomato—after it ripens, it starts to rot. Fortunately, in recent years, delivery vehicles for getting the prospect's name into the hands of the sales channel have been reduced from weeks and days to hours and even real-time notification by E-mail.

The single greatest variable in converting sales inquiries into revenue for your company is overcoming the lack of follow-up by sales. Companies that have direct control over their salespeople have gravitated to a no-nonsense stance on follow-up. Paraphrasing one company's inquiry follow-up policy, "All responders will be followed up 100 percent, or you can go work for a competitor with lower standards for serving customers."

Many companies with a long-term sales cycle believe speed is not always of the essence. They hope weekly sales lead distribution is sufficient. What these companies fail to realize is that many of their competitors are using speed of response as a competitive difference. If they follow up better or faster than their competitors and begin the one-to-one sales relationship, the other guy has a harder time playing catch-up. Response time sets the stage for the future of the sales relationship.

I recommend the safe approach. Get the lead into your sales channel's hands as soon as it is humanly and electronically possible. Make sure all profile information and the source of the inquiry are shown. Encourage the sales or telesales organization to make a follow-up call quickly. Establish the rules of sales follow-up engagement with your sales force: the representative must follow up within a defined number of hours or days. Reports back to the company must be filed within five to ten days.

Post sales inquiries on your corporate extranet. This can quickly advance the sales process and reduce the time required for salespeople to reenter the name into their contact management systems. The process of tracking sales lead inquiries has moved quickly from paper to electronic distribution via laptops. Now, personal digital assistants (PDAs) are standard vehicles to accept the "E-lead."

Direct marketing departments also are benefiting from electronic and extranet inquiry distribution. They get real-time reports showing sales inquiry follow-up and qualification for the entire channel or for a single salesperson. As the need for marketing results has grown, so has the need for instant information pertaining to the percentage of sales inquiries that have been followed up, converted to sales, lost to competitors, and so on.

Successful "indirect channel programs" are those with close contact schemes that drive the prospect into the waiting arms of the closest channel partner. After the lead is sent out to the channel, second and third mailings are sent to the responder to build on the initial interest. Phone calls also are used, under the guise of seeing if the prospect needs more information, to gently push the prospect home to the channel partner. The difference is that marketing departments are taking an active role in relationship building. The amount of time and money invested in a sales inquiry relates directly to the short- and long-term value of the customer and the profit margin on each sale.

Establish a Lead Fulfillment Strategy That Advances the Sale

Fulfillment is a necessary transfer of detailed information about the product or service to advance a prospect through the sales cycle. The nature of fulfillment is changing as we have moved from printed literature fulfillment to CD-ROMs to Web pages and now to literature files delivered via E-mail. Urgency to deliver information into end users' hands has driven some of these changes. But the goal of fulfillment literature is still to answer enough of the prospect's questions that he or she will call to speak to a sales representative, take a sales representative's call, or go to the Web to request a contact or place an order.

Several factors come into play when considering fulfillment. First, prospects have a lot of information already, so overloading them with every data sheet and brochure on your product is not necessarily the best way to advance the sale. Second, it takes time and consistent contact to build trust and confidence in your product. Fulfillment is not a one-step process. Instead, it should be considered a multi-step process in which you are providing a natural flow of information as potential customers move toward a purchase. For example, they receive product overview information first, followed by case studies, then spec sheets and application stories, next reference accounts. Then they request a demo or evaluation, and finally make a purchase. E-mail systems make it easy and inexpensive for a direct marketer to set up this chain of communication. Thinking through the strategy in advance is essential for success.

Marketers realize that end users often forgo slick and pretty four-color literature for instantly available information from the Web. This can reduce the need to print literature and will save hard-copy fulfillment costs. Print on demand, first touted in the early 1990s and now reaching considerable sophistication through digital technology, is being used to reduce the amount of literature that is printed and stored. Companies whose print budgets run into millions of dollars, plus storage and shipping costs, have found print on demand and the Web to be invaluable in reducing the cost of fulfillment. Printing companies attempting to regain lost business (from long print runs) are offering print on demand. They also store the material, inventory it, and ship it. The more aggressive printers guarantee that the customer will never run out of literature.

Case Study: The Role of Printing in a Web World

Company XYZ had an annual printing budget of $15 million for collateral materials. Totaling eleven million pieces, the materials required almost 50,000 square feet of space for storage and literature assembly. The fulfillment labor budget topped $5 million a year (including storage), and the postage and shipping costs added up to another $5 million.

As the company evaluated its $25 million-plus investment in printing, storage, fulfillment, database management, and shipping, it sought to reduce its quantity of printed materials by 30 to 40 percent by using print on demand. This would reduce the amount of literature that was thrown away because it was outdated. It would also dramatically reduce storage costs. The company implemented an aggressive campaign to make the same printed information available on the Web, further reducing demand for printed materials and the costs associated with them.

The company saved $10 million a year on printing, labor, postage, and storage and reports a low risk and high payoff for changing the way it makes information available. End users have expressed no complaints about the product literature, according to the company's senior marketing director.

Rules for Fulfillment

- Make it easy for the prospect to request information. Again, give prospects a wide choice of request options—the Web, a toll-free number, or traditional business reply mail. If you are driving prospects to the Web, give them a choice to receive your literature either electronically or in hard copy. Many prospects still want printed literature.
- Do not limit fulfillment to one vehicle. Just as you should not limit response options, make sure the actual information is available through the most convenient media for the widest possible audience. If they want it mailed, faxed, or electronic in a PDF file, do so.
- Send out your literature fast. If you use printed literature, respond the same day—or within twenty-four hours from your fulfillment house. You only get one chance to make a first impression. The speed of your response reflects the quality of your organization and sets the tone for future sales follow-up. One sure strategy for fast fulfillment is to have your literature in stock, and on the Web, ready for distribution.
- Send only what was asked for, not the entire line of literature. People do not like sorting through literature for products that do not apply. Further, it is expensive for you as the marketer.
- Put a message on the envelope that says, "Here is the information you requested." This helps the literature move through the mailroom.
- Put in "where to buy" information. A list of local distributors and sales offices helps. The closest direct-sales representative helps even more. Because this information changes constantly, it is best to include it in a laser letter format so it can be updated as needed. Include names of sales representatives and list the territories they serve.
- A personalized letter is essential. The anonymous "dear responder" letter is no longer sufficient.
- Include a business reply card with your fulfillment literature. Response packages are routed to several people within an organization. You want to make it easy for everyone on the routing list to request additional information about other products. You also want to make it easy for the primary prospect to request additional information—or even better, request a contact with a sales representative.
- Preprint the prospect's name and address on the reply card in your fulfillment kit. Doing so will increase response. In some tests, reply cards that were not preaddressed (recipients had to write in their own names and information) got a 1 to 3 percent response. That increased to 5 to 8 percent when the prospect's name was preprinted.

Summing Up

The first four steps in response management are capture, qualification, distribution, and fulfillment. Although not the glamorous part of direct marketing, they are critical. How you begin the sales relationship with responders, how you determine what their needs are, how you decide if they should be contacted by a salesperson, and the way you send them a response to their inquiry all shape the future of the sales transaction. It is crucial to think through and plan these activities before a lead generation program is rolled out—not after responses start coming in.

CONVERTING LEADS INTO REVENUE

A database is only a means to an end. The end is direct contact, dialogue, and involvement with individual prospects leading to increased sales and brand loyalty.

—STAN RAPP/TOM COLLINS
The Great Marketing Turnaround

Relationship marketing is like dating before marriage. A man walks into a singles bar and goes up to the first beautiful woman he sees. He asks her, "Will you marry me?"

"Of course not," she retorts. "We've never even dated."

"Well, if that's all that is required, will you go out with me?" he asks.

"Of course not. I don't even know you," the woman snaps.

*"Well, then, may I have your phone number so I can introduce myself?"
the man pleads.*

"Of course you can. What took you so long to ask?" she replies.

Too often, marketers and salespeople try to marry their prospects before they have even dated. They forget that people are naturally afraid—afraid of making mistakes, afraid of failure, afraid of embarrassment, and afraid to buy. Thus, before prospects will buy from you or your company, they must trust you. They must have confidence in you and believe your product will deliver what you promise. The most effective way to gain people's trust is to introduce yourself to them in small increments over time. In personal relationships, it is called dating. In marketing, it is called relationship marketing.

Relationship Marketing

M. H. "Mac" McIntosh, president of the Mac McIntosh Company (a nationally recognized sales lead management consulting firm), has talked up his philosophy for years. It is not enough, Mac says, simply to find a prospect, send him or her literature, and pass the name along to the channel. The company must build long-term relationships with prospects until they buy. Mac has three rules about relationship marketing:

> Rule 1: Companies do not buy. People buy from people.
> Rule 2: People buy from people they like, trust, and remember.
> Rule 3: People will not buy until they are ready.

McIntosh communicates this to his clients. Although research shows that 45 percent or more of responders buy from someone within a year, they will not buy unless you stay in contact with them until they are ready to make a decision. To be successful, you need a "feed, water, and weed" process that separates out dead leads and nurtures the seedlings. McIntosh's approach is one of intense continuous contact with the prospect until the prospect makes a buying decision. Vendors providing outsourced response management, such as AdTrack and Saligent (now Protocol), Inc., sometimes call this close-contact strategy "inquiry nurturing."

Regardless of the term used, relationship marketing is a series of communications that build positive awareness and trust in future buyers. The better you implement your relationship strategy, the more likely sales will shift in your favor. Nationally, less than 25 percent of all sales inquiries are followed up. If you can beat the national average, you will be viewed as more responsive than your competitors. Further, implementing a comprehensive follow-up program is the surest way to pick up additional revenue—revenue commonly left on the table. Nine guidelines for implementing a relationship marketing program follow.

Know Where Your Prospects Are

Maintain your database to know where your prospects are and when and where they move. Each year 20 percent of Americans change jobs. The database must accommodate adds, changes, and deletions. Although someone may not buy your product for his or her present company, if you follow the prospect to a new job, it can create a sales opportunity. Alternatively, that person's successor might have a completely different perspective on your product or solution, creating another sales opportunity.

A simple way to clean the database is to use a periodic survey mailing. The mailing says, "We don't want to waste your time or clutter your mailbox with information you don't care about. Please let us know if you want to stay on our mailing list, what you want to hear about, and who else in the organization we should be contacting." This same strategy can be used to maintain your E-mail databases.

Create a Special Theme

After a prospect has inquired, move him or her into a separate "nurture" category. Create a campaign identity that signals to these prospects that they are special to you. You know them and you care about helping them succeed with your product or service. A campaign theme like "Recipe for Success," "Working Together for Success," or "Case in Point" can be converted into a logo and used on each contact with prospects.

Stay in Contact

Use simple, easy-to-read correspondence formats: postcards, newsletters, electronic newsletters, dynamic E-mails, embedded video attachments to E-mails, and letter packs are all inexpensive and easy to read. It is more important that you stay in contact consistently, with relevant information, than to dazzle a prospect with your creativity.

Keep It Relevant

Find out what your prospects need to know and how much information they can take in at once, then send only the relevant information. Respect their time by not cluttering their in-box or computer with information they do not care about. One way to find out what prospects want is to ask them during the qualification process. They can check off areas of interest on a reply device or on your website registration form. Another technique is to conduct a formal survey using telemarketing, printed mail surveys, and electronic surveys.

Use the Personal Touch

You can easily mix business messages with personal recognition. When you recognize a prospect's birthday or do something that is directly personal, you have moved a long way in building rapport. Everyone wants to feel special. Everyone likes to be surprised. Add a special touch to your program. Collect birth dates, anniversary dates, first-response dates—then use them to put a smile on your prospect's face.

Educate Prospects About Your Product

You can use education as a tool to help prospects overcome their fear, uncertainty, and doubt about your product. Show prospects how other companies are using your product or service. Show them how your unique features could save them millions of dollars or thousands of hours.

Be Persistent

Rapport does not develop overnight. It takes seven contacts for the best insurance salespeople to close business. Why should it take any less for you? Don't give up. By the time you are tired of your contact program, your prospect is probably just taking notice.

Use Feedback to Refine Your Program

To make your contact program dynamic, ask for prospects' feedback. What do they want more of? How do they want you to communicate with them? Give them what they ask for. For example, using dynamic E-mail serving software, you can send a personalized newsletter to Prospect A that is entirely different from the newsletter sent to Prospect B. If Prospect A is interested in machine oils and maintenance strategies, his or her newsletter focuses on these topics. If Prospect B is interested in equipment financing and machine resale values, the newsletter is tailored accordingly.

Ask for Permission

Seth Godin, author of *Permission Marketing*, says we must move from a marketing strategy based on interruption to one based on permission. Ask your prospects if they want to hear from you, how often they want to hear from you (frequency), and how they want to hear from you (E-mail, fax, standard mail). It is better to let prospects say no and to respect that request than to annoy them with messages they do not care about. They are already overwhelmed with information, and their E-mailbox is considered personal space. You can win more favor as a seller if you respect the wishes of your prospects than if you bombard them with sales messages.

Give your prospects the chance to remove their names from the mailing list. Offer them options such as "Please remove me for the next six months," "Please remove me from your database—I am not the decision maker," and "Please send me only new product announcements."

Nurturing the Relationship

Inquiry nurturing, or incubation, as some of the response management firms describe it, has developed out of a need to shield sales representatives from raw inquiries not ready for follow-up. The process entails filtering all sales inquiries by routing them through an outbound telephone contact process for profiling before sending them to the sales channel.

Response management firms and outbound teleservice departments then can sort sales inquiries into data buckets (what I like to call prospect ponds) based on what the sales managers define as qualified. These criteria may include time frame for purchase, size of opportunity, whether the purchase is budgeted, whether the responder wants to see a representative, title of responder, and so forth, as described in Chapter 7. Think of this process as a fish hatchery. As a prospect becomes more qualified for the sales organization, it is advanced to ponds that are closer to the front line.

Julia Biolchini, strategic marketing consultant for Saligent, Inc. (Protocol), says, "It used to be clear where the function of marketing ended and sales began: marketing created demand . . . and sales followed up to generate sales. It isn't so clear anymore." In a white paper abstract from articles that have appeared in *Marcomm Choices* and *DM News*, she makes the case that field sales representatives are increasingly specialized and therefore expensive. She contends that because their time is so valuable, many companies are turning to outside vendors to interact with prospects in the early stages of the sales cycle. These third-party groups nurture the relationship until the prospect is qualified and ready to meet with a sales representative.

Opinions differ as to how much nurturing and incubation is enough. Some believe all responses should be held back from the sales channel and released only when the responder has been contacted and is ready to buy. Others believe that as long as sufficient profile information has been uncovered to qualify a sales inquiry, the lead should move into the sales channel without outbound calling. The main difference is cost. Do you spend $7 to $10 per inquiry to qualify each one by telephone, or do you initially use a qualification form to capture 50 to 60 percent of the information and then only call the responders who have not answered any

Pros and Cons of Response Nurturing

Pros

- Every responder has a conversation with a representative of the company.
- Unqualified inquiries are eliminated and not given to salespeople.
- Long-term buyers are not given to the sales force until the prospect indicates a readiness to buy.
- Long-term buyers are not lost. While salespeople focus their time on immediate buyers, marketing focuses its resources on staying in contact with long-term leads.
- Because marketing only gives immediate-need leads to salespeople, there is usually 100 percent follow-up.
- Sales may increase because salespeople only spend time with immediate-need people.
- Lower-cost vehicles (mail and phone) are used instead of a salesperson to qualify prospects.
- Sales-literature use may decline, because responders who do not pass the screening calls do not receive literature.

Cons

- Buyers may move to immediate-need status sooner than planned. So, the lead may not be given to a salesperson in enough time to close the sale.
- Most nurturing programs totally shield salespeople from buyers. This may slow the sales process if the salesperson already has knowledge or prior contact with the buyer.
- Not all responders need to be fully screened. If full profile information has been obtained via the initial response device, why spend money to call and confirm the obvious? An answer lies in the fact that basic information such as a phone number or the spelling of a person's name could be incorrect. The better the job you do in screening leads, the more confidence salespeople will have that your leads are "golden."

qualification questions? The decision of whether to telephone qualify each sales lead hinges on the value of the product and its average sales price. Can you afford to invest extra dollars to call all (or a majority) of the responders? Can you afford not to?

To build an effective inquiry-nurturing system, you must develc file of information from all responders to help the salespeople make inl sions about whether to follow up immediately. A sophisticated data that tracks the profile of the responder and the time frame for a potenti ment to purchase should also be in place. The value of making outbound calls to all who have inquired but are not fully profiled must be assessed is to determine the responders' lead status.

Don't assume that a response that is not fully profiled is not a sales opportunity. Qualified responders may not have filled in profile information because they were pressed for time. Think about how many times you have said, "I just want the information. I don't want to take time to answer all these questions." Your sales prospects think the same way. Mailings and telemarketing calls can be used to identify responders who want to see a salesperson immediately. Also, create a decision tree that, based on answers to qualification questions, determines who is qualified and who is not.

Some marketing information management systems, such as Protocol's product, automate the marketing- and inquiry-management process for companies that do not use an outside service. Of course, almost any sales force automation software package claims to have some sort of timing and nurturing system. The best nurturing systems, whether from a software package or from a service provider, help the salesperson stay close to the responder until a decision is about to be made. "Staying close" means scheduled periodic E-mails, postal mailings, and outbound calls to check in with the prospect.

Nurturing systems sound good, and they have their place in the scheme of the sales cycle. Some salespeople like a nurturing system—usually salespeople getting so many raw leads a month that they cannot follow up on all of them. Check with salespeople who receive few inquiries, and their hunger often dictates a different response: "Give me the lead now, and I'll decide if it is qualified."

The Rule of 45

Sales-lead conversion ratios have been documented in independent research reports for more than thirty years, starting with the pioneering "Did-You-Buy?" studies of 1966 by Mike Simon of Inquiry Handling Service—the first corporation to manage sales leads as an outsourced service—then the Advertising Research Council reports of the early 1970s, and the Cahners Advertising Research Reports of the 1980s and 1990s. The same figures consistently emerge: 26 percent of business-to-business responders will buy within six months; another 19 percent will buy within seven to twelve months. Overall, 45 percent of all responders will buy someone's products or services within a year of the initial inquiry date. That is, 45 percent of business-to-business inquiries convert to sales. This is the Rule of 45 (introduced in Chapter 7). Variables that affect these numbers are the buying cycle for a particular product, sales follow-up (less sales follow-up means fewer sales), and cost and complexity. The higher the cost and greater the complexity of the product, the longer it will take for inquiries to convert.

Follow-Up: The Great Variable

Gil Cargill, noted sales training consultant and nationally recognized speaker, says that when it comes to the sales process, "If you keep doing what you have been doing, you'll keep getting what you've got." Gil applies this to many issues in the sales process, but he applies it particularly to the lack of follow-up of sales leads by the sales channel. Follow-up is the great variable in converting leads to sales. To most impact sales revenue, make follow-up mandatory for all sales leads.

Telesales: The Secret Weapon

Although other parts of the average business have been dramatically automated, downsized, and electronically rejuvenated, the sales process has changed little in the past thirty or so years—despite cell phones, personal computers, personal digital assistants, and sales automation programs. But winds of change are blowing through the sales processes of most businesses. Most significant are the rise of office-based sales representation in the form of telesales departments and the automation of transactional sales to eliminate outside, on-site sales visits. This is driven by senior management's ardent desire to lower sales costs and reduce the sales force or even eliminate all staff salespeople.

In their book *Rethinking the Sales Force*, Neil Rackham and John R. DeVincentis foresee tremendous change ahead in sales: "By some estimates, at least half of today's selling positions will be gone within five years. Every aspect of sales is changing." With the advent of the Internet and the openness with which new sales models are being discussed, old distribution models are under attack. Sales jobs are disappearing. In their place are consultative sales positions with titles such as sales engineer, technical specialist, or even accountant. The sales representative has given

The Rule of 45 in Action and How Follow-Up Rate Affects Sales Revenue

A formula to forecast the projected sales results from a lead generation campaign follows:

Sales Results = (number of leads) × (45%) × (your average market share) × (follow-up percent) × (ASP: average sales price)

1,000 leads × 45% = 450 will buy from someone

Best case: 450 leads × 40% market share = 180 sales your company would get if your sales force did 100% follow-up. (The difficult number to confirm is the percentage of inquiries your sales force will actually follow up.)

Realistic case: 450 leads × 40% market share × 20% your sales force actually follows up = 36 sales your company gets

Best case: Sales of (180) × ASP of $10,000 = $1,800,000 in total sales

Realistic case: Sales of (36) × ASP of $10,000 = $360,000 in total sales

Difference is value of follow-up factor = $1,440,000

Leads = 1,000   Conversion in 12 months = 45%   Total Sales by All Vendors = 450

	Total Sales	Market Share	Follow-Up Rate	Sales by Your Company	ASP	Revenue
Best	450	40%	100%	180	$ 10,000	$ 1,800,000
Realistic	450	40%	20%	36	$ 10,000	$ 360,000
Lost Sales Due to Follow-Up Ratio						**$ 1,440,000**

way to a sales team for consultative and, especially, enterprise sales. Depending on the product and its availability, some outside salespeople are being eliminated because customers are not willing to pay for advice they do not need. As price and delivery take on new importance among buyers, the Internet and inside salespeople are becoming viable sales options.

In the last ten to twenty years, many experiments with "inside sales" have met with varying degrees of success. The word *telemarketing* has become tainted with negative connotations. Many say that putting *tele-* in the name of any corporate function dooms the department to failure. Now, though, inside sales functions—whatever they are named—are coming into their own with the help of the Internet and E-commerce. And in the typical company president's office, the executive team is relishing the opportunity to reduce the sales department, historically untouchable. The cost to field an outside salesperson who will sell $500,000 to several million dollars worth of product a year ranges from $90,000 to $250,000. If an inside person can do the job for $50,000, you know the choice the president will make. The outside sales force will be downsized. Telesales has tremendous advantages over outside sales. The inside person can reach out nationally, regardless of geography. He or she can make one hundred calls a day and talk to twelve to twenty customers, as opposed to an outside sales representative's three to five calls a day within a limited region.

For sales that do not require a personal touch from several people within the selling organization (a typical consultative or enterprise sale), companies are adopting the more economical inside-sales approach. Depending on the product, inside salespeople are generating more revenue than outside sales personnel. This is being accomplished with the cooperation of customers, who often do not need or want face-to-face time with a salesperson. If the sales transaction can be reduced to comparing prices on the Web, viewing Web-based demonstrations, and making a couple of phone calls that last minutes instead of hours, customers are happier and so is the marketing organization.

How to Avoid Inside Sales Failure

There are many ways to go wrong with inside sales. The following paragraphs explore how business-to-business direct marketers typically err in this arena and recommend how to overcome each problem.

Problem: With sales competition increasing, training is more important than ever. You have fewer opportunities than ever before to build a relationship and make a good first impression. Fielding an untrained salesperson would be unthinkable, but an appalling number of people are put on the phone to talk to customers and prospects without product training or training in phone skills, sales skills, negotiation skills, handling problem callers, and other important information.

Recommendation: The training program should be comparable to that for outside salespeople. Based on the lifetime value of each customer, invest an appropriate amount of time and money in your telemarketing staff to evaluate current sales skills and to tailor an advanced sales-training program.

Problem: Too often, the salespeople in an inside department report directly to the vice president of sales for the whole company. In a larger company, they typically report to the national sales manager. These executives would never have ten or twenty outside salespeople as direct reports. It is well understood that outside salespeople need personal attention; they require a sales manager and a coach for every four to eight salespeople.

Recommendation: Hire a telesales manager who knows the metrics and has the training necessary to be successful in this high-stress job. The manager-coach needs to be extremely capable, because the rejection telemarketers face can be crushing. Also, I do not suggest putting the losing outside sales manager from the last downsizing in the position of managing the inside salespeople. They need—and deserve—a professional telesales manager.

Problem: The goals and focus for inside salespeople keep changing. "We want them on the phone, but we don't know what we want them to do," is a common comment from management. "Maybe they can qualify leads," calls out the marketing manager. The customer service manager says, "Maybe they can take a few service calls." At the same time, the sales manager chimes in, "Could we have them sell those products my salespeople never seem to make quota on?"

Recommendation: You must describe a significant mission with a defined return on investment. Don't hire people and then fire them because no one thought of the obvious. Give them territories and products to sell. Segment them from other channels. Don't have them overlap with outside salespeople unless their mission is merely to support outside salespeople with activities like lead qualification.

Problem: You're considering hiring students for inside sales. Why not send students out with your company president next time he or she visits a customer? Wouldn't think of it? Of course not. So why hire students to take and make calls for you?

Recommendation: Most business-to-business companies aren't selling magazine subscriptions, so don't hire inexperienced students to answer the phone or make calls to the most important people you know—current and future customers. Hire professionals, or don't start up a department. Make sure they are true salespeople who know the definition of a quota.

Problem: Too often, if a new telesales department doesn't produce within ninety days, all the salespeople are fired. I know of a company that spent hundreds of thousands of dollars to launch an inside telesales operation. The company president said the department needed to be up and running in forty-five days, and the $400,000 sales automation program ninety days after that. He promised the vice president of sales a year to make it work, but he and the board grew restless after five months and decided to reduce the inside group from thirty-five to ten. The whole exercise cost $1.5 to $2 million, including all the start-up expenses for hiring, training, equipment, office space, departure packages, and canceled lease space.

Recommendation: It takes six months for an average outside sales representative to be consistently productive. Why would you expect anything less from inside sales representatives? Don't judge them too quickly or too harshly.

Problem: If you want people to sell, you must give them individual incentives to perform and control the behavior you need. Treat them like salespeople, with a comparable incentive plan. Don't treat and reward them as a team unless you are also offering individual incentives. Group incentives encourage mediocrity. If an inside salesperson does not carry a personal quota, you do not have a salesperson.

Recommendation: Create a plan that will get the inside salespeople in step with corporate expectations for revenue. Month by month and quarter by quarter, they should produce and be rewarded in line with all other salespeople in the company.

Problem: We'll get customer service to sell! Nope, it will not happen. Customer service people are averse to risk and want to make customers happy—not sell them something. If their income is at risk for more than 10 percent of their total compensation, they typically rebel. If you put a major incentive program in front of them and tell them how many "big bucks" they can earn, they will look at you as if you have lost your mind (which you have). They will go back to their jobs and ignore you.

Recommendation: If you have products that make sense for a customer service person to offer, you might pull it off. Never tell customer service people they are selling; tell them that they are serving the customer. Better yet, start up a true inside sales department that is motivated to sell.

Problem: Too many companies put people on spare phones and define them as a telemarketing department, with no measurement system. Without a measurement system to monitor the phone activity, including average answer time, abandon rate, number of minutes on the phone, and other data, your productivity for these people will be half of what it could be.

Recommendation: Tele-anything needs an ACD (Automatic Call Distribution) system to measure productivity. Without this, your representatives are working for the phone company, consuming telephone time, rather than working for you to sell your products. Measure total hours on the phone per day per person, completed calls, dials per day, dials per hour, records consumed, orders taken, abandon rates, and wait times.

Closed-Loop Lead Tracking Systems

Everyone wants a closed-loop sales-lead tracking system. Many of the service bureaus promise that they can deliver the process and the mechanism. The sales force automation companies promise that because they are such an integral part of the sales process, they too can deliver a closed-loop tracking system.

According to lead management expert Jim Obermayer, "A closed-loop sales inquiry tracking system is one in which the initial inquiry is placed in a database. The inquiry is then distributed to the sales channel, and the final disposition of the sales inquiry is reported." The final disposition may be that a sale was made, or a sale was in process. The report also includes information on inquiries that have not been followed up.

If everyone is claiming credit for delivering a closed-loop inquiry management system, why are so many people still looking for one? The answer is in the execution. It is easy for someone to draw a chart showing sales inquiry entry into the company database and a number of people and computers that count inquiries and sort by source and lead quality. However, without feedback from the sales channel, the loop is not closed.

It used to be that only salespeople could close the loop. With the advent of sales inquiry nurturing programs, "Did-You-Buy?" and follow-up research from marketing, companies no longer depend solely on the salesperson's feedback. Today, *closed-loop* simply means someone in the company applies a disposition determination to the sales leads. Specifically, were the leads contacted? What happened? Are they going to buy? If so, when? What is the opportunity worth?

As mentioned earlier in this chapter, 45 percent of all inquiries turn into sales within one year. With few exceptions, the follow-up rate of sales inquiries by salespeople averages 25 percent or less. Clearly, if follow-up of sales inquiries is increased, sales also will increase. This is the common-sense reason why companies want a 100 percent closed-loop system. However, companies typically fail to close the loop because the department that creates the sales inquiry—marketing—does not control the sales department, which follows up inquiries and reports on their disposition. The solutions address leadership and the sales process, not marketing.

Closing the loop is not the job of a single department. Sales alone cannot complete this difficult task, because it takes too many touches to contact all inquiries. If human nature takes its course, salespeople will secure the easiest sales. Often, they will give up after the first phone call. More aggressive marketers are reevaluating the wait-and-see attitude about sales inquiries and deciding that follow-up is also part of marketing's job if salespeople and their management fail to execute.

Nurturing is more than husbanding the inquiry until the prospect wants to see a sales representative and then handing off to sales. From a direct marketer's standpoint, closing the loop also includes recording the final disposition (whether the responders bought and what they bought), evaluating the success of the activity generating the sales inquiry (is the return on investment 10 to 1? 20 to 1? 40 to 1?), and making adjustments to do more of what works and less of what does not work. In the end, evaluation of program effectiveness and the quest for continual improvement of profitability fuel direct marketing.

The need for closing the loop and for evaluation is behind the rise in a relatively new category of software known as marketing automation software (MAS). This software—which will be further discussed later in this chapter—caters to marketers who have to prove the return on the marketing dollars they spend. Early adopters of MAS have been companies with product categories such as technology and software, in which marketing spending may be 20 to 25 percent or more of yearly revenue—just for traditional marketing communications activities. Although the old standby business-to-business category of "industrial products" still spends only 2 percent of its annual revenue on marketing communications, even these companies are asking why their communications dollars cannot be held accountable.

I do not endorse any particular marketing automation software product, but I have noticed that Protocol's High Yield Marketing product and MarketFirst eMarketing software offer the sophistication that high-tech, high-marketing-spending companies need to evaluate and increase the effectiveness of their marketing investments and campaigns.

Outsourcing Versus In-House Response Management

Many argue that the decision to outsource sales response management pivots on the issue of control, and that as companies outsource, they lose control. But control should not drive the decision to outsource. Drivers should include economics, technology, and an understanding of what portion of the solution needs to be outsourced. If, within your organization, the decision to bring in a third party truly does hinge on control, you can achieve control more effectively with third parties than with in-house people who may only be handling response management part-time. The decision to outsource should be based on the following:

- **Quantity of responses.** If quantity is less than five hundred per month, keep the process in-house.
- **Number of literature packages and combinations.** More than twenty packages creates a lot of confusion. Consider outsourcing.
- **Number and complexity of the sales channel partners or salespeople who will receive leads.** Do you send a lead to a reseller based on closest zip

code or longitude/latitude (favored by those who have thousands of resellers)? Is the lead sent to a reseller based on product? What about grandfathered accounts? National accounts? The more complex the distribution arrangements, the more beneficial it is to keep response management inside—unless you can set up hard and fast rules about lead assignment.

- **Reporting.** Do you need complex reports with charts and graphs? Why build when you can buy? Outsource.
- **Web enablement.** Same as above. Outsource.
- **Complementary services** such as inbound and outbound telemarketing. Let a service provider take the risk. Outsource.

Let's start with the economics of scale. If you serve a small, definable market with only a few hundred inquiries a month flowing to a small direct-sales group, you could choose to use an outside service. However, the cost would be high. If your product is a high-cost, capital-intensive business-to-business product, outsourcing may be worthwhile. If the product is worth less than $200, you may need to think twice before using an outside firm to manage the inquiry at a cost of $2.50 to $5.00 each.

Using an example of three hundred inquiries a month, at the best of times you'll only get sixty inbound calls a month. If you can prequalify most of the inquiries by asking profile questions, the salespeople can do the rest. These salespeople will say, "We know all our potential customers."

This scenario is not economically attractive for most service houses. Data entry of the names takes a few hours a month, and fulfillment is not time-consuming. You are only a $500 to $1,000 per month account, so the response management company that will want your business is usually small and unsophisticated. In this example, you could perform the function in-house reasonably well.

The metrics and needs change, however, after you surpass a thousand inquiries per month. The volume is such that you can keep several employees busy at an outsourced service center. The outsourced center will likely provide better technology and faster turnaround than your in-house service. After all, this is what they are paid to do.

Most response management companies will handle inbound telemarketing, respond with fulfillment packages within twenty-four hours, and send sales leads out to the field by mail or E-mail. Outbound telemarketing is usually part of their offering; you can have unqualified sales inquiries called, qualified, and even nurtured until the prospect is ready to see a salesperson. In addition, the vendor can produce reports, charts, and graphs from virtually any perspective, using a relational database.

For example, you need a report, with accompanying charts and graphs, on inquiries regarding your new product line that came in between January and June. You also want a report of responders with the title of purchasing agent who can spend $50,000 and are interested in leasing in the fifteen western states. Delivering this level of information could be difficult for a small response management company. In contrast, the larger service firms would ask whether you want the report the same day or the morning of the next day. Your own information technology department might say, "Of course I can give you this report. Would end-of-month be okay?"

I have not even touched on managing sales territories by zip codes or longitude/latitude or managing literature inventory so you do not run out. You should also consider Web enabling for secure access to the inquiries and a historical trace of inquiries that includes "same name" of responders, "same company," and a history of how many times they have inquired. These complex situations are best managed by an experienced service provider that focuses on these problems for many clients (see Figure 8.1).

Have I found in-house services that rival outside service companies for technology and turnaround? Yes, but they have usually been in companies that have a high inquiry volume (more than three thousand a month). Also, in these instances, the product being sold is capital equipment that costs thousands of dollars. The company's marketing staff knows how to sell management on the benefits of using the return on investment of inquiries to control marketing spending. The company has dedicated data-entry people, telemarketers, and fulfillment staff. The in-house department also creates its own reports and is not dependent on the corporate information systems department.

Often, whole departments are formed for timely processing of inquiries. Is there a cost savings? If you count everything—the people and the overhead associated with space, equipment, computer programs, and so forth—probably not. If your inquiry volume rises and falls in dramatic sweeps, from 2,000 one month to 5,000 the next, the inside people will experience corresponding dips in productivity. That is a polite way of saying fulfillment and sales lead distribution could oscillate between twenty-four hours and several weeks for data entry and fulfillment turnaround. If you are trying to decide which way to go, it probably means you are doing it inside now and are considering going outside. Review Figure 8.1 for the capabilities you need and can expect from a competent response management company. If the vendor has these capabilities, chances are it will offer a range of more sophisticated abilities, too.

Figure 8.1 Basic Requirements of a Response Management Company

Description
Relational database
Web-enabled for secure access to inquiries by the sales channel
Web-enabled for secure access to the inventory database
Historical trace: inquiry/prospects/company contact
Competitive screening/blocking
Duplicate identification and alternative fulfillment
National account or grandfathered account identification
Inquiry ranking or scoring
Sales-lead nurturing capability (scheduled mailings and callbacks)
Inbound telemarketing service
Outbound telemarketing service
Territory assignment by closest zip code
Territory assignment by longitude/latitude
Hot-lead notification to the sales channel by fax
Hot-lead notification to the sales channel by E-mail
Hot-lead notification to the sales channel by extranet
Report on inventory status of all collateral
Report: Total leads by product, 12-month running
Report: Total leads by source, 12-month running
Report: Total leads by source type, 12-month running
Report: Total leads by sales territory, 12-month running
List of sales leads by territory/region/country (manager's report)
Qualified sales lead report: Leads listed by qualification status
Sales report of inquiry conversion
Creation of charts and graphs from report results
U.S. Post Office address standardization capability
Fax on demand
Ability to create custom "pick lists" based on individual responder's need (from BRC, etc.)
Distribution of sales leads by closest zip code or longitude/latitude
Multiple lead distribution: same lead to different sales channels

Marketing Automation of In-House Response Management

"Marketing automation" has a ring to it, doesn't it? The word *automation* implies benefits for the overburdened marketer that every other department in an average company already enjoys. Most departments have had software programs creep into their daily functions with positive results. Demand is growing to automate the marketing department so prospects found through marketing communications can be properly managed and integrated into relationship marketing systems. Before the advent of marketing automation software, few programs in the marketplace could automate sales inquiries for in-house management.

Marketing automation is the engine that runs the campaign and the response management system that closes the infamous inquiry loop from the sales channel. Marketing automation can do the following:

- Consolidate sales and marketing information (data) into one database system for ease of access and interpretation.
- Manage marketing and sales campaigns for ROI calculations.
- Track and send literature to responders.
- Track inventory of collateral materials.
- Route sales inquiries to the chosen channel by segmenting sales territories by zip code and longitude/latitude.
- Manage inbound and outbound call-center activity.
- Create call scripts.
- Manage and report on the ROI of marketing and sales campaigns.
- Provide qualified sales leads, not simply inquiries.
- Provide deep profile information and reports about the responder and ultimately those who buy from you and those who buy from competitors.
- Be a central repository or even the engine for data mining.
- Provide intelligent marketing assistance.
- Feed the sales force automation (SFA) system and be integrated into a companywide customer relationship management (CRM) solution.

Although reviews of MAS programs have been mixed, most industry experts welcome MAS as a better way to manage sales inquiries in-house. Robert Mirani, in the magazine *Sales & Field Force Automation*, makes a strong case for tying marketing automation to CRM. He explains, "Marketing automation will allow businesses to present more timely, more relevant marketing messages to customers, based on information from multiple systems (CRM) delivered across multiple channels, all as part of a closed-loop system."

Rich Bohn, also in *Sales & Field Force Automation*, approaches the hype surrounding this field with hesitation: "First of all, most of them [marketing automation providers] are focusing on efficiency issues rather than effectiveness issues." He believes that too few of the available programs help salespeople sell. Bohn is pushing for "relationship marketing capabilities" in his reviews of sales or marketing automation products. He writes, "I welcome any attention marketing automation software developers might bring to the problem of generating and warming up sales leads." To succeed, ". . . programs have to shift their function from efficiency of marketing campaigns to effective relationship marketing efforts."

Bohn is right when he implies it is not enough to enter a campaign name and costs into a computer and track the number of leads generated. You also need the ability to predict and report on the return on investment. This issue leads back to the ever-elusive loop-closing that marketers feverishly pursue.

The need for a marketing automation program comes down to a requirement that software handle core sales lead management activities. Companies that do not use an outside inquiry-management vendor—75 to 90 percent of all business-to-business companies—usually patch together a process using a combination of software. Individual software programs cover database management, telemarketing, zip code and longitude/latitude programs, inventory management, and more. Each program performs its function, and few are integrated. None adequately manages campaigns or reports on marketing ROI. Nevertheless, the need to turn to third parties will probably diminish in the coming years as MAS takes a stronger hold and CRM becomes a reality.

Summing Up

Response management is the inescapable discipline that campaign managers must master to become successful. It is no longer acceptable to assume that the sales force will handle or follow up leads. Marketing managers must play a leadership role in the design and management of inquiry follow-up processes. The management of the lead-inquiry process is where the business-to-business direct marketer can significantly impact sales revenue and increase the ROI of lead generation campaigns.

Whether you take the process outside of the company or develop an internal solution, you need a system. You must strive to control the portals of entry into the company for all inquiries and use the Rule of 45 as a leverage point. Nurturing and incubating the inquiry is a fact of life as sales channels shrink and marketing takes on an increasingly important role in the sales cycle.

Those who master this part of marketing will be more secure in their careers. Company presidents and sales managers increasingly will look to the marketing professional for help in forecasting and managing not only the prospect but also the customer, so true lifetime value is obtained from every viable prospect.

## 9

EXECUTION EXCELLENCE

Many times the difference between failure and success is doing something nearly right . . . or doing something exactly right.

—Vince Lombardi
Football coach

Just as a professional football player must constantly practice the fundamentals of blocking, tackling, and catching to maintain a level of excellence, the professional direct response marketer must practice the fundamentals. The "E" in the fourth phase of the S.U.R.E.-Fire planning process stands for Execution Excellence. This phase of the S.U.R.E.-Fire process is designed to help you implement the fundamentals of direct marketing with precision and excellence. Seven fundamental direct marketing concepts go into execution excellence:

- Promote a compelling offer. (See Chapter 6.)
- Target your message accurately.
- Create relevant and arresting creative concepts.
- Write motivating messages.
- Control production costs.
- Test and measure your results.
- Analyze your results for future improvement.

Thus, the next three chapters will give you a comprehensive review of direct marketing basics—everything from list selection to results analysis. No matter how many years I practice my craft of direct marketing, I constantly return to the fundamental concepts and rules of the business. When I return to the basics, I am able to find new strategies and new ideas for my clients. Also, when I implement the fundamentals of a campaign with excellence, the campaign is more successful.

Moving Beyond the Rule of 40-40-20

Direct marketing legend Freeman Gosden, founder of Smith Hemmings Gosden, taught thousands of students, including me, the most basic rule of direct marketing: 40 percent of your success is based on your offer, 40 percent of your success is based on your list, 20 percent of your success is based on your creative. After twenty years, I have learned that Gosden's rule is correct. When a lead generation campaign contains a compelling offer and is delivered to the right audience, the message could be produced on a napkin and the campaign would generate response. Gosden's 40-40-20 rule explains why a No. 10 two-color letter is still the standard in business-to-business direct marketing, even in this era of electronic marketing. A business letter can easily be sent to the right audience. It can present your offer clearly and make your call to action. A simple letter package can generate response without fancy graphics, clever headlines, or reply gimmicks.

However, the world of business-to-business direct marketing is competitive and complex. Developing and supporting a brand for your product is now a de facto standard of direct marketing. Integrating your direct marketing campaigns with your general brand advertising messages is a must. Thus, professional direct marketers need to know how to use all media (print, mail, electronic) for lead generation. They also need to know how to manage a wide range of campaigns, from down-and-dirty letters to complex, high-end, integrated multimedia appeals.

Traditional direct marketers were taught to consider cost-effectiveness first. They are drawn by economics to the low-cost No. 10 letter pack or text-based E-mails. The new direct marketer realizes that business-to-business lead generation is about more than cost. Each advertising impression, regardless of medium (print, direct mail, or electronic), is an opportunity to develop your brand personality and increase awareness level. Therefore, more investment in direct response concepts that are highly creative, unique, interesting, colorful, and provocative serve a powerful dual function: response generation and brand development.

Maximizing Results by Pinpointing Delivery of Your Message

Between 40 and 50 percent of the success of a lead generation campaign stems directly from pinpoint delivery of your advertising message. If your message is not seen by the right prospects, you will not generate response no matter how clever your concept or compelling your offer. Leads can be generated only from those people who have the potential to be interested in the product or service you are selling.

Accurate media and list selection is at the heart of any lead generation campaign. Without it, you are wasting marketing resources, and your campaign will fail.

Media choices in the marketplace range from E-mail to broadcast advertising. In this chapter, I concentrate on the three media that business-to-business direct marketers use most commonly: direct mail lists, print advertising, and electronic advertising (including E-mail, newsletter sponsorships, and banner advertising). The selection of media for a business-to-business campaign requires mathematical and artistic skills. The mathematical side is the evaluation of media numbers and audience composition statistics, and comparisons of cost per contact and cost per thousand measurements. The art component relates to the experience and judgment required to interpret media data and editorial information.

S.U.R.E.-Fire Strategies for Selecting Direct Mail Lists

Let's begin with selecting direct mail lists, because the principles learned here carry over to print and electronic media. The selection process is based on several media principles.

The marketing universe is made of two groups of people: those who read and respond to direct mail and those who do not. Some people will accept direct mail solicitations, read them, and transact business through the mail. Conversely, many other people do not like direct mail and do not do business through the mail. This principle colors all list selection strategies. Identify and use those lists that contain names of people with a proven propensity to be mail-responsive. Mail-responsive people shop by mail, subscribe to magazines through the mail, receive newsletters through the mail, and frequently read and respond to direct mail solicitations. This same principle applies to E-mail lists as well.

Your current customers and recent responders are your best prospects. Customers and responders know your company and your products; they have either bought from you or have expressed an interest in doing so. They will respond to your direct mail campaigns. This is why building and maintaining a database of both customers and prospects is so valuable.

Your competitors' customers are great prospects, too. People who have bought from your competitors or responded to your competitors' solicitations have shown interest in your product category. Unfortunately, your competitors' customer or prospect lists are rarely available on the open market. From time to time, they can be obtained through an exchange between two companies. Because a company rarely has 100 percent market share, exchanging customer or prospect lists gives both companies a source of high-quality names and sales opportunities they otherwise would not have.

External suspects that look just like your current customers are apt to act like them, too. The closer you can get to obtaining mailing lists with names of people who "look like" your customers, the better your direct response marketing results will be. This assumes the look-alikes are mail-responsive. Exact look-alike names are developed through profiling and modeling, which require gathering demographic, firmographic, Standard Industrial Classification (SIC), revenue, and other data to build a detailed portrait of your customers and prospects. Then mathematical models are developed that enable you to see the relationship between each of these independent data elements and a dependent variable such as responsiveness or purchase behavior. You use the rules of the model to select names from third-party list sources for use in future campaigns.

Past response behavior is predictive of future behavior. A list of people who have responded to past direct response advertising solicitations is an attractive one because these people have already shown a propensity to respond by mail. Thus, lists of subscribers to magazines or buyers of products from catalogs are excellent. These kinds of responder files are called subscriber files, controlled circulation files, or mail-order buyer files, depending on their origin. Responder lists are available as a one-time-use rental for $50 to $350 per thousand names. Responder lists generally contribute the majority of names used for a direct mail sales lead generation campaign.

Compiled files usually offer more names, but have a lower propensity for response. Compiled lists—such as members of trade associations, trade show attendees, business owners drawn from public records, or business addresses from the Yellow Pages—offer the business marketer a larger quantity of names than response lists. However, they are not compiled from mail-based sources, so names in the file may not be responsive to mail. Compiled files often are used when a direct response marketer wants to reach all businesses in a category or industry or all businesses of a certain revenue size. Compiled files are good at providing the business mailing address but weak at providing contacts at the business location. The exception is any compiled file that uses outbound telemarketing to collect information into a database, such as the IRG Technology Database (www.IRG.com).

Develop a Target Audience Profile

Before you can conduct a search for any mailing list, you must profile your target audience. The more accurately you can define your target, the better results you will get from your list selection process. A target audience profile is a detailed description of who you are going to send your campaign to. For some industries, such as high technology, medicine, law, and engineering, you can order lists based on many of the criteria described above. Other industries, like human resources, moving and storage, and public parks provide only a few selection criteria. Your profile should contain these details:

- **Job Title.** What job titles within a given company do you want to reach in your campaign? For example, the titles may be human resource director, chief financial officer, and operations manager. It is all right to include more than one title, but rank them in order of their importance to you and your sales staff.
- **Job Function.** What are the job responsibilities of your target audience? For example, they may be network systems administrators responsible for server security or supervisors of plant operations responsible for plant productivity and profitability.
- **Company Size.** Companies can be specified by numbers of employees, such as any company with more than five hundred employees, or by sales revenue, such as any company with revenue between $10 million and $100 million.
- **Standard Industrial Classification Code.** The SIC code is the two- or four-digit number that categorizes all businesses in the United States, now being replaced by the North American Industry Classification System (NAICS). A listing of NAICS and SIC codes can be obtained from the U.S. Census Bureau. What specific NAICS/SIC codes will you focus on? For example, do you want to target manufacturing industries, service companies and distributors, while excluding retailers and consultants?
- **Geographic Location.** Can you sell nationwide? Are there states, cities, or even zip codes that you want to focus on?
- **Products Specify, Influence, or Purchase.** What other products, including your own category, does your target audience specify, influence, or authorize the purchase of? Look first for your exact category. If it is not listed, consider selecting related product-specification criteria. For example, if you are selling to design engineers, these individuals typically specify semiconductors. However, if this selection is not available, use chip design equipment as an alternate selection.
- **Current Products Installed.** What products, systems, and equipment would your target audience already have installed that would indicate they are good prospects for the product you are trying to sell?

Conduct List Research

In Chapter 2, I recommended that the search for direct mail lists begin with either the Standard Rate and Data Service *SRDS Direct Marketing List Source* directory or with a qualified list broker. The SRDS directory describes the more than 50,000 mailing lists available for rent. You will find 90 to 95 percent of all mailing lists within its pages. Besides list descriptions, you will find names of professional list brokers.

When you are responsible for a lead generation campaign, it is worth investing your own time in research using the SRDS directory. Doing your own list research will give you insight into your marketplace as well as confidence that all logical and viable list options for your campaign have been thoroughly investigated and assessed. Your goal is to create a comprehensive table of all the direct mail files (mailing lists) that are possible candidates for your campaign.

If you are a newcomer to business-to-business direct marketing, I suggest you do your own list research and use a list broker. The hands-on learning will be invaluable. The benefits of using professional list brokers to do your list research are time savings, the expertise they bring from working with many clients, and their familiarity with lists of many kinds. If you are a seasoned pro, you will likely rely on the quality research of your list broker.

What to Look for When Conducting List Research

Start by searching for all lists that closely resemble your customers or can reach your target audience profile. Look first for subscriber lists from controlled circulation publications, paid-circulation publications, as well as mail-order response lists from buyers of books, newsletters, and products or services related to your category. In addition, look for all compiled lists that deliver your target. Keep your eyes open for other lists you might find in related categories. For example, you would find lists targeting meeting planners in the Travel, Advertising and Marketing, and Business Executives sections. The Travel section contains lists targeted at travel agents which you might consider because travel agents are sometimes involved in meeting planning.

Evaluating List Quality

To evaluate the quality (potential responsiveness and deliverability) of each mailing list, you need to become familiar with reading SRDS mail list descriptions (see Figure 9.1). Each listing has eleven sections, as follows:

Figure 9.1 SRDS: Each Listing has Eleven Sections

All listings in this catalog are organized in exactly the same way to make it easier for you to use SRDS and easier to compare list choices. For example, rates are always noted in paragraph 4–SELECTIONS WITH COUNTS. The 13 paragraph headings used throughout this catalog are outlined below.

Market Classification (product, industry, SIC, profession, service, demographics, consumer market, etc.)

TITLE OF LIST
– Media Identification Code
– Name of owner, membership identification (such as DMA), address, telephone, fax, e-mail, website address

1. PERSONNEL
– Name of individuals in selling or service function
– Branch office identification–brokers, authorized agents or list managers

2. SUMMARY DESCRIPTION
– Descriptions of characteristics:
– Type and kind of pattern
– Special features
– Response and characteristics
– List arrangement
– Average unit of sale

2A. DATACARD DESCRIPTION
– Promotional service paid for by the list manager/owner

3. LIST SOURCE
– When, where, and how developed or derived
– Source of names:
– For a published source
– For a response source
– For a roster source

4. SELECTIONS WITH COUNTS
– Updated by SRDS date
– Counts thru date
– For total list and list parts:
– Total names
– Price per thousand
– Combination rates–discounts
– Minimum order requirement

4A. OTHER SELECTIONS
– 5-digit ZIP
– Sectional Centers
– State
– County
– City

– Business List
  • SIC or Type of Business
  • Title only
  • Name and Title
  • Size of Business
  • Other selections available
– Consumer List
  • Sex
  • Age
  • Income
  • Other selections available

5. COMMISSION POLICY
– Agency commission, broker's commission
– Cash discount policy
– Deposits, if any, with amounts and conditions
– Credit conditions

6. METHOD OF ADDRESSING
– Complete and detailed information concerning addressing methods, impression selections and rate differential, if any
– Availability of lists on magnetic tape, disk

7. DELIVERY SCHEDULE
– Availability
– Time lag or delay
– Guarantees and/or special considerations

8. RESTRICTIONS
– Conditions of availability
– Conditions regarding re-use or security

9. TEST ARRANGEMENT
– Rates
– Premiums
– Minimum number requirement
– Conditions

10. LETTER SHOP SERVICES
– Services performed
– Mailing instructions

11. MAINTENANCE
– Updating procedures
– Guarantee, if any, on delivery
– Refund conditions
– Duplication considerations

Key to Abbreviations in Listings		
Abbreviation		**Word(s)/Title**
Acct	=	Account
Adv	=	Advertising
Admin	=	Administrative/ Administration/ Administrator
Assoc	=	Associate
Asst	=	Assistant
Chm	=	Chairman
Chm Bd	=	Chairman of the Board
CEO	=	Chief Executive Officer
Circ	=	Circulation
Classif	=	Classified
Coord	=	Coordinator
Dept	=	Department
Dir	=	Director
Exec	=	Executive
Gen	=	General
Grp	=	Group
Intl	=	International
Mgmt	=	Management
Mgr	=	Manager
Mktg	=	Marketing
Natl	=	National
Oper	=	Operating/Operations
PR	=	Public Relations
Pres	=	President
Prod	=	Production
Prog	=	Program/Programming
Promo	=	Promotion(s)
Pub	=	Publisher(s)/Publishing
Reg	=	Regional
Rep	=	Representative
Sr	=	Senior
Sec	=	Secretary
Serv	=	Service(s)
Supvr	=	Supervisor
Treas	=	Treasurer
TV	=	Television
VP	=	Vice President

Reprinted with permission from the December 1999 edition of the SRDS Direct Marketing List Source.

- **Section 1: Title of List and Personnel.** In this section, you will find the name and contact information of the list owner or manager. You will recognize leading publishers such as Cahners, Chilton, CMP, and IDG, as well as leading list compilers such as Dunhill, Dun & Bradstreet, and American Business Lists.

- **Sections 2 and 3: Summary Description and Source Description.** When you read the summary description, look for key words that are included or not included, such as *subscribers to, buyers of, purchasers of booklets, individuals who have purchased by mail,* and *responsive.* When reading the source description, look for key words such as *controlled circulation, direct mail, mail-order buyers, Internet qualifications form, space ads,* and *direct response.* You want to know where the mailing list came from. Is this a compiled file or a response file? If the list is compiled, how is it compiled? If a file has any type of "mail-responsive propensity," what key words draw your attention to that fact? The absence of these key words or if the description is blank is a red flag that the names are not from a mail-responsive source. (See Figure 2.2.)

- **Section 4: Selections with Counts.** This section shows you the total universe count, the total number of names available, as well as the count by various selections. Examine your selection options. How closely can you target your audience? Check the approximate number of names per selection option. How many names can you reach for each selection criterion? Note that the numbers listed are not mutually exclusive. As you combine selection options, the total number of names you receive is reduced. Look at the base cost of the list and the cost for each selection and compare the cost per thousand of each file you plan to use for your campaign. (See Figure 2.2.)

- **Section 4A: Other Selections.** This section tells you what other options you have, including state, SCF (first three digits of zip code), zip code, number of employees, and dollar volume. (See Figure 2.2.)

- **Section 5: Commission, Credit Policy.** This section tells brokers and agencies what their commission will be when a file is rented. The list research and rental process takes time, so managers provide a 15 to 20 percent commission to individuals involved in the rental process.

- **Section 6: Method of Addressing.** This section tells you the format options you have. Options include four-up cheshire labels, pressure-sensitive labels, diskette, E-mail, CD-ROM, internal bulletin-board pickup, cartridge, or magnetic tape. This information is an important production detail. (See Figure 2.2.)

- **Sections 7, 8, 9, and 10: Delivery Schedule, Restrictions, Test Arrangements, and Letter Shop Services.** These details are important for production planning. How long will it take to get the list? What restrictions of use are on the file? This section is where you can see if the file can be rented to a competitor. What is required for approval of the file? For example, often a sample of the mailing piece must be reviewed before approval is granted. Also, some files require the use of their own letter shop for confidentiality.
- **Section 11: Maintenance.** This crucial item gives you an indication of the quality of the file. The more frequently the file is updated, the better the deliverability. You are seeking lists that are maintained and updated at least monthly or semiannually. An absence of maintenance information should raise a question in your mind.

The listings in *SRDS* are sometimes abbreviated. Therefore, it is imperative to contact the list owner or manager directly and request a data card. Data cards give a complete description of a mailing list. Figure 9.2 is a data card for *Human Resource Executive Magazine*.

Additional List Evaluation Strategies

Understanding the source of the names and having strong confidence in the delivery of your target are part of list selection. Other list-evaluation methods, especially for controlled circulation files, are to look at both the Business Publishers Association (BPA) statement and an actual copy of the publication.

Look at the editorial description in section 2 of the *SRDS* listing. This lets you see if your target would subscribe to and read the publication.

Look at the publication's subscription form. Check how many different types of qualification questions are on the form and the detail of each qualification question. If you were a member of your target audience, how would you answer the questions? Some technology publications, such as *Internet Week*, ask twelve qualification questions. Other publications ask only four qualification questions. The more qualification questions on the subscription form, the better.

Compare the selection options listing in the *SRDS*, or on a mailing list data card, to the publication's qualification form. You want to see if the selection options you are given match the qualification form. Can you make fine selections to pinpoint your message, or has the list owner lumped various selection options, reducing the accuracy of your targeting? It is important to know the sacrifices or trade-offs you need to make in targeting—if any.

Figure 9.2 Data Card: Detailed List Description, Selects and Counts

---

HUMAN RESOURCE EXECUTIVE MAGAZINE

-------------------- DATE --------------------

44,489	Active Subscribers	$140/M
42,782	* Trials, Inquirers	$95/M
	Counts Thru 01/2000	

2/01/00   UPDATED
2/25/00   CONFIRMED

--------------- UNIT OF SALE --------------

N/A

Published by LRP Publishing.

HUMAN RESOURCE EXECUTIVE MAGAZINE is the most widely read and respected magazine among the top executives in the human resource field. That's because it provides timely, comprehensive and accurate coverage of a wide variety of topics important to high level HR/Personnel professionals. They read the magazine to keep abreast of the latest HR issues and developments. Note that over 85% of the subscribers are director level or higher. These are the people actually running human resource departments.

-------------------- GENDER -------------------

% N/A
CANNOT SELECT

HR topics covered by HUMAN RESOURCE EXECUTIVE MAGAZINE include: Increasing HR Efficiency, Internets and Intranets Training, Measuring Employee Performance, Motivation and Productivity, Retirement & Pension Programs

-------------------- MEDIA --------------------

100% CONTROLLED
     CIRCULATION

Additional Selections:
  Inquirers Phones @ $50/M
  Diskette @ $25/F
  Company Size For Trials/Inquirers- Please inquire

--------------- ADDRESSING ---------------

4-UP CHESHIRE OR MAG TAPE

* Selects limited to company size.

--------------- SELECTIONS ---------------

A/B Split $50 Min.

$7.00 NUMBER OF EMPLOYEES
$7.00 JOB FUNCTION SELECT
$7.00 BUS/INDUSTRY TYPE
$7.00 SCF
$7.00 STATE
$2.50 KEYING
$25.00 MAG TAPE
$8.50 P/S LABELS
$5.00 A/B SPLIT

The HUMAN RESOURCE EXECUTIVE MAGAZINE mailing list is one of the most effective HR and Training lists on the rental market, with an excellent history of successful mailings by many direct mail marketers. Subscribers have told the publishers they have purchasing responsibility for benefits and insurance, HR development and training, personnel and recruitment, compensation, employee relocation, awards/incentives and information systems.

----------- MINIMUM ORDER -----------

5,000

-------- LIST OWNER/MANAGER --------

Job Function:

President	2,508
VP Human Resources	11,095
Assistant VP Human Resource	1,026
VP Personnel/Training/Benefits	6,527
Asst VP Personnel/Training/Benefits	919
Director of HR/Personnel	14,901
Manager of HR/Personnel	6,892
Consultants	397
Other	239

--------------------WEBSITE--------------------

www.chessielists.com

CHESSIE LISTS
13321 NEW HAMPSHIRE AVE
SUITE 202
SILVER SPRING MD 20904
MISSY FERRELL
PHONE: 301-680-3633
FAX: 301-680-3635

Business/Industry:

Agriculture/Forestry/Fishing	435
Mining/Construction	1,026
Manufacturing/Distribution	12,802
Transportation Communication/Elec/ Gas/Sanitary Services	3,163
Wholesale/Retail	4,132
Finance/Insurance/Real Estate	5,526

Figure 9.2 Data Card: Detailed List Description, Selects and Counts (continued)

Services	13,299
Public Administration	4,121
Number of Employees:	
25,000 or More	3,692
10,000–24,999	3,192
5,000–9,999	3,485
2,000–4,999	6,085
1,000–1,999	6,072
500–999	6,891
150–499	7,493
Under 150	4,892
Not Classified	1
Co Size for Trials/Inquirers:	
25,000 or More	191
10,000–24,999	239
5,000–9,999	299
2,000–4,999	792
1,000–1,999	1,163
500–999	2,078
150–499	6,313
Under 150	31,707
Trials/Inquirers W/Phone	39,741

State:

AL	560	AK	50	AR	442	AZ	298
CA	3,907	CO	595	CT	797	DE	153
DC	647	FL	1,849	GA	1,433	GU	0
HI	116	ID	145	IL	2,694	IN	1,050
IA	545	KS	475	KY	528	LA	488
ME	222	MD	1,003	MA	1,481	MI	1,597
MN	1,214	MS	345	MO	1,148	MT	97
NE	422	NV	222	NH	199	NJ	1,556
NM	143	NY	3,423	NC	850	ND	91
OH	2,306	OK	429	OR	396	PA	2,382
PR	0	RI	196	SC	513	SD	91
TN	941	TX	2,765	UT	273	VT	71
VA	1,201	VI	0	WA	723	WV	205
WI	1,145	WY	59				

100% Contact name

99% Business address

Turnaround: Allow 5 work days

How Cleaned: Annual requalification

Updated weekly.

Last Update: 02/2000

Request a media kit and look at the BPA statement. For mailing lists from magazines that sell advertising, request a media kit and a BPA statement from the publisher. A media kit can be obtained by contacting the publication's local advertising representative, found on the magazine's editorial masthead. Do the BPA statements give you a clearer understanding of who subscribes to this publication? Are you confident this mailing list will deliver your message to the target audience?

Ranking Lists

After you have a comprehensive list of potential mailing files, I recommend that you rank each mail file as A, B, or C. "A" files are your best-targeted files. For a list to rank as an "A," it must give you a tight match between selection criteria and your target audience profile. "A" files must also be highly deliverable; therefore, they come from data sources such as controlled-circulation publications, newsletters, or mail-order companies, which have a vested interest in keeping their lists current and clean. "A" files must also be mail-responsive. Your house files, such as customer lists or prospect lists, are always considered "A" files.

"B" files are lists that are targeted by category but do not offer all of your selection options. "B" files have high deliverability and are from mail-responsive sources. What separates "A" and "B" files is the degree of selection. A "B" file might only have selection options such as recent subscriber, gender, or book buyer. In contrast, an "A" file would offer at least job title, company size, and revenue selection.

"C" files are mailing lists that are questionable as to list quality, accuracy, deliverability, or mail-responsiveness. I generally rank compiled files, such as an American Business List file compiled from public records, as "C" files. Although compiled files can reach your target audience, their original source is not mail-responsive and accurate delivery of an individual is difficult. Caution is advised.

After you have ranked each file develop a table that ranks the lists. Structure your table to track the counts (the quantity of names available for each list). Include one column for the total universe of names available and a second for the number of names available based on your selection criteria. Counts for each category can be obtained from your list brokers or by contacting the list manager. Also include columns to track the selection criteria that can or cannot be used for each file; a simple yes or no is adequate. Figure 9.3 is a sample of the list ranking and evaluation form used as part of the S.U.R.E.-Fire planning process for my clients.

After your table is complete, based on your lead generation goals and program budget, start with your "A" lists. Select those lists first for your campaign. If you need more names, then rent the "B" lists. Continue with C-ranked files, as needed.

Figure 9.3 List Ranking and Evaluation

LIST RECOMMENDATION		
List Name	**Selects**	**Quantity**
A-Ranked Lists		
Beyond Computing Magazine	Top MIS/IT titles	1,635
CIO Magazine Subscriber List	Industry: Education	7,800
College Administrators on Campus Magna Pub.	Top MIS/IT titles	2,932
College and University Administrators and Deans ALCNY	Top MIS/IT titles; 1,000+ students	899
Data Communications (CMP)	Industry: Education	4,500
LTS High Tech Database	Top MIS/IT titles; Industry: Colleges/Univ.	6,234
	A Lists—Primary Subtotal:	**24,000**
B-Ranked Lists		
Informationweek	Industry: Education; MIS/IT	7,825
Technology and Learning	Grade Level: College/Univ; Job Funct/Title: Tech/Comp Co-ord.; Dir. of Tech. Programs; District Admin.	10,500
The Journal Technological Horizons in Education	Administrators	9,325
	B Lists—Secondary Subtotal:	**27,650**
C-Ranked Lists		
College Administrators on Campus Magna Pub.	Pres./Chancellor; EVP; Bis. Officer/Admin. VP	9,192
Schooltech Expo Attendees 1999	Convention/Expo attendees	6,459
	C Lists—Tertiary Subtotal:	**15,651**
	USA Universities/Colleges TOTAL:	**67,301**

Caution: Each List Is a Test

No matter how much research you do, you should consider each list a test until you have conducted a lead generation program and have a history of list performance. The testing of mailing lists is important and will be discussed in greater detail later in this chapter. If you are just starting a new lead generation campaign, spread your risk by testing several different lists within a ranking category. For example, use all your "A" lists first, then test two or three "B" lists, and test two "C" lists. There is no simple way to establish a set of rules for list selection. If you need help preparing a final list recommendation, use the services of a professional list broker or direct response media expert.

Selecting Print Media with Excellence

Print media selection is similar to list selection. Your goal is to identify publications that will deliver your advertising message to the highest concentration of the target audience most cost-effectively. Direct mail enables narrow targeting. In contrast, print media sends your advertising message to all subscribers of the publication. The exceptions are publications such as *InfoWorld*, *PC Week*, and *Time Magazine*, which offer demographic or select category editions. For example, *PC Week* offers the flexibility to place advertisements in targeted versions such as a Network Edition, Unix Edition, or Value Added Reseller (VAR) Edition.

There is a tremendous benefit to using print media to generate leads. Print delivers direct response advertising messages to a large audience at a lower cost per thousand than is possible with direct mail advertising. Print builds brand and company awareness by repeatedly exposing your advertising message to a publication's readership. Well-crafted direct response print ads also generate sales inquiries through Web traffic and phone inquiries.

Print media for business-to-business marketing is more powerful when part of an integrated media strategy that involves telemarketing, direct mail, and electronic media. Although print ads generally are not the highest-responding media source in a lead generation campaign, the awareness and credibility they create can increase the results of the other lead generation media. If you run a print ad campaign in conjunction with a direct mail campaign, the print ads alone may not generate thousands of responses. When your direct mail package arrives sporting creative design and concept similar to the print ads, a prospect is likely to think, "I've seen that. I've heard of that company. I wonder what this offer is about?" The suspect opens and reads your direct mail. This same scenario holds for telemarketing and E-marketing.

Fundamentals for Evaluating Print Media

The first step is to seek an overview of the various print media options available to you. Note the publications within your industry in the classification groupings found in the front of the *SRDS Business Publications Advertising Source*. Then turn to your industry and read the editorial description for each publication. Even if you are familiar with every publication in your industry, reading their editorial profiles will give you insight into the target audience each can reach. As you read each description, build a table that lists all the publications that reach your target audience. If you build an integrated media plan, your research on direct mail lists will provide considerable insight into a given publication's circulation composition.

Item 18 of each *SRDS Business Publications Advertising Source* listing provides valuable information about each publication's total circulation with breakouts by territorial distribution (circulation by geography) and the business analysis of the circulation (circulation by industry and title). Add to your table the publication's total circulation and its targeted circulation. Targeted circulation refers to the number of people who subscribe to or receive a publication who are also in your target audience. If you do not find this number in the *SRDS* directory, you will need to request the BPA from the publication's media representative.

Confirm circulation details by reviewing BPA statements or Audit Bureau of Circulations (ABC) statements. These statements reveal the composition of the circulation. Circulation numbers are audited every six months, so you can have confidence in their accuracy. Some BPA statements are detailed; they show you by job function and industry exactly how many subscribers the publication has. Others only provide an outline of the subscriber base.

Check advertising rates in Items 5 and 6 of each publication's *SRDS* listing. You will generally find advertising rates presented as a base black-and-white charge by ad unit size. In Item 6, you will find the additional charges for two- or four-color ads.

Using circulation figures and ad rates, you then develop a cost-per-thousand (CPM) comparative analysis:

1. To determine the publication's cost-per-thousand reach, divide the total circulation by the cost of your advertising rate, given the size of your ad (full page, half page, one-third page).
2. Divide the targeted circulation by the cost of your advertising rate, given the size of your ad, to determine the cost-per-thousand targeted reach of each publication.

This number enables you to compare the efficiency of each publication in delivering your advertising message to your target. Generally, the larger the circulation, the lower the cost per thousand. Don't make a media decision solely on total circulation CPM analysis. Some magazines that look cost-effective can only deliver a small percentage of the target audience. Using target audience CPM, sort the publications in your media analysis table from lowest to highest.

You should also evaluate each publication's editorial calendar for how well it matches the needs of the target audience. An important media strategy is to place your print advertising in at least the issues that have editorial or special features that will attract your target audience. Another reason for reviewing editorial calendars is to learn how much editorial coverage is given to a specific topic that may be relevant to your product. Clearly, the more coverage the better.

Look at the past three to six issues and track down how many times each of your competitors placed an ad in each publication. This will tell you how much competition you face, and how much you need to invest to have an equal share of voice. In business-to-business marketing, readers rely on advertising as part of their education; it keeps them current on trends in their industry. Publications that have a lot of advertisers also tend to have a lot of readers.

Selecting the Best Publications for Your Campaign

I rely on a combination of the following factors to make the final print media selections for my clients:

- **Editorial quality, coverage, and appropriateness.** Does your target audience want or need to read this publication? How well produced is the content of the publication?
- **Target audience CPM cost-effectiveness.** You want to invest your marketing budget wisely, so consider selecting publications that have the lowest target audience CPM. Don't use low-CPM publications that have substandard editorial quality or coverage rate.
- **Budget availability.** How much can you afford to invest? Within your budget, you need to balance reach and frequency. How large an audience will you reach, and how many times will you expose your message to them? For lead generation print campaigns that have the additional objective of generating brand awareness, frequency is more important than reach. It takes three to seven exposures to an advertising message to create an impression in the reader's mind. It is better to concentrate your media dollars on a core target audience and create impact with multiple impressions than to use a single exposure to a large number of people.
- **Placement options.** Where your advertising message falls within the pages of the publication impacts both readership and response. The back cover, inside front cover, and inside back cover enjoy highest viewership and readership. Generally, the closer your ad is to the front of the publication, the better the viewership. Right-hand pages enjoy better readership than left-hand pages. These high-viewership positions generally cost 10 to 20 percent more than the publication's standard advertising rate. It is better

to maximize your opportunity for readership and response by negotiating a good position than to risk your advertising investment on an ad that will not be seen.

One S.U.R.E.-Fire strategy I use to maximize readership and response is to place a bind-in reply card next to my client's print ad. You probably have noticed how magazines tend to fall open to the ads with reply cards. This tactic increases response and grabs readers' attention.

Selecting Electronic Media to Generate Sales Leads

Electronic advertising (E-mail, newsletters, and banner advertising on websites) is sparking great excitement among business-to-business direct marketers. Direct response marketers can now instantly send messages out at a very low cost and measure the results by medium, by offer, and by campaign. Electronic media enable business-to-business direct marketers to initiate, advance, and complete sales transactions faster than ever.

New electronic media options seem to crop up daily. As of this writing, four primary electronic direct response media are available to the business-to-business direct marketer: opt-in E-mail lists, electronic newsletter sponsorships, key word sponsorships on major search engines, and website banner advertising. The Standard Rate and Data Service publishes a monthly directory of electronic media options called *SRDS Interactive Advertising Source*. The following overview will help you select the best electronic medium for your lead generation campaign.

Opt-In E-Mail Lists

This media option is maturing rapidly and will soon offer the ability to target narrowly, just like direct mail lists. New opt-in E-mail lists (of people who have agreed to accept E-mail messages) are growing at a rate of 100 percent a year. As of December 2000, there were roughly three hundred commercially available business-to-business or high-tech opt-in E-mail lists totaling more than 15 million names. Most of these electronic lists of E-mail addresses do not offer as many selection criteria as direct mail lists. Generally, you can rent names with selection criteria such as geography, title, and company size. And while direct mail lists are sent to a third-party mailing house or data processing bureau for merge/purge before mailing, most E-mail lists require that you provide your message to the list owner, who serves (sends) the message to the list.

The criteria for selecting E-mail files are similar to those for selecting direct mail lists. Factors for selection include:

- **Source of names.** How and where were the E-mail addresses collected? Did they come from an E-mail transaction, or were they collected from a print-based transaction? How closely do the names match your target audience profile?
- **Opt-in.** Did the names give their permission to receive E-mail? If not, sending messages to this list may provoke return mail calling you a spammer.
- **E-mail responsiveness.** Are the names E-responsive? People who transact business over the Internet are likely to continue doing so.
- **Frequency of usage.** How often do the names receive E-messages from marketers? If there is high use, this may mean the names are very responsive. However, like all lists, overuse can lead to wearout.

E-mail lists are priced between $250 and $550 per thousand. They can be bought for testing in quantities of as few as five thousand names. Clearly, the attraction of E-mail for the business-to-business marketer is the low cost per contact and the immediacy of message delivery and response. Businesspeople, though, are beginning to perceive the E-mailbox as a personal space—one that they do not want jammed with unsolicited E-mail. It is also important, before a large rollout, to test a small quantity of rented opt-in E-mail names to prove their viability.

I predict that many more E-mail files will become commercially available, but that response rates to opt-in E-mail lists will continue to decline as usage increases. It will become necessary to build your own files of people who have given you permission to send them messages.

One media strategy to consider when building an integrated direct mail and E-mail campaign is to look for sources of files that have both E-mail and direct mail names. Then separate the files into two groups: names that have both an E-mail and a physical mailing address and records that only have a physical address. To maximize the impact of your campaign and stretch your budget, send your direct mail only to the records that do not have an E-mail address, and send E-mail to all the E-mail records. This keeps you from investing in a higher-cost contact medium (direct mail) when you can send a lower-cost E-mail message.

Electronic Newsletter Advertising

A second type of electronic lead generation medium for the business-to-business direct marketer is newsletter advertising. You pay the producer and deliverer of an electronic newsletter a fee for an advertisement and a URL link in the newsletter. The newsletter is then sent to a group of E-subscribers who have agreed to accept

Figure 9.4 Electronic Newsletter Advertising: Reaching Your Target Electronically

From: Network World <news@caserta.itwpub1.com>
To: Russell Kern <rkern@kerndirect.com>
Sent: Wednesday, February 09, 2000 10:27 PM
Subject: inSite: 2/9/00

Russell Kern, this weekly newsletter highlights vendor resources, downloads, demos, white papers, and other special offers found on Network World Fusion (http://www.nwfusion.com).
We hope you find this information "insightful" and useful.

1) RISK-FREE Voice over IP migration to converged networks
2) CHECK POINT EXPERIENCE, User Conference & OPSEC Expo
3) The new 3Com® 10/100 PCI NIC with 3XP

1) RISK-FREE Voice over IP migration to converged networks
Quintum's Tenor MultiPath VoIP Gateway, 3 time award winner, offers transparent auto-switching between IP and PSTN to assure PSTN-quality voice and reliability. Check out our industry-first MULTI-PATH CALL CONNECTION GUARANTEE. Call 1-877-SPEAK IP for more information, or check out our website at: http://www3.nwfusion.com/click;930589;0;0;2;0;?http://nww1.com/go/930589.html

2) CHECK POINT EXPERIENCE, User Conference & OPSEC Expo
Are you a FireWall-1 user? VPN-1 User? MetaIP or FloodGate-1 user? Don't miss this Internet Security event, the first ever user conference hosted by Check Point, the leading security software provider. March 15-17, 2000 in San Francisco. The theme of the conference is Experience, share yours, learn from others! http://www3.nwfusion.com/click;930599;0;0;2;0;?http://nww1.com/go/930599.html

3) The new 3Com ® 10/100 PCI NIC with 3XP
Combining an integrated 3XP processor for exceptional performance with on-board encryption chip for maximum security, this groundbreaking 3Com innovation enables you to utilize the powerful new security features of Windows ® 2000. For a limited time, an evaluation unit is available for $59.
http://ad.doubleclick.net/clk;900120;3846483;d?http://www.3com.com/securenic

Plug into this FREE online seminar and discover how to unlock the power of new broadband services. Register today!
* Please note that the vendor promotions described here do not necessarily reflect the opinions of the editors of Network World.
Network World Fusion is part of IDG.net, the IDG Online Network.
IT All Starts Here: http://www.idg.net
This information update is brought to you as a reader service from Network World. If you wish to discontinue receiving the inSite newsletter, don't reply to this e-mail, but send a message to
    listinsite@gaeta.itwpub1.com
with
 unsubscribe rkern@kenrdirect.com
in the message subject

the newsletter. If the E-subscribers read the ad you placed in the newsletter and it interests them, they click on the URL link and leap directly to your landing page. Figure 9.4 shows a sample of newsletter advertisements.

Key Words on Search Engines

When business prospects are searching the Web for information, they usually type a key word into a major search engine like Yahoo! or Alta Vista. Search engines sell specific search words to business-to-business direct marketers. When a particular word is typed into the search engine, the marketer's banner ad appears. This technique is powerful, because it enhances "right time, right place, right message" advertising. You are able to place your direct response advertising in front of interested prospects exactly when they have a demonstrated interest in your product or service. Strategies for key word buying include buying all names relevant to your product category, your company name, and the names of your competitors.

Website Banner Advertising

The last major category of electronic media is Web banner advertising. In 1997, this new advertising method attracted a lot of attention, but the medium quickly lost its luster. Response rates declined from a high of 5 percent in 1997 to a mere 0.5 to 1 percent in 2000. Although advertisers are exploring new animated techniques, such as media-rich video banners, most business prospects only click on a banner ad if it is relevant to them or if they are in the market for the product. Like TV commercials, banner ads are becoming less and less effective at attracting attention. Therefore, a clear and compelling offer is crucial to banner advertising success.

Researching and placing banner advertising can be complicated. The SRDS has a directory of websites that offer banner advertising. Visit each potential website and review its structure, navigation, and editorial content. This should be followed by a review of traffic counts plus a CPM analysis. Companies like WebConnect and DoubleClick can help you develop media plans and place your media buys.

Measurement: The Key to Program Effectiveness

John Wanamaker, former president of Sears, said, "I know that half the money I spend on advertising is wasted, but I can never find out which half." Some advertising ideas, media, and offers work better than others. You must be able to measure your results from each ad and media source to identify winners and losers. Direct response advertising strategies that track response by source code enable you to measure response rates. These measurements let you identify your best performers.

Measurement is the backbone of direct marketing. The fundamental creative principles of using calls to action and source codes within each direct response advertisement provide the mechanism for the business direct marketer to measure response by media, by creative concept, and by offer. The Internet, with its built-in tracking systems for capturing clicks, is the direct marketer's dream come true. The Internet offers real-time response measurement of promotions combined with the flexibility to rapidly change campaign elements such as copy or offers at a relatively low cost.

Fundamentals of Measurement

As simple as it seems to count results, it is amazing how difficult it can be for organizations to capture data. Many companies fail to make one individual responsible for tracking results. Millions of marketing dollars are spent with no clear measurement of return on investment (ROI). The reasons include lack of technology resources, poorly designed procedures, untrained call-center agents, and no tracking codes.

If you want to measure the results of each aspect of your lead generation campaign, you must code and track your results accordingly. The most important aspect to track and measure is your testing. You want to be able to measure what media, list, offer, or concept "pulled better" than another. That is, the direct marketer measures not only the quantity of each response, but the quality of each. You want to know the percentage of responses that are qualified leads for the sales force to call on, the percentage of qualified leads that result in a sales presentation, and the percentage of sales presentations that result in closed business. For responses that are not initially qualified, it is important to know how long it takes to nurture them into qualified leads.

Only by tracking and capturing these data can you establish acceptable standards and measure the return on your marketing investment. If you refer back to Chapter 2, you can see that the S.U.R.E.-Fire planning process is circular. The numbers required to develop program size projections are the same numbers that must be tracked in your direct marketing programs. Also, as discussed in Chapter 7, the method and process of capturing response must be planned out long before a lead generation program is implemented.

Another fundamental aspect of measurement is knowing the flow of response by media. To measure your response, you must be able to accept the lead flow from your campaign within the given time period or you will lose leads and sales opportunities. Each direct response medium generates response at different rates. Figure 9.5 compares three media.

Figure 9.5 Response Time Frames by Medium

Medium	Time to Deliver	First Response	Peak After Receipt	Last Response After First Response
E-mail	1 hour–5 days	5 minutes	2–3 hours	2 days
Direct mail	1–10 days	1–2 days	10 days	6–8 weeks
Print	30–60 days	1–2 days	20 days	6–8 weeks

Results must be measured daily. After your campaign is launched or placed into the mail stream, you need to track the first day or hour of response. If you are running an E-mail campaign, you want to know which lists or offers are working. If you spot a winner, E-mail lets you quickly remail.

Before your campaign begins, establish a set of projections for response by medium, offer, and creative using the data provided in Chapter 2. Results will vary by company, market, and campaign, but at least you can set a benchmark. As you track results daily, you will be able to compare actual data to your projections.

If results are less than projections, you have some options. If you dropped small test quantities of mail or E-mail, you can choose not to implement the rest of the program. If your E-mail message is not working, you can rewrite it. If you have not assembled all your direct mail components, you can choose to revise an element. One of the most important steps to take, if possible, is to get on the phone and see why suspects are not responding. Sometimes you cannot change the result of a program after it is under way. That is why testing is such an important part of the S.U.R.E.-Fire planning process.

On the positive side, if response is better than expected, you can prepare future programs based on your campaign findings. You will be able to read your results with confidence after you have received at least 50 percent of your response. With E-mail, that takes only a few hours. For direct mail, allow about ten days after the first response. With print, you need to wait about twenty days.

The Power of Testing

Every direct marketing campaign should contain at least one test. Testing reduces your risk. The entire S.U.R.E.-Fire planning process is about risk reduction. Testing allows you to set up small pilot campaigns and measure results before rolling out to a larger market or universe. It allows you to approach future advertising situations with more confidence. It also gives you the ability to predict future marketing results based on past marketing data. Before any significant marketing dollars are spent, you can make go or no-go decisions about various aspects of a campaign based on fact rather than conjecture.

Testing increases marketing effectiveness. Direct response testing enables you to identify ineffective lists, media, offers, campaign concepts, or ad headlines. Identifying a failure quickly is as valuable as identifying a winning approach. You can cut your losses. Armed with this information, you can invest your marketing funds more shrewdly and choose marketing approaches that you know are effective.

Knowledge is the greatest asset a direct marketer gains from testing. Testing lets you conduct experiments in the marketplace. You want to test media and lists constantly, since they affect 40 to 50 percent of your results. If your budget and program are sufficient, you also want to test at least two offers in the beginning stages of your programs.

What to Test

Test the big differences and variations. Start testing the factors that can make a dramatic impact on your results, especially offers and lists or media. The major tests for a lead generation campaign are:

- offer (type, positioning, presentation, value)
- list and media (category, source, selection criteria)
- message, copy, and creative concept (idea, headlines, copy, visuals, layout)
- splash and landing page (copy, offer, flow)
- registration page (design, copy, number of qualification questions, offer)
- format (size, shape, elements)
- conversion and relationship marketing follow-up communications

Offer Testing

The fastest way to improve your program results is to improve your offer. There is a direct correlation between offer and response that impacts both the quantity and quality of response. Testing offers must be a central and ongoing part of your lead generation programs.

If you or your company is new to two-step lead generation, one of the most valuable offer tests you can conduct is a comparison between a soft (educational) offer and a hard (request an appointment) offer (see Chapter 6). This test can establish a benchmark between response rates and the impact on lead quality of a soft offer and a hard offer. Other offer tests you should consider are:

- product literature offer versus educational offer
- hard offer ("Have a salesperson call me") versus soft offer ("Send for your free guide")
- type of soft offer (value-add website, book, guide, CD, checklist, video, self-assessment, ROI calculator)
- offer title (title A versus title B)
- premium offer (sweepstake, limited quantity gift) versus educational offer
- single offer (guide only) versus multiple offer (guide, CD, and checklist)
- limited time ("order by March 31") versus open-ended

To determine what type of offer test to conduct, consider your marketing objectives. Do you want to build a database for the future, or do you want to only generate highly qualified leads? If you want to build a database, focus on finding the softest offers that generate the highest response without too much degradation of lead quality. If you want only high-quality leads, focus on testing various hard offers. If you want to improve a current program, consider adding a super-soft, premium offer to lift response—but be sure to measure the impact this kind of offer has on lead quality.

List and Media Testing

If you do not reach the right audience with your message, you will not generate response no matter how strong your offer is. List and media testing must be a continuous process. Business-to-business direct marketers have smaller universes than consumer marketers. For a specific kind of product, a core group of lists or publications can be tested and proven more effective than secondary sources. However, the financial dynamics of generating additional sales or propelling business growth may force the direct marketer to continually search for and try new lists or publications to produce more sales leads. By measuring the performance of your lists and media through testing, you can make marketing investment decisions with knowledge of the performance of each list or media option. The most important list and media tests to run are as follows:

- Media selection, including list A versus list B, magazine A versus magazine B, E-mail list A versus E-mail list B, and website www.xyz.com versus website www.abc.com.
- Media type, including direct mail versus E-mail, print versus direct mail, telemarketing versus direct mail, and banner advertising versus E-mail.
- Selection within a given medium, particularly direct mail lists and E-mail lists. These tests may include title selection test (network administrators

versus technology executives), title slug (office manager) versus title supplied, employee size selection (fewer than 100 employees versus 500-plus employees), hot line or recent subscribers versus older names, full-run edition versus demographic selection of a magazine, and key search words on Web search engines (your company's name, your competitors' names, your product name, category functions).

Start with media selection, so you can avoid investing in nonperforming media. Then compare the cost-effectiveness of lead generation by media type. This information can help you focus future investments wisely. Finally, test selection options and refinements to various lists and media. Media and list testing are easier than offer testing, because the tracking or response can be accomplished by a change of tracking code rather than a printing plate change.

Figure 9.6 reports the measurement and analysis of list tests for a direct mail campaign. Both response rate and lead quality are tracked. Using an index, you can compare results between lists while taking into consideration both response rate and lead quality. The index formula is:

Index = response percentage $\times$ lead quality percentage $\times$ 100

Message, Copy, and Concept Testing

If you have followed the steps of the S.U.R.E.-Fire process, you did much of the pretesting of concepts and message in the second phase. Only after your direct response advertising is sent into the marketplace will you know its actual response rate. Although the S.U.R.E.-Fire planning process reduces your risk by helping you avoid guesswork and providing market feedback on your creative, live testing gives you definitive measurements of responsiveness. Here are the message, copy, and concept tests you should consider:

- message A versus message B
- headline A versus headline B
- short copy versus long copy
- concept A versus concept B
- benefit statement A versus benefit statement B
- personalization versus no personalization
- closed-face envelope versus window envelope
- subject line copy A versus no subject line
- E-mail length: short copy versus long copy
- self-mailer versus letter package
- dimensional/impact versus flat letter package versus self-mailer

Figure 9.6 Response Analysis: Response Rate and Quality by List

Source Code	List	Total Mail Quantity	Returns	Percentage Returned	Net Mail Quantity	Total Responses	Response Rate	Number of Responses Scored	Qualified (3–5 score)	% Quality	Response Quality Index
F315TJ	List A	10,000	82	0.82%	9,918	100	1.01%	87	45	51.72%	52.2
F330TJ	List B	5,000	35	0.70%	4,965	42	0.85%	31	15	48.39%	40.9
F353TJ	List C	20,000	107	0.54%	19,893	201	1.01%	145	72	49.66%	50.2
F308TJ	List D	15,000	177	1.18%	14,823	327	2.21%	288	157	54.51%	120.3
F320TJ	List E	7,000	53	0.76%	6,947	142	2.04%	135	50	37.04%	75.7
F309TJ	List F	12,000	606	5.05%	11,394	139	1.22%	60	29	48.33%	59.0
F397TJ	List G	25,000	123	0.49%	24,877	434	1.74%	393	200	50.89%	88.8
F321TJ	List H	6,000	62	1.03%	5,938	26	0.44%	20	11	55.00%	24.1
	Total	**100,000**	**1,245**	**1.25%**	**98,755**	**1,411**	**1.43%**	**1,159**	**579**	**49.96%**	**71.4**

Your goal in message and concept testing is to identify the most cost-effective approach that generates the highest quality of leads. So test radically different approaches and measure their impact on results. If your goal is to find the most cost-effective format to generate leads, test promotion format. If you want to find the creative concept that generates the most response, test dramatic creative approaches.

Splash and Landing Page Testing

Statistics indicate that between 10 to 50 percent of prospects who hit your splash page or landing page will fill out registration information. Maximizing the stickiness of your splash or landing page—keeping prospects on your site and moving through the registration process—is critical to web-based lead generation success.

The more motivated the prospect is to obtain information from you, the higher the stay rate and the greater your compliance/fill-out rates. The source of the inquiry to your site also affects registration rates. Figure 9.7 shows the progression of interest. People who receive a printed direct mail promotion and go to a URL generally have much higher interest than prospects who happen upon a Web banner ad and click on the offer.

The purpose of testing landing page design, copy, format, and offer statement is to maximize the conversion rate from click to completion. Think about how many more leads you would capture if you could increase the completion rate within your site by 25 percent. Design and copy that stop the momentum of your responder depress completion rates. Building flow and increasing excitement keeps responders moving toward you. For example, offering a sweepstakes drawing for a Palm Pilot to all who complete your registration form is a great way to lift completion rates. Visitors stay at sites that entertain, surprise, reveal, educate, provide interaction, or have movement. Valuable landing page testing ideas include: splash page before landing page versus straight to landing page, long copy versus short copy, design A versus design B, headline A versus headline B, and restatement of offer versus additional premium offer.

Figure 9.7 Landing Page Interest Level by Source

Ad Banners	Website Links	Newsletter Links	E-mail Promotions	Hard-copy Direct Mail

Low Interest ————————————————————▶ **High Interest**

No matter what you are testing, your landing page should reflect the creative message and offer that stimulated readers to visit your URL. When readers go to your URL and see your landing page, you want them to feel that they have come to the right place.

Registration Page Testing

Many of the comments on splash and landing page design apply to the testing of your registration page, which may or may not be designed into your landing page. The goal of the registration page is to capture a sales inquiry. Anything you do to make it more difficult or time-consuming to complete makes it more likely a responder will click out. Make it simple, quick, and easy to use, and prospects will hit the submit button. Test registration design, form format, question order (what qualification questions in what order), short (two questions) versus long (six questions), pull-down menus, and alerts that tell readers the mandatory fields to fill in before submission.

Eric Morley, outbound Internet marketing manager at VeriSign, Inc., reports that reducing the number of qualification questions on your registration page can more than double compliance rates. Compliance rates include both the percentage of people who submit the registration form and the percentage of questions they complete. He suggests that fellow direct marketers only use two questions instead of six, saying, "Make the beginning of the sales inquiry process as fast and simple as possible. Don't overburden your prospects. After you have captured the E-mail address and two data items, use relationship marketing strategies to develop a full prospect profile over time."

Format and Size Testing

This aspect of testing involves the size, length, and layout of your direct response advertisements. When you test either format or size, you must go back to your marketing objectives. If you are looking to optimize cost, determine the smallest space you can buy or simplest kind of direct mail you can send and still generate leads. If you are looking to build your brand, establish a presence, or maximize response, test big space units or large formats.

In my experience, a bind-in reply card adjacent to your print ad is the best way to get your ad seen and maximize response opportunities. Frequency is more important than reach. I prefer to run in fewer publications using a bind-in plus a print ad rather than to run in twice as many publications without the bind-in. As for direct mail, the No. 10 business letter package may be industry standard, but if the budget is available and the product justifies the investment, I like to use big packages. Large formats stand out among the contents of a mailbox.

For print ads, test right page versus left page, full page versus half page, and forward magazine placement versus back cover. Also test devices such as bind-in reply card versus no reply card or coupon versus no coupon. For direct mail, test size, shape (standard and nonstandard size), and color (white mail versus promotional mail). Banner advertising calls for testing animation (none versus lots), size (full, half, and square button), and position (top of page, bottom of page, left side).

Conversion and Follow-Up Strategy Testing

In this area of testing, you focus on specific follow-up campaign elements (such as your follow-up E-mails) as well as your overall approach to follow-up once an inquiry is captured. For example, after prospects hit your website and fill out your registration form, what happens next? Do they get an automatic E-mail confirmation? Do they get a telephone call? Test your copy on this follow-up. Measure how many responses each version generates. Do you make your prospect a second offer to keep the relationship moving toward a sale? Test that. What happens? Do you make a follow-up phone call? Test your script. What about your printed literature fulfillment package? Test the effectiveness of the letter that accompanies the literature. What offer are you making in your kit? How many responses do you get after the literature is sent? Do you need to call every prospect?

Guidelines for Conducting Direct Marketing Tests

When you begin to test, you should follow these guidelines to keep your tests valid (interpretation based on *Direct Mail and Mail Order Handbook* by Richard Hodgson):

- **Test only one variable at a time.** Your test must be "apples to apples." For example, test list A against list B, but hold the offer and the package constant. If you change too many variables, you cannot accurately interpret results.
- **Select a random sample of the universe.** Random sample selection is a complex and serious topic. To select a random sample from a direct mail list, you must have a computer select names from the entire list. In E-mail advertising, you cannot select sample populations the same way, because E-mail messages typically are served by the list owner. Be sure to ask each

E-list provider if it offers testing options. For print advertising, you can run split tests on circulation. One half of the subscribers would see ad number one, and the other half would see ad number two. For banner advertising, you can run rotational tests on viewership. Request that ad number one and ad number two rotate, each appearing half the time.

- **Select a sample size that will give statistically valid results.** Select a proper sample size based on your predicted response, accuracy level, and confidence level in your accuracy. A rule of thumb is you need 50 to 100 responses in a given test cell to have valid test data.
- **Track the sample used for testing.** First, code the file so you know what names or records were used for your test. This lets you hold out or include these names in future campaigns. Codes can include the promotion month, package type, offer, and list source in a series of alphanumeric digits. When creating a code, remember not to make it hard on your responders. You want them to be able to enter the code into a registration form or read it to an operator over the telephone. Highlight your code by calling it a priority code or reservation number. People know marketers track results, so make it easy for them to find the codes you want to capture.
- **Test twice.** If you are going to make a big decision based on your test, consider two rounds of testing to see if you get the same results.
- **Try to keep everything equal.** If you are conducting a mailing, drop on the same day. Mail from the same mailing house. Reduce as many variables as you can. The mailbox and marketplace are imperfect laboratories.
- **Wait until you have all your results before making major decisions.** Don't rush to judgment after preliminary results. Wait until you have all your results so you can do a proper comparative analysis between tests.
- **Don't follow your test results without taking other factors into consideration.** The world is constantly changing. War, economic shifts, major events, time of year, and weather all affect test results. Don't follow your test results blindly. Take all business and world factors into consideration.
- **Test the big stuff.** Don't get test-happy. Test the things that truly will make a difference in your response, conversion, and bottom line.
- **Track your response codes.** Determine in advance the code scheme and collection method for each test. Keep a logbook for each test code.
- **Track your test results.** In your logbook, jot down a summary of each test you conducted and why you conducted it. Without a log to refer to, you will be amazed at how quickly you forget what you did, why you conducted a test, and what your marketing assumptions were. Spell out your

test results using probability tables. A logbook entry might go something like this: "This test got a 2% result. The sample size was 10,000. At a 95% confidence level, the expected response range was 0.X% to 0.Y%. Apply test results to rollout." If you have a positive test result, show what will happen using the low number in your response range when you roll out that test to a larger universe.

Summing Up

Effective media selection and evaluation are essential to Execution Excellence, the fourth phase of the S.U.R.E.-Fire planning process. Media selection covers the range of direct mail lists, print media, and electronic media. Sending a powerful offer to the wrong group of prospects minimizes your results. Circulation and cost-per-thousand analysis, mail-responsiveness analysis, and source and editorial analysis represent half the selection process. The other half comprises budget allocation to maximize frequency and judgment about the quality of each list or publication.

Testing is a major issue in judging the results of campaigns. Every lead generation campaign should include at least one test. Choosing the variables to test is also important, in that a number of factors, such as message, copy, format, offer, registration page, and size, affect the success of a campaign. Testing variables and following up with refinements are central to getting the most out of a campaign.

## 10

THE STRATEGY OF
CREATIVE EXCELLENCE

It's not creative unless it sells.

—DICK LORD

Copywriter, D'Arcy Masius Benton &
Bowles advertising

Direct response advertisements are the gasoline that fuels your lead generation engine. Your direct response print ads, mail packages, E-mail messages, and banner ads are the most visible outcome of the S.U.R.E.-Fire planning process. Outstanding direct response creative can provide you with a double benefit, establishing the credibility of your company while attracting qualified sales prospects. In this chapter, you will learn how to combine the work you have done throughout the S.U.R.E.-Fire planning process with the fundamentals of creative to manage the development of excellent direct response advertising. The resulting advertising maximizes the return on your marketing investment by generating leads while developing your brand image at the same time.

Effective direct response advertising presents your offer and product in a fresh manner, one that appeals to both the emotional and logical side of readers' minds. Effective direct response ads pull readers into your story while describing benefits and promises that overcome their natural reluctance to respond. Even in this era of interactivity and dynamic E-mail, the fundamentals of creative excellence are timeless. These fundamentals include a benefit-oriented headline, well-written body copy, an easy-to-read layout, attention-getting visuals, and a strong call to action.

Although facts are an important part of creative, facts alone seldom compel a person to respond. In a 1970s study of 137 managers conducted by Dr. F. Robert Shoaf and sponsored by *Steel* magazine, Shoaf concluded, "The large majority of buying decisions are made on an emotional basis." Don't think of your audience as business machines set on cold, hard, logical facts. Instead, advertise to business buyers as the human beings they are—people who may be unpredictable, warm-hearted, stubborn, intelligent, fickle, and well intentioned.

To create direct response concepts that appeal to your target audience as people rich with emotion and desire, follow the most basic principle of marketing: listen to the market, then give it what it wants. The fourth phase of the S.U.R.E.-Fire planning process includes two main creative steps to accomplish this.

Step 1: Use the information collected from your strategic planning (SWOT, USP statement, product positioning, buy cycle analysis, and win/loss analysis) together with the findings from your one-to-one interviews as the foundation for preliminary creative concept development.

Step 2: Using qualitative and quantitative research methods, ask the marketplace for opinions about your preliminary creative concepts. Listen to the feedback and interpret your findings. Then, based on your findings and your knowledge of the market, select concepts for campaign implementation.

By following these two steps, you will increase your chances of implementing a successful lead generation campaign. My clients have experienced increases in response rate between 50 and 2,000 percent after following the S.U.R.E.-Fire planning process. The main reason for these increases is that the process reduces subjectivity in selecting offers, messages, and creative concepts for campaigns.

Developing excellent direct response creative advertising requires managing the creative process. You must know how to give strategic direction and inspire preliminary creative ideas. You need to integrate research results into the final production of a concept. It is also important to apply the fundamental creative guidelines of direct response to all print ads, mail packages, and electronic communication.

Integrating Strategic Planning and Research Results into the Creative Process

Managing the concept development and final production of your direct response advertisements is the key to execution excellence. Keeping creative concepts strategic—using the results from the prior three phases of the S.U.R.E.-Fire planning process—requires teamwork and constant attention to your findings.

There are seven creative development steps within the creative aspect of execution excellence. The first five steps are required to prepare for the research phase. The last two steps are needed in final program implementation.

1. **Rough concept and idea generation.** In this step, the original ideas for your print ads, direct mail packages, websites, or banner ads are developed.

2. **Preliminary evaluation of concepts.** This step begins when you start to evaluate each rough idea and compare it to your strategy.

3. **First round of refinement.** Preliminary concepts are improved and modified to stay focused on strategy.

4. **Second round of evaluation and refinement.** This is the iterative process of creative development. All preliminary creative ideas are reviewed and evaluated again. Good ideas move forward. Concepts that are off-strategy are discarded. Concepts that are kept may need additional improvement or modifications that were not noticed before.

5. **Preparation of concepts for research studies.** After you have produced your concepts, you will need to prepare them for your research studies. See Chapter 4 for details.

6. **Final creative selection based on research results.** In this step, your creative judgment must be combined with market feedback to guide selection of creative.

7. **Production of finished artwork for campaign implementation.** After you have selected a concept for your campaign, careful supervision of the many creative details is required to produce superior artwork.

Experience has taught me that it is easy for creative concepts to get off-strategy. Therefore, I have developed a set of guidelines to keep creative development on track and close to the insights gained from all the earlier steps of S.U.R.E.-Fire planning.

Before your concept work begins, hold a meeting with your project managers, research team, and creative resources. A lot of marketing information was collected throughout the process, and it is important to hold a review session. You should have the project managers review the findings from the SWOT and the sales cycle and buy cycle analyses. Write key conclusions on a summary sheet. Show the group the USP you have developed for the company or product. Review where the product that you will promote is located on the product life cycle positioning curve.

Then have the research team review the findings from the one-to-one interviews and the message map. Ask the team to identify the four to six key ideas, problems, or approaches most relevant to the market and to interpret or expand on any of the gray areas discovered thus far. Your goal in this meeting is to agree as a team on the four to six problems, concerns, or solutions that are most urgent to the market. You need to focus the preliminary stage of the creative concept process on these areas.

Using the results of your review meeting, give your creative resources clear written direction. This is the single most effective way to keep the creative process on-strategy. It gives the creative resources a reference to determine whether their ideas are on-strategy or not. I suggest you provide a written list of four to six creative approaches that you want the creative resources to explore and ask them to develop at least two creative ideas or concepts for each. It is also helpful for them to have copies of key documents created earlier in the process as background information (one-to-one interviews, interview summary, SWOT planning session notes).

For example, Figure 10.1 is the message map resulting from the one-to-one interviews for a backup and recovery software product called Replica Network Data Management (NDM), from Stac Software, Inc. From this message map, the creative team was given this list of strategic approaches:

Reduce IT workload: install & forget
Easy for users to restore to any stable state by themselves
Utility to make migrations and upgrades easy
Nontraditional way to protect workstation data that does not require
    tape storage or operator intervention
Reduce the risk of losing workstation data

If you are creating a direct mail lead generation campaign, have your creative resources focus first on the exterior of the envelope. When you send direct mail, you have less than a second to persuade a prospect to pick up the envelope and rip it open. If your concepts fail to motivate a prospect to open the envelope, everything inside is wasted. That is why the S.U.R.E.-Fire planning process devotes a considerable amount of time to creating and testing envelope concepts. You want to find the envelope concept that has the highest likelihood of getting opened. After you have identified the best envelope concept, you can write and design the internal components (letter, brochure, and reply device).

This same creative and research process applies to direct response print advertisements. Your goal is to create the strongest advertising concept, headline, and visual concept possible, using the research process. You can write the body copy and produce the final art after you have identified a winning candidate.

Treat preliminary creative ideas like babies. Evaluate them gently. They are not fully formed. They need time to grow, they need to be nurtured, and they need attention to become strong concepts. Therefore, when you review preliminary creative

Figure 10.1 Message Map: Snapshot of Marketplace Hot Buttons

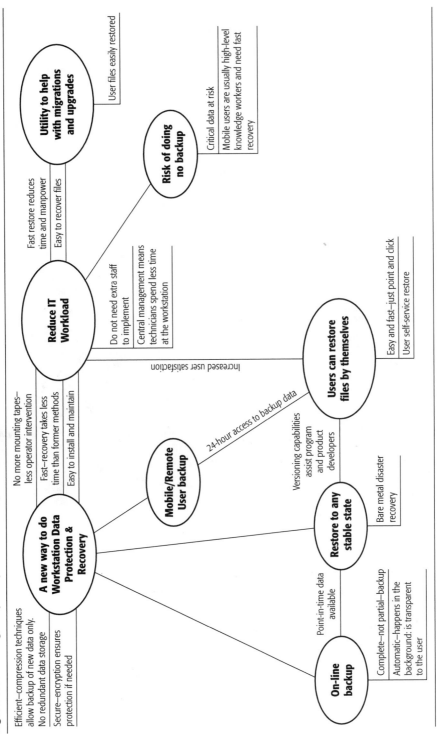

Stac Software, Inc.: Reprinted with permission.

ideas, look for the positive and provide encouragement on how each idea can be improved. Many times the best ideas come in the second round of creative refinement. The rough ideas generate a creative opportunity for recombination, or they may inspire stronger concepts. It is important to give your creative resources time to think, distill, and improve. The creative process is not a precise activity. Be patient.

Evaluate each preliminary concept from three perspectives. First, how accurately does it communicate the desired strategy? Managing creative resources

Figure 10.2a Concept Presented to Focus Group

Epicor Software Corporation: Reprinted with permission.

Directions to creative:

During the focus group, the participants suggested that the photo used in the image was too old-fashioned. The black and white image of an older building looked too stable and boring . . . it did not convey a dynamic image that would appeal to high-growth companies. Also, participants thought a few bullets used with other images were more attention-grabbing. So, change the bullets as indicated below:

- Locate an image that shows a more modern, high-tech building. Make sure the image is in color.
- Replace "multi-unit accounting capabilities" bullet with "Integrated financial, customer service and sales modules."
- Replace "Powerful FSX and Crystal Reports" bullet with "Up-to-the-minute information."

requires walking a fine line between inspiring outside-the-box thinking and guiding the creative process to keep on-strategy. Your creative strategy list is developed to help keep concepts on the right track. If a concept is off-strategy, it must be set aside. Second, how well does it grab your readers' attention? Is it arresting, provocative, or compelling? If an idea will not stop a reader, it will not generate a response. Finally, how relevant is the concept to your target audience? Ideas or images that are arresting but not relevant generally are not well received by the market. The result is low response rates.

If an idea has no merit or does not pass this preliminary screening, kill it rather than waste time trying to fix it. Remain open to testing concepts that make you uncomfortable. Original creative concepts come from combining old ideas in new ways. Don't set yourself up as the judge. Let the marketplace do that job. Let the research process evaluate the validity and impact of a creative concept.

Provide specific direction for creative refinement. In concert with your research team, evaluate and critique each concept, then give direction for refinement in writing. This forces you to be clear and specific. Figures 10.2 and 10.3 are some examples of creative ideas, why they were liked or rejected, and how they were refined.

Figure 10.2b Concept Refined After Focus Group

Epicor Software Corporation: Reprinted with permission.

Before showing your concepts to focus groups, make them look as accurate as possible. After each idea has been through a round of refinement, polish the details. Refine elements such as typography, color choice, artwork selection, offer wording, and layout. As you prepare your concepts for your research, try to be as precise as time and money permit. Most participants in focus groups cannot imagine how a rough concept will look when finished. They react to exactly what they see.

The creative guidelines and checklists in this chapter and the next are useful in two ways. First, they will guide the development and evaluation of your preliminary

Figure 10.3a Concept Presented to Focus Group

Stac Software, Inc: Reprinted with permission.

Directions to creative:

During the focus group, the participants said they would be very interested in a tool that would help them upgrade and migrate workstations. However, they did not like the image. The graphic made no sense to them. Please do the following to revise this image:

- Locate an image that shows many desktop computers . . . which conveys the feeling that it would take a lot of time to upgrade them.
- Turn the headline into the subhead.
- Create a new headline . . . something like "Are you overwhelmed because you need to upgrade all these computers right away?"

concepts—the concepts you will test. Second, after you have identified the concepts for your campaign, the guidelines can help you manage final art production. I refer to these guidelines often. They constantly remind me of the fundamentals of effective direct response advertising. But creative guidelines are just that—guidelines. They are rules that require interpretation and professional judgment. You should assess their relevance and importance case by case during the creative process.

What Makes a Creative Concept a Winner?

Although many creative people in the advertising business are out to win awards, the only real acclaim business-to-business direct marketers should seek is praise from their sales departments for the quantity and quality of leads generated by their marketing programs. All else is superficial. Awards presented solely for creativity have nothing to do with an ad's ability to produce sales results. The best award a business-to-business direct marketer can receive is strong support from the sales department when it comes time to approve budgets for future direct marketing programs.

Figure 10.3b Concept Refined After Focus Group

Stac Software, Inc: Reprinted with permission.

Professional direct marketers recognize that direct response advertising messages are just an extension of the sales force in either print or electronic format. The job of any banner ad, E-mail message, print ad, or direct mail package is to sell—or, more specifically, to persuade someone to take immediate action to find out more. Every word, every picture, and every headline should be in the message for a single purpose: to drive qualified response.

But conceiving and writing a direct response ad is no simple task. It is easy to be influenced by the desire to imitate brand advertisers. Brand advertising seeks to build awareness and/or create a brand personality for a company.

Personally, I strongly believe in the long-term value of establishing a brand identity and leveraging that brand identity in lead generation campaigns. I also believe business-to-business marketers should strive to focus on both brand-development and response generation advertising. Why? Because if you place an ad, serve a banner, or send out a direct mail package that generates no response but is justified under the mantle of branding, you will receive few if any praises from your colleagues in sales. Although all sales managers want to work for a company that has great brand awareness, the daily task they face is feeding leads to their hungry sales force or dealer network. This can only be accomplished with advertising designed from the outset to generate response.

A Clear Creative Strategy Underlies Winning Creative Concepts

Effective direct response creative is not accidental. A well-crafted message is the result of clear, concise input provided to creative resources. The tool most commonly used to give creative direction is the creative brief. There are at least a dozen different creative brief templates, but the answers to at least the following questions must always be included.

- What is the objective of the advertisement? Do you want to motivate a response, influence attitudes, change perceptions, or increase company/product awareness?
- Who is the main target audience? What are their job titles and job functions? What types of companies do they work for? What are the Standard Industrial Classification (SIC) code, number of employees, revenue, and geographic location?
- What are the features and benefits of the *product* or *service* being promoted? What does someone gain as a result of buying it?

- What are the benefits of the response *offer* (call to action) being promoted? What is going to make people respond? Why should they stop what they are doing and request your offer now?
- Given the market and your research, what is the single most important message you want to communicate?
- What are the three to five most important copy points you want to communicate?
- What are the format, size, and type of advertisement (E-mail, print ad, direct mail package, banner ad) you want to produce?

Give yourself adequate time to write a brief. The rule of "garbage in/garbage out" applies. The quality of the information will influence the quality of the concepts generated by your creative resources.

Kern's Rules for Direct Response Creative Excellence

In addition to the guidelines discussed earlier in this chapter, the following rules can help you evaluate and manage the development of creative concepts. I recommend that you review each concept against this list and check off how many guidelines it achieves. If you are a seasoned pro, this list can serve as a helpful reminder or provide inspiration to push your creative ideas.

Attract Attention

Unless your headline and visuals attract the attention of a reader, nothing else can happen. If no one looks at your message, you are guaranteed that it will not generate response. Grab your readers. Draw their eyes to you. Your headline and visual must call out to them. Consider using their titles or functions in your headline. For example: "Now Human Resources Managers can provide personnel data to all employees, directly over the Web," or "Financial Executives: Learn how to stop wasting money on bad business information."

Show Them Something They Never Thought of Before

Effective creative concepts present an ordinary topic in an extraordinary way. One technique to attract attention is to get a reader to think, "Wow! I never thought of that before!" This is the single most difficult job in any creative process. Bringing together facts into new combinations to create new ideas takes time, patience, and practice.

Stand Out from the Crowd

There are two ways to separate yourself from the pack—either shout louder than anyone else or whisper. When a market is cluttered and there is a lot of competition, your advertising message has to speak loudly. It should jump out at your prospects. Color, size, visuals, and provocative headlines can be used to make your message stand out. At other times, speaking softly or being reserved draws readers toward you. It is like the teacher in a classroom full of noisy children who speaks softly until the children turn their attention toward her. A quiet story line can be telling and is commonly used in financial and insurance advertising to add credibility to a company. For example, Northwestern Mutual uses the tag line "The Quiet Company."

Create Curiosity to Find Out More

Intrigue your reader. When people are looking for answers, they are more receptive to new information. Helping people find the information they seek is more powerful than thrusting unwanted information at them. Your lead generation direct response advertising is the first step in a sales relationship. Hold back information from your audience. Pique their interest. You want them to ask you more questions. This makes them open-minded and willing to listen to your sales story. Think like the owner of the ice-cream shop: if you give people a taste, they will be motivated to buy a whole cone.

Be Specific

Facts, figures, and specific measurements give the reader confidence in your message. Details sell. Conversely, vague statements, generalities, and open-ended promises are nothing more than that. Look at this example from a mail package offering a subscription to a financial magazine:

> *Learn from the Net's 50 fastest growing companies and discover the one smartest way to invest in tech. Discover 10 fascinating on-line businesses and hear from 15 visionaries about the Internet in 2002. Just this month. FREE.*

Now compare that to the following copy. Would you be as compelled to open the outside envelope of a direct mail package bearing this message?

> *Learn about many of the Net's quickest growing companies and the best way to invest in technology. Discover several on-line businesses and hear the future of the Internet from visionaries. Just this month. FREE.*

In the first example, specifics like 50, 10, and 15, combined with words like *fastest, smartest, fascinating,* and *visionaries,* draw in readers. The specifics create interest and add credibility to the sales story.

Be Relevant

Speak to your readers in their language about something of immediate and direct interest to them. People do not read ads for fun. Instead, they allow themselves to be interrupted by ads as they are looking at a website, sorting mail, or flipping through a trade magazine. The more relevant your message, the more educational or informative your advertisement, the more you will draw in potential buyers who are looking for a solution to their problem.

Engage Your Reader

People are in constant search of entertainment: television programs, movies, plays, music, CDs. Whether at work or at home, they want to be engaged. An effective lead generation creative concept does not need to be a Broadway show, but it must engage the reader. One way to intrigue readers is to present a challenge that gets them to think for a second. For example: "How many mistakes do you commonly make when reviewing your financial statements with your banker?"

Paint a Picture in Your Reader's Mind by Using Power Words

Your copy's job is to paint a picture in the minds of readers, a picture that builds desire and shows them what they stand to gain if they simply respond to find out more. Use words that build desire or communicate action: *discover, how to, learn, act, see, new, now, hurry, free, save, love, money, avoid,* and *reduce.* Words are the copywriter's paintbrush.

Empathize with Your Readers' Problems or Fantasies

Demonstrate that you understand your readers' problems. Show them you know the daily challenges or obstacles they face. Be understanding of their difficulties and, of course, show them the solution.

Write as if You Were Standing Right in Front of Your Prospect

Your copy should be written as if you were explaining your product to a friend. What would you say to a potential buyer seated across the desk? Make your copy simple to understand. Present a logical sales argument that convinces the prospect to buy. One great way to develop compelling copy is to tape-record sales presentations made by your top salespeople to their biggest prospects. The transcripts will give you or your copywriter golden phrases and ideas for your message.

Talk to Readers in Their Language

Use your readers' words, jargon, and phrasing. Tell them stories or analogies that relate to their daily world. Your prospects have spent most of their lives learning and studying their business. Most attended college, many have advanced degrees, and most read their trade magazines to stay current. If you want to gain their trust, you must earn it by demonstrating that you know their business. Speak their language.

Overcome Your Audience's Fear, Uncertainty, Skepticism, and Doubt

Businesspeople hate to be sold. They are afraid of making a purchasing mistake. They have learned to be skeptical of salespeople's claims. Using specifics, providing testimonials, establishing the reputation of your company, and providing no-risk ways to sample your product without obligation are the fastest and most direct ways to address your sales prospects' hesitation or fear.

Make Them Laugh, but Don't Laugh at Them

People love to laugh. Look at the large number of situation comedies on television. Businesspeople love to laugh, too. Just look at the huge success of the Dilbert comic strip. Humor is a great technique to draw in your reader. It helps people let down their defenses. Humor can be effective in business marketing, but it must be used carefully. It is not appropriate for every situation or every product. As a general rule, make fun of the problem or situation your target audience faces, but do not make fun of your audience. No one likes to be ridiculed. Figure 10.4 is an example of when humor worked well.

Make Your Direct Response Advertisements Easy to Read

Whatever you do, regardless of the medium, make your headline and copy easy to read. Bouncing letters, confusing typography, body copy reversed out of a dark background, small type, and copy placed over graphic images are difficult for the reader. Businesspeople do not want to struggle to figure out your message.

Tap into People's Emotions

Motivational speaker Tony Robbins explains, "People move away from pain and toward pleasure." Psychologists also have taught us that emotions such as joy, laughter, fear, love, and pain drive human behavior and, therefore, response.

Tell and show your prospects how they are going to feel when they use your product or service. They have a problem, and they are looking for relief. Effective communication arouses human emotions and makes an impact on readers. It is human nature to want praise, appreciation, love, affection, recognition, reward, and admiration. Businesspeople want their lives to be made easier. They want to save time and avoid headaches and hassles. Does your copy promise to do this?

If you talk to your prospects about their emotions and problems, you should dangle a solution. Show them relief is just a URL or a phone call away, and you will motivate response. Stimulate the human emotions of fear, happiness, admiration, and advancement to make your creative powerful.

Figure 10.4 Use Humor: Capture Attention and Break Down Defenses

Network Peripherals: Reprinted with permission.

Tell a Story Rich in Promise

Joe Karbo, author of the bestselling book *The Lazy Man's Way to Riche$*, says people always want recognition (acknowledgment, identification, or distinction), romance (attractiveness, desirability, or popularity), reward (wealth, achievement, money, or power), and reincarnation (immortality, youth, or vitality). These four impulses are the basics of all great stories—stories that involve human emotions. Consider the blockbuster movie *Titanic*. The hero, Jack, wants to be something more than a boy from the streets. He wants respect from the wealthy. Jack falls in love with Kate and is rewarded with her devoted love. Jack dies in icy Atlantic waters only to be brought back to life during the retelling of the story by the aged Kate aboard a ship searching for the treasure of the sunken ocean liner.

But how does the marketer selling technology products, manufacturing equipment, or consulting services tell such an engaging story? How does a company tell a story that captures the attention and imagination of the reader? First, the marketer

---

A Campaign in Harmony with Customers

Chordiant Software manufactures a suite of customer interaction applications called Chordiant CCS. The company's enterprise-class software has a high price tag that is justified only by its ability to increase revenues and customer retention. This product allows companies to integrate all existing customer data and make them available to customers through any communications channel. The product has a limited market. The target audience is the top one thousand global consumer companies, which typically have extremely large customer interaction centers. The target titles for this product are executive vice president of business operations and chief information officer. Only the most senior executives can authorize the purchase given the investment required.

To generate leads for the field sales organization and build awareness for the company and its product, a dimensional campaign was developed. The campaign's story line compared the targeted top-level executives to an orchestra conductor. A top executive oversees a range of disparate units within a company. The executive is responsible for bringing units together, just as an orchestra conductor brings together the string, woodwind, percussion, and brass sections of the orchestra.

Three months were invested in building and verifying a database of top executives. Then a teaser mailing went out. It was a long, thin box that carried a quotation from the composer Aaron Copland: "At the orchestra's head is a leader who, through bodily gestures and facial expressivity, acts out the music's progress. There are subtle understandings between leader and instrument . . . all intent on achieving a single goal." Inside, the prospect found a personalized letter, a professional-quality conductor's baton, and a response card. The objective was to demonstrate to prospects that Chordiant understands the

---

can only develop a creative story line by understanding the problems, frustrations, and desires of the target audience. Second, the business-to-business marketer must use professional creative talent—people who can combine old ideas to create new ones and present products and services in fresh ways.

Clearly Promote Your Offer

An offer is the reward you wave in front of your prospect to motivate response. Without a clear presentation of a compelling offer, your advertisement will not generate response. If there are no sales leads, there will be no prospects to nurture over time.

Time and again, I have seen marketers use their product literature, their product story, and their company story as the direct response offer. These direct marketers are under the false impression that if they just say enough about themselves

---

difficult tasks they face managing diverse data sources and customer requirements. The creative also communicated that Chordiant's software solution could help improve customer interactions, thereby enhancing customer retention.

Figure 10.5
Tell a Story:
A Campaign
in Harmony
with
Customers

Two weeks later, the prospects received a large shipping box. Inside, they found a full-size violin. The story line was that Chordiant software could make their call center sound like a Stradivarius to their customers' ears. By using a Chordiant solution, the prospect company would please and delight customers who contact them.

The campaign generated nearly 13 percent response. It helped start ten sales relationships and heralded the successful launch of this start-up company. Although not every company or product lends itself to this kind of story, developing an appropriate story is well worth the investment of time and effort.

and their products they will convince prospects to respond. My experience has shown that in two-step lead generation it is best to promote the reason to respond, generate the lead, then promote product benefits and features. I recommend this strategy because prospects will not care about your company, product, or service until they understand what you can do for them. Combine this with the fact that people are busy and naturally self-centered, and you will find that success comes to business-to-business direct marketers who provide information, education, or assistance before trying to sell their product.

In a little less than one second, your direct response advertisement must stop prospects in their tracks. In the next second, it must interest them to find out more. In the third second, it must convince them that what you are offering is so valuable that they must call, fax, go to the Web, or send back the reply card immediately. Given this scenario, will you generate greater response when you force a prospect to wade through a pile of product information, or when you clearly promote your offer—an offer that costs readers nothing but gives them something of value?

A strong offer, by its nature, content, and title, self-qualifies prospects. It calls out to prospects in search of a solution, saying that your product can eventually provide a solution. For example:

Making the network connection: How to harness the power of thin-client computing.
Fifteen strategies you need to know before buying your next phone system.
The financial manager's handbook to capital asset accounting and the impact of fixed asset tax laws.

Make Your Offer Irresistible

Your response rates and lead quality are in direct proportion to the appeal of your offer. At the core of every effective campaign is an offer so irresistible that prospects will drop everything to reply to the message. Give away a free digital camera when prospects respond. Offer an important book or give a gift to the first five hundred responders. (See Chapter 6 for a full discussion of direct response offers.) Never forget, the fastest way to improve your response rates is to increase the value of your offer.

Evaluate Direct Response Advertising Like a Door-to-Door Presentation

Think about how the Avon door-to-door salesperson succeeds. She knocks on the door to find out if anybody is home—she targets the market and gets attention.

When the door is cautiously opened, the salesperson is ready with an arresting reply to the question, "Who's there?" She is prepared to address the buyer's fear. She calls out, "It's Avon, and I'm giving away free samples of new lipsticks to see how women in the neighborhood like them." She overcomes the buyer's fear using company brand credibility, and she creates curiosity.

As the salesperson secures the interest of the home owner, the door opens. The salesperson continues, "Hello, Ms. Smith. My name is Sue Seller. Avon thought it would be a good idea for me to see what women think about a new lipstick line. May I have just five minutes of your time?" She gains permission to speak.

When she is inside the house, the salesperson comments, "What a beautiful home you have, Ms. Smith." She builds rapport. "By the way, Ms. Smith, so I pick out the best samples for you, would you mind if I ask what you like best and least about the lipstick you wear now?" She determines the buyer's problem. She is quickly developing an understanding of the prospect before she begins her sales presentation. A successful salesperson knows the importance of discovering the prospect's interests and troubles before presenting her wares.

Our salesperson continues the sales process by pulling out a brochure that shows a lineup of fifty new lipstick colors. The brochure, instead of selling the product, is educational. It shows many pictures of women using the newest lipstick styles and techniques. The brochure involves the emotions, and then sells the promise. While the brochure is open, the salesperson initiates a dialog. Sue Seller asks what colors Ms. Smith would like to try, and as Ms. Smith tries the product, the salesperson begins to tell her why that sample is a unique product. She uses one-to-one communication. After the demonstration is completed, Sue Seller tells Ms. Smith about a special price and pulls out her order form: She asks for the order.

Your print advertisement, E-mail message, banner ad, or direct mail package must operate as this door-to-door salesperson does. The headline, graphics, subject line in the E-inbox, and teaser headline on the mailing surface of an envelope are your knock on the door. They must arouse attention and immediately answer the prospect's questions of "Who are you?" and "What do you want?" The body copy of an advertisement, E-mail message, or sales letter is the one-to-one communication, the place where you can speak person to person, just as if you were sitting in the living room with your prospect. Your brochure within a direct mail package is the offer demonstration. It explains all the benefits of responding to your offer. Your call to action or reply card is equal to the salesperson's order form. It is the communication that directs prospects to a specific action. It tells prospects exactly what they must do to receive the offer and what they will get in exchange for their action.

Make Your Creative Concepts Live Up to AIDA

The salesperson's acronym of AIDA—Attention, Interest, Desire, and Action—is another useful guideline for evaluating direct response creative. Consider this application of the acronym:

- **Attention.** Call out to your prospect. Use his or her name, title, and concerns. As you know, you sometimes need to yell, shout, jump up and down, or even whisper to attract someone's attention. Unless you grab the prospect's attention, nothing can happen. Look at your mailing surfaces, your print ad headlines and graphics, your E-mail subject lines, and ask yourself, What did I do to capture the reader's attention? Arresting graphics? Provocative headlines? A combination of both?
- **Interest.** Now look at your creative work and ask what strategy you are using to create interest. What are you doing to develop empathy? How are you demonstrating your understanding of prospects' problems? Finally, what have you done to position your offer and your message as providing a solution to the problem?
- **Desire.** Next, evaluate the body copy and your story line. Are you building desire by discussing the benefits of the offer? Are you tantalizing the reader with and selling the sizzle of the offer?
- **Action.** People are begging to be led. We are used to being told what to do. Therefore, the marketer needs to clearly present the offer and follow through by making the call to action easy to accomplish. For example, "If you want this free demo CD, just call, fax, E-mail, visit, or mail the enclosed reply card."

Tell Prospects What You Want Them to Do

Don't assume people know what to do. Tell them where to click, tell them what number to call, tell them what URL to go to, and tell them to return the reply card. We are trained from childhood to follow directions given to us by our teachers. Give your prospects the directions they need to receive your offer.

Thank Them for Their Time

Be appreciative of people's time. In focus groups, I have many times heard prospects say how much they like to receive free T-shirts because they consider them a thank-you gift from the marketer for taking time to look at the marketer's materials. Good manners, graciousness, and courtesy are techniques of successful salesmanship.

Summing Up

Managing the creative development process is complex. Staying on strategy requires teamwork among your research staff, creative resources, and project managers. When beginning the creative process, you should review the results of the strategic planning phase and the one-to-one interviews from the Understanding for Empathy phase of the S.U.R.E.-Fire process.

The information gathered from your strategic planning steps, such as the SWOT and win/loss analyses, can be combined with the findings from the one-to-one interviews to lay the foundation for development of offers and creative concepts. When qualitative and quantitative research methods are used, the marketplace feedback can help you select the best offers and concepts for campaign implementation.

In this chapter, you examined several sets of guidelines for managing the creative process. These guidelines included the seven creative development steps of execution excellence, Kern's rules for direct response creative excellence, the model of the door-to-door salesperson's presentation, and the AIDA standard. As you move toward implementation, you should rely on the rules and guidelines presented in this and the next chapter to produce excellent creative work.

MANAGING DIRECT RESPONSE ADVERTISING

*To communicate, put your thoughts in order; give them a
purpose; use them to persuade, to instruct, to discover, to
seduce.*

—William Safire
Columnist, *The New York Times*

This chapter contains the rules and principles that will help you achieve creative excellence. One of the best ways to manage creative implementation is to refer to the tried and true rules. From the letter strategies of Joan Throckmorton to the advertising philosophies of David Ogilvy, these guidelines are timeless. Although there are specific guidelines for each medium, all focus on the underlying issue of direct response advertising—how to use communication to motivate a reader to action. This chapter includes evaluation guidelines for direct mail advertising that I have developed over twenty years while creating more than a thousand campaigns for a wide range of clients.

Choosing a Direct Mail Package

One of the most common lead generation tools for business direct marketers is direct mail advertising. Direct mail advertising provides the business marketer with an unlimited amount of space, color, and format options to communicate a sales message. The standard components of a business direct mail package are outer envelope or carrier envelope, letter, brochure or broadside, and reply card or reply form. A direct mail package can have many additional inserts, including lift notes, buck slips, and testimonial letters.

White Mail versus Promotional Mail

Two major categories of direct mail advertising are used in business-to-business direct marketing: white mail and promotional mail. White mail is any piece of direct mail that looks like genuine personal correspondence. A standard closed-face No. 10 business envelope is the most common type of white mail. White mail generally has only the sender's company logo or name and address in the top left corner. The recipient's address is printed in the center of the envelope, directly on the surface of the envelope (as if it were typed). The envelope has first-class postage, either metered or as a stamp. There is generally no teaser copy or artwork on the surface. The envelope looks clean. The exception to this rule is that the outer surface is sometimes printed with words like *Personal and Confidential* or *Confidential Correspondence.*

Promotional mail, also called advertising mail or impact direct mail, includes all other types of advertisements sent through the U.S. Postal Service or third-party carriers. Promotional mail comes in all shapes, sizes, and colors. The most common types of promotional mail are postcards, self-mailers, envelope packages, and dimensional packages. The size and type of promotional mail used for a lead generation campaign are based on your objectives, budget, production time frame, offer, product, and the competitiveness of your marketplace.

When the daily mail is delivered to a suspect, it is usually stacked with the largest pieces on the bottom and the smallest envelopes on the top. The suspect then separates all white mail, which includes correspondence such as letters, bills, and invitations, for closer inspection. During sorting, promotional mail is glanced at, and within a split second, the suspect decides to either keep it or toss it. Never forget: suspects sit or stand near a trash can to speed their sorting process.

By definition, white mail must be opened. Readers feel that if they throw away a white mail package unopened, they might miss out on something important. The limited use of design and lack of a sales message on a white mail envelope telegraph to the reader that something personal or important is inside. Human curiosity or concern (depending on who sent the letter) drives readers to open the outer envelope and look inside at the contents before they decide to discard or save. Promotional advertising mail, on the other hand, is only opened if the suspect is persuaded in a split second that the contents of the package have value that must be secured immediately. In short, if the copy and graphics on your promotional envelope do not do this one job, your package and your marketing investment are headed for the trash.

White mail is commonly used to reach top-level executives and professionals such as doctors and lawyers, who have gatekeepers (people who open and screen their mail). It is used when there is not time to produce a promotional package. White mail communicates to people who know you, such as customers or prospects. These people want to hear from you, so you do not need to invest in a promotional package.

You may be wondering why, if white mail is always opened, business direct marketers do not limit themselves to white closed-face envelopes. There are several answers. Unless you really know your suspects, sending them a personal letter becomes a gimmick. People are not fooled, and a fake personal approach can create a negative reaction. Further, because white mail does not use pictures or words on the outside of the envelope to set up the story line inside, it does not help build brand personality. Also, packages wear out. Unless the audience is huge, most business marketers have to mail to the same prospects again and again. If you continue to send the exact same white No. 10 closed-face package to the same people, response rates will quickly decline. Closed-face personalized mailings can be more expensive than promotional packages because the outer envelope address must be matched to the personalized letter inside. Finally, marketers want to integrate their advertising. The same images and messages used in advertising can be carried over to direct mail. This integration builds awareness and increases the opportunity for success.

Choosing the Best Promotional Direct Mail Format

There is an art to selecting the style and size of promotional direct mail. Here are some guidelines to help you choose the format that is best for you.

Postcards

A postcard is a two-sided piece of mail. It can range from 3½ by 5 inches to 9 by 12 inches or even larger. I recommend using a postcard when you have a brief message to deliver, such as a trade show reminder or a sales announcement. A postcard can be effective when you are marketing to customers who already know and trust you, and when your offer is simple to understand and extremely valuable. Department stores like to use postcards to announce holiday sales, for which little copy is required. A postcard is quick to produce and less expensive than other types of mail packages because there is nothing to insert into an envelope. Large sizes and unusual shapes incur postal surcharges.

One drawback to postcards is the lack of a reply device. Your suspect has nothing to mail back to you. The biggest downside to using a postcard is that it only gets "postcard attention" from a suspect. Quick to read, it is even quicker to discard. Unless your offer is really a stopper, postcards get little consideration.

Self-Mailers

A self-mailer is any flat piece of mail that has been folded but not inserted into a carrier envelope. There is no limit to the size or the number of folds. Because self-mailers can be any size (check with the post office for sizes that incur a surcharge), they are versatile. Unlike postcards, self-mailers can have reply devices that help you track source code information. They can be used for many types of business-to-business marketing activities, including event announcements, trade show traffic generation, or lead generation. They are ideal when you need a lot of space to show graphics and images and make a big impact. Self-mailers can be less expensive than envelope mail packages, because there is no insertion of additional components. A self-mailer can be an effective way to stretch a limited budget.

One downside to self-mailers is that they don't produce as high a response rate as an envelope mail package. Also, they are not personal communications. Generally, there is no letter in a self-mailer. A prospect will spend slightly more time looking at your self-mailer than at a postcard, but once again, your offer statement must be clear and exceptionally compelling to drive response.

Envelope Letter Packages

Envelope letter packages are direct mail packages that contain at a minimum a letter inserted into an outer envelope. Envelope packages can also include brochures, lift notes, and reply devices. They are the workhorses of business direct marketing because they simulate personal correspondence, and they let you show and tell your story. Your letter speaks to your reader personally. If you include a multipanel brochure, it can contain headlines, copy, pictures, and illustrations to support your promise. You can also include a reply device that makes it easy for a prospect to act.

Suspects open envelopes and read the letter inside when the message is relevant to them. Even in the era of E-mail and fifteen-second television spots, people still read well-written letters. An envelope letter package can be used for many types of business direct marketing programs, including lead generation, event attendance, and direct mail sales.

The upside of an envelope letter package is that you are not limited by space. The format also encourages suspects to spend time looking at the components in your package, giving you more time to sell. Depending on the design, envelope letter packages can help establish credibility as well as build brand image.

The downside of an envelope letter package is higher production time and cost, especially for high-impact mailings that require custom envelopes. Unlike self-mailers, which only entail the production of one piece, envelope letter packages require an outer envelope plus several other components—each of which requires a certain amount of time to prepare. You also have to examine the cost of producing each element of the package and then compare these costs with the cost of other formats, keeping projected response rates in mind. I have found that even though envelope letter packages are more expensive per piece than self-mailers, they generate more response and therefore are more cost-effective than postcards or self-mailers for lead generation campaigns.

Dimensional Direct Mail

Any direct mail correspondence sent in something that is not a flat envelope, box, or tube is called a dimensional mailing. These mailings are used to get the recipient's attention. The idea is to make a big impact so the recipient will open the package—which contains items that reinforce the message or story the marketer is trying to communicate. Dimensional mailings range in cost from $5 to $1,000 per unit. They can be sent as a one-part mailing or as a series of mailings.

Dimensional mailings are good when you have a small audience that is well identified and valuable, or when you are selling an expensive product such as an executive airplane. They require time to design, produce, and assemble. The upside is that they seldom are thrown away unopened. However, if you want to use a dimensional mailing to generate leads, remember this rule: your dimensional mailing only generates attention—your offer influences response.

Getting Your Envelope Opened

Envelopes are effective when they motivate a reader to pick them up, rip them open, and look inside to see what is there. Envelopes must grab a reader's attention, provoke curiosity, be involving, and establish the seller's credibility. The look and feel of your envelope establish who you are. They set the stage for the first questions a suspect asks: "Why should I open this? Why should I give you a second of my scarce time?"

If you are a well-known corporation like IBM, Xerox, or AT&T, putting your name and logo on the outside of your envelope in the upper left corner (called the corner card area) lets your brand's value communicate your credentials. This credential factor works the other way, too. If suspects have never heard of XYZ Manufacturing Company, they will be more hesitant to open the envelope than if they know the company. Regardless, I suggest putting your name and logo in the corner area. Gimmicks and trickery are ineffective strategies for business-to-business direct marketers. If you are unknown, elements such as paper stock, envelope size, colors, image, design, and addressing method all subconsciously communicate the importance and credibility of your message and the contents inside. A high-gloss, full-color envelope sends a different message than a two-color, all-type headline sloppily offset-printed on a thin, paper stock envelope.

Following are several creative approaches you can use to help get your envelope noticed and opened. Each is an option. Only through research and testing will you know which is the best approach for your product.

- **Communicate a huge promise of what lies inside.** You only have a second. Tell your readers all the reasons they should look inside your envelope. For example:

  Everything you ever needed to know about chemical recycling inside.

- **Establish a question or pose a challenge.** If you can capture the mind of your readers and get them to think about your message for a second, you increase the chance they will open your envelope. For example:

  How ready are you for the IRS to audit your books?

- **Tell it all on the outside.** If you think of your envelope as a print ad, you will want to communicate an entire story on the outside surface. For example:

  Plant Managers. Learn how to cut the cost of uniforms by 25 percent. Discover how to improve the appearance of your workforce. Plus, eliminate the headaches of uniform inventory control.

- **Make it a mystery.** Don't say too much. People do not want to be sold. White mail works because it does not start selling until the suspect reaches the inside. The phrases "Personal and Confidential" and "Important tax information inside" are always effective.

- **Make it dramatic or unusual.** You want to stand out from the clutter in the mailbox. Consider a large format, dramatic graphics, die cuts, tear-offs, or metallic material. Anything that helps the piece stand out can make you more successful.

An Army of Salespeople in Print: The Power of Your Sales Letter

Direct mail advertising originated in the days when businesspeople actually sent personal correspondence to each other. People expected to receive a letter inside every envelope they received. Then addressing and inserting machines made it possible to send a sales letter to tens of thousands of people at once. This gave the direct marketer the ability to launch a virtual army of door-to-door salespeople to show up at each suspect's threshold.

Direct mail studies show that immediately after a person opens the envelope, he or she scans its contents and reads the sales letter. The sales letter in a direct mail package is the only enclosure that should be written in the first person. It is the element within the envelope that lets you, the letter writer, tell your story on a personal level. Write as if you were talking to a friend, one-to-one. The quality of your letter writing can affect your response by 10 to 50 percent. Never send an envelope package without a letter. Your letter is the single most important creative element in the envelope.

Make your letter as long as required to convince your readers to respond. Tell them what they will get, why they want to respond, and how to respond. Two-step business-to-business direct marketing letters tend to be shorter than consumer direct mail, because the objective is to generate a lead, not make a sale. Therefore, you do not need as much copy. Here are some guidelines for writing strong business-to-business sales letters.

- **Start with your most important benefit and embellish it.** Get your readers excited to find out how your product is going to help them.
- **Be specific.** Tell your readers exactly what they are going to get. Use exact numbers, figures, and percentages.
- **Provide proof or endorsements for your claims and promises.** Readers are skeptical. They want evidence. Include testimonials from peers or customers to prove your point.
- **Let readers know what they will miss out on if they do not take action.** People do not want to pass up an opportunity. Telling your readers what they will not get provides motivation to act now.

- **Restate your benefits in the closing of your letter.** Reinforce the benefits and all the reasons why your readers need to act now. If you kept your readers' attention to the end of your letter, give them a parting shot about how they will benefit from your offer or product.
- **Encourage immediate action.** Overcoming inertia is the biggest obstacle to generating response. Tell your readers why they must act now. Give them a time limit, or let them know how much more it will cost if they do not act.

Writing a great direct response letter is an art. Here are some techniques that add punch to letters and improve results.

- **Use a Johnson box.** The Johnson box is a message or headline at the top of your letter before or adjacent to your salutation. This technique was developed by Bob Johnson, who, using a manual typewriter, called attention to a headline by typing stars around it in a box format. Today, there are many versions of the Johnson box. The Johnson box gives your readers the first reason they should read your letter. For example:

  Stop wasting time and money ordering office supplies through a catalog. Go to www.officesupplies.com and save 40% now.

- **Salutations are necessary.** When you are personalizing your letter with a suspect's name, unless you know the title (Mr., Mrs., Ms., Dr., Rabbi), use "Dear First Name Last Name," as in "Dear Sally Johnson." When you do not personalize a letter (I call this a generic letter format), use a salutation that calls out to your reader, such as Dear Fellow Executive, Dear Customer, Dear Architect, or Dear Technology Professional.
- **Your body copy must motivate.** After your lead sentence grabs the reader's attention, your letter must immediately build credibility, overcome skepticism, present major benefits, substantiate the claims, describe specific features to generate enough value that a prospect will act. Your letter is supposed to be a personal correspondence between the author and the reader. Write in a personal tone. Write as if you are talking to a dear friend and you want to convince the person how foolish it would be to miss out on this offer. Show that you care about your readers, that you understand their problems, that you have walked in their shoes, and that you have something they must see.
- **Include a postscript.** The postscript at the conclusion of the letter is a timeless letter-writing technique. It tells the reader that there is something so important you want to make sure they don't forget about it.

Businesspeople will read the postscript of your letter. Sometimes, they will read the postscript right after they read the Johnson box headline. Readers often glance over a letter, read the subheads, and then read the postscript—all before they read the lead sentence. A good use of the postscript is to restate your offer. Also, you can drop in a selling point, which serves as a reminder of a key message covered in the body of your letter.

Twelve Letter-Writing Approaches Proven to Work

Joan Throckmorton, direct marketing specialist and president of Joan Throckmorton, Inc., has developed twelve basic creative approaches for direct mail letters. The following is my interpretation of her twelve approaches.

1. **The generic approach.** This most widely used approach is basic and straightforward. It lets you start right in with the major benefit and offer. This approach is best when used for business-to-business mail, testing a brand-new product, or offering an exciting premium.

2. **The invitational approach.** This approach is used to announce new products or to invite a prospect to an event. The phrasing may be "You are cordially invited to" or "Please RSVP by . . . ." The words "you are invited" force readers to consider if they want to come. Invitations can be formal or casual depending on your audience and your offer. This approach is ideal for driving attendance to seminars, Internet conferences, or trade show events.

3. **The Bartlett's quotation approach.** *Bartlett's Familiar Quotations* is a reference book for writers that contains wonderful quotations. Using a quotation is a fast way to gain a reader's attention and establish your credibility. You can quote a famous author or person, but it is more effective to quote a well-respected source in your field. For example:

   Now, virtually any device, from a new terminal or PC to an outdated Macintosh, can tap into programs that may be running on a server in another city or another country.
   —Don Clark
   The Wall Street Journal, November 15, 1999

4. **The testimonial approach.** Readers want to hear from others. Most people don't want to go first. They want to benefit from others' experience. Using testimonials to start your letter is a winning strategy:

I've never seen a product work as fast as this.

—Bob Smith
Any City, Any State

I was skeptical about these claims, but in just three days I was amazed at the results.

—Lydia Marie
Any City, Any State

5. **The identification approach.** This letter-writing technique is effective because it calls out to your readers and draws them into your story. People react when their name is called. The same is true when you call out their profession or occupation. When cost or list quality makes it impractical to personalize letters, a generic salutation is an alternative. Although this kind of salutation does not call the reader by name, it does confirm that the reader is in the category of people the marketer is seeking. This, in turn, increases readership. For example:

Design Engineers: Here is news on an important advancement in chip performance.

6. **The "if," or assumptive, approach.** This is a variation on the identification approach. It uses the "If you are . . . then this is . . ." copy style. This creative approach is a good way to present a self-qualifying offer. It gives you room to call out to the types of prospects you want to attract. For example:

If you are concerned with the cost of paper for your printing plant . . . then you'll want to request this free video today.

7. **The question approach.** Questions involve and engage your reader. Using questions is another effective strategy to call out to your target audience. For example:

How many of these customer service mistakes do your call-center agents make daily?

Consultants: Do you know your true client profitability?

8. **The problem/solution approach.** This creative strategy lets you admit that there is trouble but then offers your reader a resolution. I like this approach when research shows the market is looking to solve a particular problem, and the product that I am promoting is uniquely qualified to solve that problem. For example:

Capital gains taxes are on the rise. See what you can do to avoid their impact on your profits.

9. **The fantasy approach.** This works well for sweepstakes or when the benefits lend themselves to building dreams or imaginary situations.

You get the reader dreaming along with you and then propose the answer or solution:

Imagine yourself enjoying free time without a thought as to who's minding the shop. You can have this peace of mind when you use . . .

10. **The analogy approach.** Analogies help readers understand complex products. The comparison of your product to something a suspect relates to makes it easier to understand. Analogies are useful in developing empathy with your readers, too.

11. **The story approach.** People love to read a good story. However, when you use a story in business-to-business marketing, it must be relevant to your readers and pull them right into your benefits. For example:

While I was flying to New York the other day, the woman sitting next to me asked about my accountant. I told her how much money my CPA had saved my company . . .

12. **The be-a-hero approach.** Businesspeople are constantly looking for ways to increase profits or save their company time and money. Showing readers how they can gain the praise of others by bringing these benefits to their company is effective. All people want to gain the appreciation of others. They want promotions and recognition. They want to feel important to their peers. For example:

In just twenty seconds, you are going to learn how to give yourself a $10,000 raise.

The Value of Brochures in Your Package

You include inserts such as brochures in your mail package to support your sales story. A brochure adds credibility. It gives you room to dramatize the benefits you are promoting. I recommend that all business-to-business direct mail packages use a brochure, because people are persuaded to act when a story is told to them from several angles. A brochure gives you the space and freedom to use pictures, copy, diagrams, illustrations, testimonials, and examples. The size of the brochure must be determined by the value of what you are promoting and the degree of complexity of your product and offer. For example, if you are using big screen shots of a software program to demonstrate its functionality, you would need a large brochure.

You want to design and write a brochure to advance your sales story. Use pictures to help readers understand, headlines to guide them through your copy, and design to keep them on track. I like the writing and concept of my brochures to continue the creative concept presented on the outer envelope. Your brochure can help build your brand personality by using a design style and copy tone that reflect your corporate advertising and style. Here are a few rules to help you direct the development of a brochure.

- **Design a cover that people want to open.** The sole job of a brochure cover is to get people to open the brochure. Make your cover interesting, but be sure it leads the reader inside.
- **Use gatefold panels to advance the story but not to tell the main story.** Readers immediately open a brochure to the largest single flat surface. Important sales messages will get lost if they are on the gatefolds, because readers skip over these panels as they quickly unfold the brochure to see what is inside. You can use gatefolds to help advance your concept, but do not assume readers will see each panel.
- **Design the inside to show and tell the whole story.** Design and write your brochure to achieve your objective—generating response. Show pictures and tell stories that convince readers to respond to your offer—nothing more and nothing less. Make it easy for readers to follow your story by using easy-to-read typography. Support your story with photos and illustrations with captions. People are trained to read captions. Show your offer, and let your readers know what they will get when they respond. Place your clear call to action (URL, toll-free telephone number, or fax number) right next to the offer.
- **Close the deal with your reply device.** The purpose of a reply device is to make it easy for prospects to respond. Print prospects' name and address information on the reply so they do not need to write it in. You should give them the options of responding by fax, mail, website, or toll-free number; whatever is most convenient to them.

There are two kinds of reply devices. A reply card can be sent through the mail. A reply form must be inserted in a business reply envelope before it can be mailed. Whether you use a reply card or a reply form, clearly state and show your entire offer proposition. Make it easy to see your offer statement on the top of the form even when it is still folded in the envelope. Some people, in their rush to sort through mail, slice open the envelope and peek inside without removing the contents—the "envelope peek." People must get a quick snapshot of your sales proposition at a glance.

Consider the following guidelines when evaluating your reply device.

- **Make the reply device easy for your prospects to return.** Do the work for your prospects. Use printing technology to preprint their name and address.

- **Summarize the benefits of your offer.** Tell—and show—your readers what they will get by responding.
- **Tell them all the response options.** Tell them what phone number to call, what URL to visit, what fax number to use, or how to return the form by mail.
- **Create a sense of urgency.** Promote your expiration date or use a copy line, such as "quantities limited to stock on hand," to add urgency. One way to overcome inertia is to give people a deadline.
- **Request contact and address information verification.** Don't assume the name and address you rented and printed is 100 percent correct. Ask responders to make corrections and tell them where to do it on the reply form. The wording might be "Please make address corrections below."
- **Ask qualification and profile questions.** Don't be afraid to ask profile questions. As discussed in Chapter 7, lead generation is about quid pro quo: you are willing to give prospects something of value in exchange for information about themselves. A typical reply card asks five to fifteen questions.
- **Ask for an E-mail address and permission to use that address.** E-mail communication is a low-cost way to stay in contact with responders. Leave space on your reply form to collect E-mail addresses. You must get permission from prospects before you start sending E-mail messages. For example: "Please fill in your E-mail address if you would like to be updated on our products and receive our electronic newsletter."
- **Make your reply form inviting.** Make the reply form clear. It should be so easy to understand that a ten-year-old could figure out what you are offering. Make sure your type, design, and layout streamline the communication.

Lead Generation Print Advertising

In business marketing, print is a crucial advertising medium. Using print advertising for lead generation presents challenges because of conflicting marketing objectives. Most business marketers use print advertising to build brand awareness. However, these days they also want their print advertising to generate sales leads or drive traffic to a website. They must measure their return on marketing investment, which is hard to do with pure brand advertising.

Kern's Rules for Direct Mail Packages

Consider using this list of questions to help you evaluate your preliminary direct mail concepts and to aid in the supervision of your final production.

- Do you have a clear and believable selling proposition?
- Is your selling proposition based on the findings of your research and the desires of the market?
- Is your offer irresistible? Will someone stop and request it now?
- Does your outside envelope call out to your target audience?
- Do the design, color, size, shape, and appearance of your outside envelope establish credibility and reflect the quality of your company and product?
- Does your outside envelope motivate your readers to get involved with your message?
- Do your graphics reinforce your message and aid communication?
- Is the type easy to read?
- Is the copy relevant, specific, and readable? Is it personal?
- Does your copy tell readers why they must act now, not later?
- Does the package tell a dramatic story?
- Is the package written in the jargon of the reader, not the advertiser?
- Do the copy and package design guide the reader to respond?
- Is the story comprehensive?
- Does it present all the benefits, with emphasis on the most important benefit?
- Are features presented as advantages?
- Does the package touch readers emotionally and appeal to their logic?
- Do you talk to the reader in a positive and flattering way?
- Do you prove and dramatize the value of the offer?
- Do you overcome the reader's fear, uncertainty, and doubt?
- Do you reverse the sales risk by giving a guarantee of satisfaction?
- Do the letter and brochure support each other by repeating key points?
- Have you used testimonials or third-party sources to lend authority to your story?
- Does the package give a reason for immediate response?
- Did you make it easy to order and tell readers how to do so?
- Is your story consistent from beginning to end?
- Does each element in your package stand on its own yet mesh with every other element?
- Will it mail? Can everything be inserted? How will its weight affect postage?
- Can you preprint your piece to make it easy to capture tracking codes and measure response?

Professional business marketers must strive to achieve both marketing objectives. This requires wrestling with the space limitations of print, the short attention span of readers, the clutter of advertising in magazines, and the difficulty of motivating response from print advertising. The specific questions the business marketer must address are: What percentage of the message should focus on the offer versus the product and its benefits? How much space should be devoted to the headline? How much space should the visual take up, and what type of visual should be used? How much space should body copy occupy, and what should be its focus? How much space should be devoted to the presentation of the offer? What type of call to action should be used, and how strongly should it be promoted?

The blending of brand advertising with direct response techniques is a subject Stan Rapp covers in his book *The New Maximarketing.* Richard Rosen, principal of the Rosen/Brown Direct agency in Portland, Oregon, says: "All communication should be a blend of promoting the brand message, in combination with a strong promotion of the offer strategy. These days, the primary offer strategy is to drive all prospects to the Web."

The blend of brand advertising and lead generation can be viewed as a continuum with a 100 percent brand message ad on one end and a 100 percent lead generation ad on the other. Figure 11.1 shows three examples of print ads that lie on this continuum.

The 100 percent brand ad is focused on awareness, the personality of the product, and making a memorable impact. The 50/50 ad balances the presentation between awareness and response. The offer is shown, and the calls to action are apparent. The 100 percent response ad is only about the offer: why readers would want it and how they can get it. Although this ad attempts to present a personality, response is the major objective.

In today's Web-enabled, metered marketing world, 100 percent brand advertising is a major luxury for most small and midsize business-to-business marketers. There is no argument about the value of building a brand, but for average business marketers, it is unacceptable and wasteful to spend hundreds of thousands or even millions of dollars on brand awareness alone. I am a strong supporter of the blended approach to business print advertising. When you make an offer in print advertising, you can generate a lead or drive traffic. Never forget that you do not invest in print advertising to impress your board of directors or make your sales force feel good. You place print ads to help the sales process and generate a return on your investment. Using 100 percent direct response ads or an advertising approach that blends brand building with lead generation is among the surest ways to help the sales process.

Figure 11.1a Three Samples of Brand vs. Response Advertising: 100% Brand Advertising

Figure 11.1b Three Samples of Brand vs. Response Advertising: 50% Brand/50% Response Advertising

Which one of these Vice Presidents just deployed the next generation of e-service software for their website?

Trying to stay on top of stacks of Internet requests? Losing customers because you can't respond to their queries in realtime? Or are you getting a lot of hits on your web site that don't result in sales conversions?

Today it's the electronic age. And instant response is *everything*. If you can't process leads or help your customers fast enough, then they *will* go elsewhere.

@eez e-service center software is here. It's truly the next generation of e-service software. It allows you to prioritize Internet queries according to urgency, or by purchase criticality. This way, customers who are most ready to buy always receive top priority. Furthermore, you can respond to all your customers' queries in seconds, by using automatic channel selection.

The time has come. Change the way you think about e-service. To get you started, we'll send you an invaluable e-service book.

It's yours **FREE**, when you call XYZ Company at **1-877-123-4567** or visit us online: **www.xyzcompany.com/freeguide**.

@eez e-service center software will help you:

* Provide outstanding, efficient customer service
* Prioritize customer requests
* Automatically respond to your most urgent customers first

Get your **FREE** copy of "**50 Proven E-Service Techniques That Your Competition Doesn't Know...Yet!**" and learn how you can stay one generation ahead of your competition. Call now: **1-877-123-4567** or visit our website at **www.xyzcompany.com/freeguide**.

@eez e-service center software from
xyzcompany

Figure 11.1c Three Samples of Brand vs. Response Advertising: 100% Response Advertising

Are you frustrated trying to answer stacks of Internet requests?

Are you losing customers because you can't respond to their queries in realtime?

Are you getting a lot of hits on your web site that do not result in sales conversions?

Today it's the electronic age.
And instant response is *everything*. If you can't process leads or help your customers fast enough, then they *will* go elsewhere.

@eez e-service center software can help.
It's the next generation of e-service software. It allows you to prioritize Internet queries according to urgency, or by purchase criticality.

This way, customers who are most ready to buy always receive top priority.

Furthermore, it allows you to respond to all your customers' queries in seconds, by using automatic channel selection.

The time has come. Change the way you think about e-service.
To get you started, we'll send you—at no charge—an invaluable e-service guide: **"50 Proven E-Service Techniques That Your Competition Doesn't Know...Yet!"**. This important book is yours **FREE** simply by calling XYZ Company at **1-877-123-4567** or when you visit us at **www.xyzcompany.com/freeguide**.

Discover how you can:
* Provide outstanding, efficient customer service 24/7
* Prioritize customer requests by your own business rules
* Allow your website to automatically respond to your most urgent customers first
* Provide automatic channel selection like e-mail, I-mail, chat and/or voice callback

Receive your **FREE** copy ($39.95 value!) of **"50 Proven E-Service Techniques That Your Competition Doesn't Know...Yet!"**

@eez e-service center software.
Stay far ahead of your competition. Call now: **1-877-123-4567** or visit our website at **www.xyzcompany.com/freeguide**.

@eez e-service center software from
XYZcompany

Figure 11.1b (the 50/50 example) is a business-to-business ad that blends brand awareness with direct response techniques. Notice how the headline calls out to the audience. The ad tells a story backed up with facts. Then the offer is presented with a strong call to action.

When business marketers want to accomplish both branding and response, they are best served by engaging the services of a professional who knows the discipline of direct marketing. Direct marketing agencies have experience in writing and designing communications to generate response. They are less worried about how a URL or toll-free number will impact the ad's design than they are about readers not seeing the ad and not responding.

To successfully blend branding with lead generation in print advertising, you must borrow strategies from each approach. From brand advertising, you want the big idea. You want concepts that are unique, compelling, and memorable, that reflect the quality, personality, and distinctive characteristics of your product and company. From direct response advertising, you want the fundamentals of calling out to your readers, presenting your offer, and telling them what to do. The challenge a blended brand/direct response ad faces is in presenting both a product image and an offer without sacrificing the impact of either.

I will explain the fundamentals of brand print advertising relying on advice from the expert himself, David Ogilvy. Ogilvy defined the rules for effective business print advertising. One reason he was a great advertising man was that he spent many years with Gallup Research before forming his agency. This gave him the opportunity to witness and measure the impact different advertising techniques have on response. He knew that his clients invested in advertising to generate sales. The high points of his advice follow. These rules, found in *Ogilvy on Advertising*, apply to advertising and direct marketing as much today as when he first developed them.

- Your headline is the most important element in your ad. On average, five times as many people read the headlines as read the body copy.
- Long copy sells more than short copy.
- Testimonials increase credibility and sales.
- Overcome readers' delay. Make an offer.
- Headlines work best when they promise a benefit.
- Specifics sell more than generalities.
- Photographs that arouse curiosity or tell a story work best.
- Show the end benefit of your product. Before and after campaigns increase sales.
- Color is more memorable than black and white.
- Write to people in the singular, not as if they are in a stadium.

- Write in short sentences with words that can be easily understood.
- Avoid superlatives. Bragging and boasting convince nobody.
- More people read captions than body copy.

Relying on ideas like Ogilvy's, I have developed the following guidelines for managing the development of a business-to-business print ad that can provide dual brand and response function.

- Does the ad have a high degree of visual attraction? Does it act as a magnet, drawing in readers? Brand ads need a strong graphic design that is attractive to look at and helps build credibility and quality for the advertiser.
- Does the ad attract the right prospect? Through the use of words or pictures, the ad should call out to the target audience.
- Do the ad copy and visual invite readers into the situation or story? Can readers put themselves in the situation and have empathy or desire for what is going on?
- Does the ad promise a reward? Is the benefit clear to the reader?
- Are promises and claims backed up with facts and specifics? Facts provide the proof readers require.
- Does the ad present the sales story in a logical order? Does the ad set up an argument or promise and then, in a logical process, persuade the reader?
- Does the ad address the reader on a personal level? Is the copy written as if the reader were standing right in front of you?
- Can you read the ad easily or have you used fonts or visuals that obscure the copy?
- Does the ad focus on the promise, the offer, and the service provided by the product and not on the advertiser? To gain prospects' trust, you must be of service to them before you try to sell them on your company or product.
- Does the ad reflect your company's character and tone? This is one of the most important rules of brand advertising. Your ad must reflect the quality of your product, company, and customer service.
- Is your ad memorable? Will it stick in the reader's mind? Over time, will it build a positive impression for your company and product?
- Are the layout and format flexible in accommodating additional concepts yet consistent in overall look? Can the layout help to build recognition among your target audience?
- Does the ad establish and build a distinctive personality for the product or company?
- What percentage of the message is devoted to building awareness and brand personality versus generating response?

The New Standard: Electronic Direct Response Advertising

What makes the Internet and its interactive features so exciting to business-to-business direct marketers is that the techniques for generating clicks come directly from the fundamentals of direct response marketing. Most of the rules and guidelines just covered for the development of effective direct mail packages and print ads also apply to electronic direct media. Electronic direct response media differ from hard-copy media in important ways, however.

- People interact differently with a computer screen than with hard copy; they read in a different eye path. On computers, the path is from top left across to top right, then down to bottom left, then over to bottom right. In print, people's eyes scan from top left to bottom right, then back up to top right then down to bottom left. Further, people's eye path is limited to what they can see on their screen until they scroll down. Thus, the marketer must take into consideration the most common screen size.
- Electronic direct marketing is dynamic. You can change, personalize, and customize continuously. Therefore, you should think about not just the first communication but the communications after prospects respond.
- With a click of a mouse, prospects respond to or discard your message. Response is immediate. This lets you test creative, offers, and messages— and measure results—within hours of creating a promotion. Most importantly, it means that you can test many small promotions quickly before you commit to a rollout concept.
- The cost of sending a message is a fraction of printed direct marketing. However, this means that every marketer will flock to the medium, creating clutter. This competitiveness will reduce the medium's effectiveness over time.
- Unlike print, which lets you tell a long story, the electronic medium demands quick information, which is what readers want from it. Readers have short attention spans. You must use headlines and short copy phrases to meet their expectations.
- Electronic direct response advertising has a short life span. E-mail response happens within hours. Banner advertising wears out in two weeks. If the members of your target audience do not respond to your message the first time, they likely will not respond when they see it a second time. Repetitive exposure does not build response.
- The E-mail in-box is a zone of privacy. Businesses and businesspeople are much less tolerant of unwanted, unsolicited communications in their

in-box than in their postal mailbox. This is why I suggest that you ask permission to send E-mail to your customers and that you use opt-in E-mail lists as discussed in Chapter 9.

Developing Direct E-Mail

When you are developing a direct E-mail message, review the rules of direct mail packages. Consider the primary purpose of E-mail: the quick delivery of important messages from people you know inside and outside your organization. Unlike hardcopy direct mail, E-mail demands brevity. Get right to the point and state your offer. E-mail messages with four or fewer sentences have a 30 percent higher response rate than E-mail messages with seven sentences and a series of bullet points. An E-mail message is just a short teaser letter delivered on screen. The rules of good letter writing apply, but you must be succinct.

Think of E-mail as a simple two-part direct mail package. The "subject line," which appears in the recipient's in-box, is the equivalent of an envelope teaser. The "from line" is your corner card. It imparts either credibility about who sent the message, or uncertainty. For example, if you were to receive an E-mail message from your best friend, and the subject line said, "Ten things I need to tell you," you would almost certainly open and read the message. If you were to receive a message from an unknown company, ABC Ltd., and the subject line said, "Become a millionaire," you might not even open it. You would be skeptical about who sent you the message, the importance of the message, why you should open it, and why you should respond to it.

Techniques to Boost Your E-Mail Effectiveness

Think about the "from line." It speaks to your credibility. Who are you? Does the reader know you? Does the reader want to read what you have sent? If you have no credibility, you are at the mercy of the recipient. This is where the value of brand awareness and a multimedia approach to business-to-business marketing can work in your favor. You might advertise in the appropriate trade magazine for four months to build awareness, then send to the opt-in E-mail list a message that ties back to your campaign. This approach could be much more effective than cold E-mailing. Another strategy is to use your company name first in the subject line, followed by key words in your message. For example: "Kern Direct: Leads, Response, Sales."

Be careful with the subject line. You should arouse curiosity here. Always remember that people do not like spammers, and they are fearful of downloading viruses. Be specific and call out to your audience. Here are a few sample subject lines for a company that markets website analytical software: "Web Optimization"; "Clicks to Customers;" "Beyond the Click Stream."

Don't use loaded words. Using the following words in your subject line will make your message look like spam: *money, sex, girls, free, opportunity, sale, power, new, invest, maximize, profit, buy,* and *special.* Don't use dollar signs and exclamation marks. Avoid using all-capital letters.

Make your E-mail message easy to read. Minimize the air at the top of your message, but space your text to keep readers moving. E-mail is a fast medium. You need to write in short sentences. Keep the message driving to the action desired. Start by reminding the recipient of the relationship between you. For example: "As a customer of XYZ Company, our user conference is ideal for you to . . ." Present your offer as early in your message as possible. Give your reader a reason to keep reading. Make your message useful and fun. The best way to educate is to entertain.

If you are sending E-mail to people who know you, do not violate their trust. Be honest in what you say. Don't overpromote. If you are sending to opt-in lists, establish your credibility quickly in your message. For example: "More than 90% of our clients are *Fortune* 500 companies." Unless your copy delivers benefits and provides facts and specifics backed up by proof statements, your message is just a click away from "delete."

Follow proper opt-in and opt-out etiquette rules. Provide a way for responders to opt out of future E-mail, and respect their requests.

E-mail can be an unforgiving medium. Keep potential technical problems in mind. Watch out for formatting issues. Because everyone has a different mail system, you will have to format your copy for the lowest common denominator. Don't attach large pictures or documents; you'll waste your reader's time on downloading and opening messages. Provide the entire URL link to make it easy for the reader to hyperlink to the URL automatically.

Using Web-Page Banner Ads

When banner advertising first appeared on the World Wide Web, it generated greater than 5 percent click-through rates because of its newness. Response rates have fallen to less than 1 percent because consumers are bombarded with banner ads. The most effective banner ad campaigns appear on sites that offer pinpoint delivery of your target audience or appear during a keyword search with a major search engine.

Your goal in placing banner ads, as in all direct response advertising, is to generate qualified response. This means you need to measure not just click rates but also lead quality and conversion to sales. If you do not have the technology in place to track these metrics, I suggest you seek the services of companies such as DoubleClick and WebConnect.

The following are some guidelines for creating direct response banner ads. Compare these to the sequences in Figure 11.2.

- Think of a banner ad as an animated outdoor poster. Keep copy short and make visuals strong.
- Don't let your animation overshadow your text. People read text—they do not read animation.
- Use your animation to attract attention or create a story.
- You only have one-tenth of a second to motivate action, so never forget the power of putting your offer up-front and early in your banner ads.
- Show or tell viewers exactly what to do to receive your offer: "click here," "pull down here." Don't assume they know what to do.

The Splash or Landing Page

Your splash page (also called a jump page) or landing page is the page to which your readers are transported when they enter a reply URL or click on your banner. A landing page contains a registration form, whereas a splash page does not.

Figure 11.2a An Example of a Good Banner Ad

Reprinted with permission from VeriSign—The Internet Trust Company at www.verisign.com

Figure 11.2b An Example of a Good Banner Ad

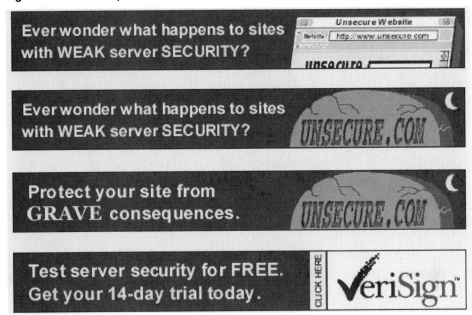

Reprinted with permission from VeriSign—The Internet Trust Company at www.verisign.com

Figure 11.2c An Example of a Good Banner Ad

Reprinted with permission from VeriSign—The Internet Trust Company at www.verisign.com

Your goal is to capture a lead. If someone hyperlinks from a banner ad to your landing page and never fills out the registration information, you have not generated a sales lead. When you are using the Internet as a response medium, do not make your splash or landing page your company's home page. You do not want prospects to get distracted. Keep them focused on completing the inquiry process by eliminating any ancillary information until they have submitted their registration information.

The design and copy on the splash or landing page should link back to the copy or promotion that initiated the visit to the URL, and should be simple and easy to read. Restate your offer. Give your reader a reason to complete the response process. Keep the number of profile questions to a minimum. After you capture the response, you can always ask for more information. Request permission to contact them in the future. Don't assume that since they have inquired they want to hear from you. With the raised interest in privacy, it is important to ask.

Summing Up

Understanding the differences and similarities between direct response advertising approaches is the best way to manage for creative excellence. Your suspects' mailboxes are filled, print advertisements are everywhere, and E-mail is on the rise. Getting your creative message to stand out is not a simple task. Still, you can count on people being on the lookout for messages, products, and services that can improve their condition.

In this chapter, I presented guidelines to help you direct the development of several types of direct response advertising (mail packages, print ads, E-mails, banners, and splash pages). Use these guidelines to evaluate your work, and ask your creative resources to use them to evaluate their own work before they submit it to you. Direct response marketing is a complex business, and there is no good reason to leave the basics of the business to memory. Scrutinize your work to see how it stands up to comparison with the guidelines, but don't limit your thinking or be rigid. Fresh creative approaches come from challenging the status quo.

Finally, in this era of electronic direct marketing, don't let the technology get in the way of the principles of response. Prospects respond because they want something from the advertiser, not because your banner animation was so clever and entertaining. Entertainment helps, but prospects want to be educated, they want to succeed, and they want their problems to be solved. Text and copy sell. Your electronic advertising must deliver on these fundamentals.

THE INTERNET: THE MARKETING MEDIUM OF THE FUTURE

The Internet is the greatest direct marketing medium ever invented.

—SETH GODIN
Permission Marketing

The Internet will challenge marketers to move faster, think more strategically, and hone their problem-solving abilities dramatically. The call to improve response rates and build relationships with prospects and customers using the Internet will be all-pervasive.

The power the Internet brings to marketers rests on several noteworthy factors:

- It costs virtually nothing to contact someone.
- The speed of testing is a hundred times faster than with traditional media.
- Response rates are five times higher.
- You can implement continuous marketing using copy alone.
- Frequency is free. You can identify and talk with individuals over and over again.
- There are no printing costs.

Future Shock: Responsiveness Will Shape Marketing Strategy

In the marketplace of the future, if you as a marketer do not make it easy for a buyer to transact business with you, that buyer will go elsewhere without leaving his or her desk or picking up a telephone. Competitors are just a click away for customers and potential customers.

Traditional direct marketing techniques forced marketers to bear the cost of distribution. They were responsible for the expense of items such as printing, lists, and postage. Now, with the Internet, the recipient bears a large burden of the cost of distribution. The consumer pays for Internet access. This shift in economics affords direct marketers the resources to conceive and implement highly targeted, personalized messages.

Accordingly, marketers will need to create a balance between interrupt advertising and permission marketing. This will make permission-based E-mail databases the key asset of the future. The only way marketers will be able to build these databases is to capture initial responses through traditional, intrusive interrupt media such as print, broadcast, direct mail, and prospect-based E-mail. Marketers who focus on getting prospects' permission to provide them with information will be able to spend less and obtain better results than ever. Marketers can gain permission from prospects by demonstrating that their marketing activities provide value.

Interactive advertising will require marketers to apply the strategies of direct response marketing universally. Every marketing professional must begin to think like a direct marketer. The call to action of the past, which was "Call our 800 number," has changed to "Visit our website" or "Click here." The website is becoming the offer's delivery vehicle. This change will push marketers across industries to learn to design and implement communications that generate response in all media: television, print, mail, and Internet.

With this new pressure to drive response to the website comes increased pressure to track and optimize advertising performance. Because the Internet simplifies measurement, senior managers will continue to insist on high accountability from all marketing programs. Soon it will be unacceptable to remain ignorant of the return on investment (ROI) on each advertising message, medium, and offer.

Shortening the Measurement Cycle

The other change the Internet is effecting involves the time it takes to measure results. E-mail and banner programs make it possible to test and measure campaigns within hours, as opposed to weeks, at a very low cost, and with near-instant access to results. This speed of access to results is changing the concept of direct response marketing in terms of campaign testing, analysis, and management. Speedier time to market—the result of faster testing and measurement—will force marketers and their agencies to build more comprehensive test strategies. These strategies will have to focus on lead quality and long-term customer value in addition to response.

The Internet's speed also makes it a desirable arena for testing and research of off-line media. Offers can be tested "live" in the marketplace and proven before roll-out to traditional media. Marketers who use the Internet this way will increase their campaign's chances of success as well as their confidence in the campaign.

Data analysis and analytics also will become important skills for marketers in the future. Marketers will need to know how to read Web log files and review statistical reports to uncover insights about customers and their interests. With these new abilities comes the challenge of developing or finding resources to leverage the data in relevant, effective ways. The Internet and the efficiencies of marketing automation, combined with the power to code, track, report, and analyze marketing campaigns in real time, will force marketers to integrate segmentation strategies and personalize offers and messages throughout the sales process.

Taking Advantage of a New Medium's Capabilities

The Internet's capabilities and its growing use for marketing will shape future business-to-business marketing strategies. In the next two to three years, several major trends that leverage the power of the Internet will emerge:

- Customer relationship management (CRM), or one-to-one marketing, and the integration of E-mail message management.
- Permission marketing as standard practice.
- Data mining integrated with analysis of prospect behavior and customer behavior information derived from Web logs.
- The convergence of voice, video, and data delivered by networks and TV broadcasts for delivery of an entirely new type of interactive commercial message.
- Increased use of promotions and loyalty strategies to turn browsers into buyers and to keep customers coming back.

Customer Relationship/One-to-One Strategies Will Gain Importance

Making the back end of direct marketing work—specifically, converting prospects to customers, repeat selling, up-selling, cross-selling, and retaining customers—is where marketers must focus their efforts. These back-end marketing activities generate long-term profits for most businesses.

In the past, back-end marketing campaigns lacked the glory and luster of customer acquisition programs. In the next two years, CRM software systems will become commonplace and revolutionize back-end activities. The information captured in CRM systems, in concert with E-mail message management systems, will make it easier for marketers to use one-to-one marketing strategies to nurture customer relationships. CRM software will empower marketers to identify the financial value of each customer relationship. No longer will sales leads pass to field sales organizations without the marketer knowing the disposition of the prospect. CRM systems will help marketers determine whether the prospects bought, how much they spent, and what marketing tactic helped generate the revenue. CRM software also will help marketers learn about the future needs and wants of customers. Marketers will be able to use past purchase behavior as a predictor of future behavior. Armed with this knowledge, they will be able to launch personalized campaigns to enhance the business relationship.

One-to-one marketing requires four key steps, as outlined by the Peppers and Rogers Group in its report *The State of OneToOne Online*. The four steps are Identify, Differentiate, Interact, and Customize. The Internet, when combined with CRM applications, makes this possible. The Web will continue to enable marketers to collect information on customer behavior and store it in a centralized database. The Web also makes it easier for customers to sign in and provide information on themselves and their preferences so you can interact with them using customized messages and techniques.

The core customer-communication tool of the future will be E-mail. "Survey: Retention-Based E-mail to Surge," in the June 2000 issue of *Direct*, reports that Jupiter Communications estimates that E-mail volumes will increase from 3 billion in 1999 to 268 billion in 2005. The latter figure represents almost a thousand messages per man, woman, and child in the United States. With this barrage of messages, consumers will continue to disregard or delete E-mail received from unknown senders. Therefore, the fundamental concepts of direct marketing will continue to shape the marketing landscape. For example, marketers will have to know how to write copy that is compelling to read, and offers will need to be integrated into all promotions. Permission-based E-mail databases will become standard.

According to Jupiter Communications, only 14 percent of consumers want to receive E-mail from companies that have not previously contacted them. As of 2000, though, nearly 50 percent of marketers are using E-mail as a prospecting strategy. Conversely, an IMT Strategies, Inc., study, *Permission E-mail: The Future of Direct Marketing*, reports that more than 50 percent of prospects feel positively about permission E-mail and look forward to receiving E-mail from companies they have granted permission to.

Clearly, direct marketers will still rely on nonelectronic media to generate initial response. At the same time, the trend toward using E-mail for cultivation and retention is supported by the Jupiter report. The dynamics for this shift are evident: each E-mail contact costs $6, as opposed to $18 for direct mail. As streaming media technology (video and audio delivered over the Internet) emerges, marketers will be able to send interactive E-messages to customers to help them use products better and to learn about new product opportunities. This new E-message platform will help build customer loyalty.

Permission-Based Marketing Is Here to Stay

The rapid rise in E-mail volumes, combined with consumer attitudes about the personal and private nature of their E-mail in-box, means that gaining permission to send messages will become a core objective for all marketers. This will require marketers to foster a new mind-set, moving from "I will send everything I have on my product and company to you—relentlessly—to beat you into marketing submission" to "I respect that you don't want to speak to everyone. I realize you have a limited amount of time, money, and attention. I will only send you messages when you have actively expressed to me permission to do so."

Having to respect prospect and customer wishes directly challenges the marketer's belief system and financial desire to sell to everyone, right now. But data gathered between 1997 and 2000 clearly show that when marketers follow the path of permission marketing, response rates are five to ten times greater.

Seth Godin, creator of the permission marketing concept, has explained the three main factors that make permission marketing a must. First, "human beings have a finite amount of attention." People cannot watch or read everything, remember everything, or do everything, and as noise increases, everyone must be more selective about what gets their attention. Second, "the more products that are offered, the less money there is to go around." Every time you buy a Coke, you don't buy a Pepsi. As more companies enter the market, others must exit. Third, "there is a Catch-22 in marketing. The more they spend, the less it works. The less it works, the more marketers spend." Because there is a finite amount of time and money, marketers are all fighting for a share of mind and wallet. But increased spending leads to more clutter, which leads to less attention.

Permission marketing requires that you send messages that are anticipated, personal, and relevant. When someone is thrilled to receive your message because it has specific interest or value, you have his or her attention. When your message is personalized both by being addressed to an individual and by containing information that shows you really know that person, your message gains more credibility. When you are able to create and send messages relevant to that individual—that address specific concerns—you have completed the circle of permission-based marketing. This is why one-to-one marketing and permission marketing are kindred strategies.

Although the concept of permission marketing is easy to understand, marketers will have to struggle with creating tens of thousands of anticipated, personal, relevant messages. How will they do it? How will they bucket, group, segment, and aggregate their database into manageable groups? Further, how will they create and write a meaningful message for each group? Lastly, and most importantly, how will they track whether all this unique writing really improves results? Do the time, money, and effort put into permission-based marketing campaigns pay off?

Marketing automation software packages are the key to implementing and measuring permission marketing programs. Companies like Annuncio Software, Broadbase, E.piphany, Kana, Responsys.com, and MarketFirst Software all sell leading applications. Peter Tierney, chairman and president of MarketFirst, says, "The Internet is the ultimate marketing platform for economical interactive personalization. Applications that enable dynamic interactions with consumers are essential tools for any competitive marketing organization. These applications will increase marketing velocity while improving responsiveness and relationships with customers."

The power of a solution like MarketFirst is that it enables marketers to implement permission-based marketing communications quickly and easily. This type of application enables you to implement an automated E-mail communication flow that has content inserted that is relevant to each individual. Further, this program enables you to host value-add websites that by their structure of interactive questions help you learn about each recipient and improve your communications program by tracking and reporting on response behavior. Then, it becomes possible to send different messages or different actions to different prospects according to their interests and purchase behavior.

Data Mining Will Drive Future Marketing Programs

The trend toward data mining is changing the face of business-to-business marketing. If used throughout your organization, data mining unleashes the power in your data. Data mining lets you use data from marketing programs to locate your most profitable customers and win over prospects faster and more cheaply than in the past. Many successful organizations are turning to data mining for better decision making. Relying on powerful analytical techniques, data mining enables you to turn raw data into information you can use to transform the way you interact with your customers—and to gain a marketplace advantage. It enables your organization to make changes up front that can help you reach your goals and better understand the dynamics of your marketing campaigns.

For example, you can optimize advertising based on traffic, cost, or revenue measures. You can identify which search engines and portals refer qualified prospects to your website. You can also determine your least effective website pages, the pages that cause visitors to hit the browser's "stop" button and/or exit the site. You can find the factors that cause a visitor to buy on your website. Finally, you can recognize which banner ads and directory listings are most effective in driving visitors to your website.

To achieve these goals and optimize the effectiveness of complete closed-loop direct marketing, you will need to capture website traffic information and leverage legacy (off-line) demographic and transaction data. Software such as Accrue Software's Hit List provides a powerful Web analysis solution of both on-line and off-line data, practically in real time. Hit List can help you optimize the effectiveness of your Web initiatives, make merchandising decisions based on data stored in all areas of the enterprise, and increase revenue and customer satisfaction.

Data mining requires a continuous effort to combine your business knowledge with the data you have acquired. Once you have the knowledge, you discover tremendous insights into your business problems and identify new opportunities. Armed with these results, the true power of permission marketing and CRM management over the Web becomes real. With a comprehensive data mining and campaign implementation program, you can:

- suggest additional products to individual customers at the time of purchase based on their unique profile and likelihood to buy
- reduce customer defection by providing individualized services (with personalized content, special offers, and loyalty programs) based on the recipient's value to your organization
- determine what type of visitor is in session and dynamically adjust site content to match his or her interests
- develop Web marketing strategies and new campaigns that target people most likely to respond and become profitable customers
- direct individual Web visitors to the most relevant content and offers, based on their likelihood to respond
- get your visitors to stay on your website longer by responding with custom content or offers designed to keep them interested
- dynamically present pricing discounts to potential buyers, based on their likelihood to purchase

- identify the major paths through your site and make it fast and easy for visitors to get the information they want
- present Web content, ads, and special offers to individuals—based on their likelihood to respond—as they explore your website

Mastering data-mining software that can deliver these kinds of solutions will be an important task in the next two years. Data mining and analysis are powerful tools that take time and diligence to master. The investment of effort will be well worth it.

Convergence of Television and the Personal Computer: Broadband and Streaming

A convergence of video, voice, and data delivered over the Internet as well as by television is in the making. Streaming media will enable marketers to deliver thirty-, fifteen-, or even five-second interactive commercials or messages to customers' desktops. Instead of a prospect passively reading your company's literature or browsing your website, you will be able to use the power of voice and video to demonstrate and persuade. Further, marketers will be able to add interactive features to help potential buyers or customers learn more about their company or even ask for immediate, live help.

What impact will this have on marketers? First, the complexity of marketing communications will increase. Marketers will have to make it easier and quicker for potential buyers to interact with their company. You, as a marketer, will need to be ready twenty-four hours a day, seven days a week to do business with prospects when they want to do business with you. This will impact staffing strategies in your inbound contact center. Second, streaming media will require every marketer to become a video and audio communications specialist. Print or text messages will no longer be enough. Marketers will learn to use the power of video and voice to deliver messages on their websites and in their E-mail messages. Marketers who embrace these new technologies will leapfrog their slower competitors because consumers will spend more time with companies that use streaming media. These marketers will have more power to influence the purchase decision and enjoy more control over long-term communication with customers and prospects.

Wide acceptance of convergence depends on rollout of a technology called "broadband," which delivers E-messages at speeds ten times greater than 28K modems can deliver. The high speed enables video and voice to synchronize and appear natural to consumers. Currently, most midsize and large corporations have high-speed connections to the Internet through DSL (Digital Subscriber Line) and T-1 line technology, so now is a good time for business-to-business marketers to integrate and test streaming media in their marketing mix. The coming technology is exemplified in the offerings of a company called WebRadio.com. Go to www.webradio.com to get a glimpse of the future.

As part of the trend toward convergence, the value of your corporate and product brands will play an increasingly important role. In an environment in which any marketer can send commercials to every television set or to any computer, whom will buyers trust? This brings us back to the rules of relationship marketing and permission marketing: people do business with companies they know, like, and believe. Awareness, personality, and confidence that result from brand building will improve your results.

Where do you start with streaming media? Begin with your own customers. Think about how you can use a video presentation delivered directly to customers' desktops to make them feel better about your company or to persuade them to do more business with your company. Maybe what you need is a new product introduction, a message from your top executive, or some additional education to help your customers extract more value from their current investment.

The second place to consider using streaming video is on your own website. How can you make your website come alive? How can you help potential buyers feel good about your company and have confidence in your product or service as soon as they hit your site? The University of California at Berkeley estimated there were more than 30 million commercial websites in 2000. Streaming video can help your site stand out from the pack.

The third place to consider using streaming video is at events. How can you bring live events to the desktops of customers and prospects? Live video webcasts require planning and technology. Companies that embrace these strategies will stand out from their competitors, though, by providing valuable information conveniently.

Promotions Make a Comeback Thanks to On-Line Competition

In the past, promotions were not part of the business-to-business marketer's toolbox. The Internet is changing that, because the cost of cultivating a lead has decreased. Automatic Web-based capture and qualification systems make sorting through high volumes of mixed-quality responses more economical. With the increase in competition, marketers must consider more dramatic offers to motivate response behavior. Promotions work because they play into the human motivators discussed in Chapter 6. Prospects do not want to miss out on a chance to win something of value. Business-to-business marketers must know how to use promotions to generate site traffic, repeat visits, and repeat purchases. Promotions, when done well, can compress a customer's buying time. When done poorly, a promotion can attract nonbuyers and cost the marketer plenty.

Promotions can give your advertising the extra edge needed to stand out from the crowd by grabbing readers' attention. There are many types of promotions, including price discounts and prize giveaways (e.g., sweepstakes or free gift with purchase). When you promote a chance to win $25,000, many more people notice your message. The more eyeballs that look at your message, on-line or off-line, the greater the product's chances in the marketplace.

Prize promotions can also build traffic. Relied on for years by retailers such as McDonald's, they now are being rediscovered and exploited by dot-com companies and E-marketers. For example, a search engine called iWon.com gives away $10,000 every day—and $10 million on tax-filing day—to generate site traffic. There are many ways to structure a traffic-building promotion. The most common promotions are games in which the more you visit, the more chances you have to win.

Sweepstakes can lift direct mail response rates by 30 to 100 percent. The same is true with Internet-based communications. A well-planned sweepstakes can lift response rates to both E-mail and banner advertising campaigns. Sweepstakes can also help build databases, which are the foundation for one-to-one permission-based marketing programs. Offering automatic entry into a drawing upon submission of a response form that contains demographic or marketing-based questions is a proven strategy for identifying prospects and collecting information that can be used to differentiate messages in the future. For example, in the June 12, 2000, issue of *iMarketing News*, Student Advantage reported that its "Spin, Click, and Win" promotion eliminated inefficiencies in data collection because it eliminated the handwritten data collected in the course of traditional off-line promotions. The contest also required students to interact with the product and learn about the company and the rewards it offered.

A prize promotion can use a contest of skill instead of a "chance to win." For example, you can promote a write-in that requires the prospect to read your materials. This reinforces a particular product or service benefit. In such a promotion, the entry form may state, "Please provide the three most important benefits of our product on your entry form. These benefits can be found on our website or in our product literature."

Promotions help draw readers' eyes to your advertising, but a promotion alone cannot do the entire marketing task. Although promotions and sweepstakes are important tactics, they *cannot* build brand loyalty, build an image for a company, or compensate for low levels of advertising. Only advertising can build an image for a company, although the right promotion can reinforce brand image and increase immediate action. Unless the advertising level is appropriate for the marketplace, a promotion will not have any long-term effect on the brand franchise.

The Internet Streamlines Use of Incentives for Loyalty Building

With the dramatic increase in on-line shopping and purchasing, marketers will need to learn loyalty-building strategies to generate repeat purchases and create loyal customers. In the airline and hospitality industries, loyalty programs have long proven themselves as ways to influence consumer decisions. Now, the same principles are available to business-to-business marketers, thanks to the Internet. Companies such as ePrize can help you custom-build and administer your own loyalty program. You can either provide your own rewards or establish a structure with Flooz dollars, the Internet currency that can be exchanged for products at more than sixty on-line stores. Other promotion companies, such as Netcentives and MyPoints.com, offer points-based loyalty and shopping rewards programs that can be incorporated into marketing programs.

Summing Up

The future is bright for direct marketers. The Internet is the most powerful marketing medium ever created. Marketers can now build more personal relationships and communicate more personally, more often, and at a lower cost than ever before. There are several important trends that marketers should embrace in the next two to three years:

- The wide deployment of CRM software systems to track sales results.
- The general adoption of permission marketing philosophies.
- The use of increasingly sophisticated campaign automation software to drive fast, personal E-communications.
- The increase in knowledge of data analysis and data mining. These tools let you use data from marketing programs to turn data into action-producing information, locating your most profitable customers, winning over prospects faster and cheaper than in the past, and transforming your customer interactions.

- The convergence of voice, video, and data over public and private networks. This convergence will make it possible to deliver interactive commercial messages to prospect and customer desktops.
- The resurgence of promotions to help drive traffic and increase customer loyalty.

It is always hard to predict the future, but I am confident these trends will grow during the next few years. As you use the S.U.R.E.-Fire direct response marketing planning process to create and implement direct response programs, I encourage you to monitor these trends and to test new technologies as they become available.

APPENDIX
MAIL SURVEY: VALIDATE
RESEARCH QUANTITATIVELY

—STAC SOFTWARE, INC.

Reprinted with permission.

Workstation Data Protection & Recovery Questionnaire
Estimated completion time: 7–10 minutes

1. In what industry is your company? *(select only one)*
   - ❑ Education
   - ❑ Utility
   - ❑ Retail/Wholesale
   - ❑ Manufacturing
   - ❑ Healthcare Provider/Health Insurance
   - ❑ Finance/Insurance
   - ❑ Government
   - ❑ Other_____
     (please specify)

2. How many employees does your company have?
   - ❑ 1–99
   - ❑ 100–499
   - ❑ 500–999
   - ❑ 1,000–4,999
   - ❑ 5,000+

3. How many personal computer workstations are there in your company?
   - ❑ 0–199
   - ❑ 200–499
   - ❑ 500–999
   - ❑ 1,000–1,999
   - ❑ 2,000+

4. How many personal computer workstations is your department responsible for supporting?
   - ❑ 0–199
   - ❑ 200–499
   - ❑ 500–999
   - ❑ 1,000–1,999
   - ❑ 2,000+

5. What is your job function? *(select only one)*
   - ❑ Senior mgmt. of information systems (CIO, VP, Director)
   - ❑ Management of information systems
   - ❑ Staff of information systems
   - ❑ Other_____
     (please specify)

6. Which of the following messages grab your interest most?
   Please rank (*1 = grabs interest most, 6 = grabs interest least*). **Please use each number only once.**
   - _____ Sit back and relax. Now you can backup thousands of desktop and mobile PCs without lifting a finger.
   - _____ Are notebook backups taking so long it feels like a lifetime?
   - _____ Would you like to find a solution that helps you upgrade a room full of PCs in days instead of weeks?
   - _____ Now you can recover desktop or mobile PCs with just the click of a mouse. It's that easy.
   - _____ Chances are your end users are not backing up their PCs to the server . . . or any other device. Find out about an automatic way to protect workstation data.
   - _____ Your laptop has just been stolen. Now it's easy to recover lost or stolen data.

7. How important are the following business challenges to you?
   Please rank (*1 = most important, 8 = least important*). **Please use each number only once.**
   - _____ Helping users restore files is a resource drain.
   - _____ Upgrading workstations and migrating to new software is a resource drain
   - _____ There is risk of losing business critical data that is stored on workstations
   - _____ Mobile workstations add a level of complexity to data protection activities
   - _____ Workstation backup and recovery takes too much time; it's slow
   - _____ It's difficult to restore a workstation to a stable state or point in time
   - _____ End users do not backup their workstations or critical data on the server as they should
   - _____ Recovery efforts are often incomplete; some files and user information like address books & settings are non-recoverable

1   Version 1

8. Consider that each of the envelopes below arrived in today's mail at the office. Based on the wording and images on the front of the envelopes, which one would you be **most** likely to open? Which one would you be most likely to open next, and so on? *Please assign a number, 1 through 6, to indicate your preference (1 = the envelope you are* **most** *likely to open and 6 = the envelope you are* **least** *likely to open). **Please use each number only once.***

_____ Image N

_____ Image L

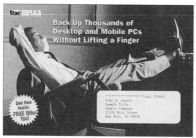

_____ Image Q

_____ Image J

_____ Image G

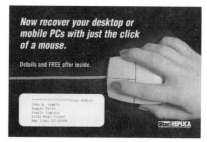

_____ Image H

Version 1

9. What does your company do to protect, backup, and recover data and programs that reside **on the user workstations**?

❏ There is no stated policy for workstation backup and recovery
❏ **Users backup** files to a centralized server
❏ **Users backup** files to workstation devices (tape, Zip drive, removable disk)
❏ We use a centralized, automated system for workstation backup and recovery: **no user intervention required**
❏ We use application server/thin client technology: there is no data on the workstation
❏ Other_____
                (please specify)

10. How satisfied are you with your current method of workstation backup and recovery?
❏ very satisfied   ❏ satisfied   ❏ neutral   ❏ dissatisfied   ❏ very dissatisfied

11. Does your company plan to **significantly** change the way workstation backup and recovery is done now within the next 12 months?
❏ yes   ❏ no

12. How interested would you be in receiving the following free of charge?
Please rank (1 = most interested, 6 = least interested). ***Please use each number only once.***
_____ Demonstration software/self-running presentation that you can run on your computer or the Web.
_____ Free 60 day software trial.
_____ Free 20 workstation licenses and 30 days free support.
_____ "Microsoft Office 2000 Administrator's Desk Reference." Book & CD-Rom covering all versions of Office and addresses real concerns when deploying, configuring, and troubleshooting (998 pgs. 8/99).
_____ "Centrally Managed, Backup and Disaster Recovery for Desktop and Mobile PCs." White paper discussing how on-line workstation backup, data protection & recovery can lower IT workload and keep end users satisfied.
_____ "A River Runs through IT." Article discussing disaster recovery strategies, prioritizing and analyzing the company's needs, data backup methods, alternate computing arrangement (CIO mag. 4/98).

13. How interested would you be in receiving the following free of charge?
Please rank (1 = most interested, 5 = least interested). ***Please use each number only once.***
_____ T-shirt
_____ CD travel case made from recycled circuit boards
_____ Wrist watch with a rotating "Dilbert" second hand
_____ Entered in a drawing for a Palm Pilot
_____ Entered in a drawing for a paid trip to a major computer convention

14. How interested would you be in the following type of software?

Backup	❏ Very interested	❏ Interested	❏ Not Interested	❏ Never heard of
Data protection	❏ Very interested	❏ Interested	❏ Not Interested	❏ Never heard of
Recovery	❏ Very interested	❏ Interested	❏ Not Interested	❏ Never heard of
Restore	❏ Very interested	❏ Interested	❏ Not Interested	❏ Never heard of
Repair	❏ Very interested	❏ Interested	❏ Not Interested	❏ Never heard of
Migration utility	❏ Very interested	❏ Interested	❏ Not Interested	❏ Never heard of
Self-healing	❏ Very interested	❏ Interested	❏ Not Interested	❏ Never heard of

15. Assuming there is a new method to protect and recover workstation data, what are the most important benefits you would like it to provide?
Please rank (1 = most important, 8 = least important). **Please use each number only once.**
_____ Less IT time spent helping users restore files
_____ Upgrading or migrating workstation software could be done more quickly and with less effort
_____ Reduced risk of losing business critical data that is stored on workstations
_____ Data on mobile PCs would be protected
_____ Faster backup and recovery
_____ Easily restoring a system to a stable point in time
_____ Workstations would be backed up without relying on the end users to take action
_____ Complete recovery of all user information, including personalized settings

16. Assume you were looking for a new workstation data protection and recovery system, what factors or product features would **grab your attention** most and cause you to take a closer look at the software?
Please rank (1 = most attention grabbing, 8 = least attention grabbing). **Please use each number only once.**
_____ Easy to use: requires minimal IT support
_____ Can run on existing network; no additional bandwidth required
_____ Centralized administration and operation
_____ Automatic backup: users do not have to take any action to make it happen
_____ User self-service restore: users can restore files without IT support
_____ Backup takes place on-line; no external workstation devices needed
_____ Ability to recover an entire PC system (bare metal) including data files and personalized user settings like screen savers, address books, and internet bookmarks
_____ Mobile user support: when mobile users sign on to the network their system is automatically backed up

17. Do you receive the majority of your own mail?
❏ yes   ❏ no, another person filters my mail before I see it

Thank you for your time. Your responses will be kept confidential.
Please return the survey in the enclosed postage paid envelope by December 8, 1999.

If you would like to receive additional information about workstation data protection and recovery software from our client, please provide us with the following information:

Name: _____   Title: _____

Company: _____

Address: _____

City, State, Zip: _____

Phone: _____   Fax: _____

E-Mail: _____

Version 1

RESOURCES

Annuncio
2440 West El Camino Real, Suite 300
Mountain View, CA 94040
Tel: 877-993-6060
www.annuncio.com
Marketing automation software

Acxiom Corporation
1 Information Way
Little Rock, AR 72202
Tel: 501-342-1000
www.acxiom.com
*Parent company of mIn, on-line research
service for mail lists, E-mail lists, and
interactive media*

Adscope, Inc.
P.O. Box 50610
Eugene, OR 97405
Tel: 800-478-2241
www.adscope.com
*Competitive ad tracking service for high-
technology industries*

AdTrack
Tel: 800-735-3237
www.adtrack.com
*Sales-lead development and response-
management services*

Advertising Age—Leading National
Advertisers
711 Third Avenue
New York, NY 10017
Tel: 212-210-0100
www.adage.com
*Comprehensive ad spending estimates of
major marketers*

BK Marketing & Associates
Los Angeles, CA
Tel: 310-839-8920
Direct marketing research and consulting

Broadbase Software, Inc.
181 Constitution Drive
Menlo Park, CA 94025
Tel: 800-513-8027
www.broadbase.com
*eCRM software: e-marketing, e-commerce,
and e-service*

Cargill Consulting Group, Inc.
6101 W. Centinela Ave., Suite 340
Culver City, CA 90230
Tel: 800-405-4732
www.cargillsells.com
Sales productivity improvement services

Corporation Strategies & Solutions
20315 Ventura Boulevard, Suite C
Woodland Hills, CA 91364
Tel: 818-347-3191
www.sandlerstrategies.com
Sales training and consulting

Direct Stock, Inc.
10 East 21st Street, 14th Floor
New York, NY 10010
Tel: 212-979-6560
www.directstock.com
Photos and illustrations stock books

DoubleClick, Inc.
28 West 23rd Street
New York, NY 10010
Tel: 888-727-5300
www.doubleclick.com
Internet advertising planning, placement, and tracking

Data Specialists, Inc. (DSI)
625 Dallas Drive, Suite 450
Denton, TX 76205
Tel: 940-383-1314
Mail survey data tabulation services

The Image Bank
Tel: 800-TIB-IMAG (800-842-4624)
www.theimagebank.com
Photos and illustrations stock books

iWon, Inc.
One Bridge Street, Suite 42
Irvington, NY 10533
Tel: 914-591-2000
www.iwon.com
Internet portal—cash giveaways to drive traffic

Kern Direct Marketing
20300 Ventura Boulevard, Suite 210
Woodland Hills, CA 91364
Toll Free: 800-335-4244
Tel: 818-703-8775
Fax: 818-703-8458
www.kerndirect.com

www.sure-fire.net
S.U.R.E.-Fire direct response advertising agency

The Mac McIntosh Company, Inc.
1739 Havemeyer Lane
Redondo Beach, CA 90278-4716
Tel: 800-944-5553
www.salesleadexperts.com
Sales-lead management consulting services

MarketFirst
2061 Stierlin Court
Mountain View, CA 94043
Tel: 650-691-6284
www.marketfirst.com
Permission-based marketing automation software

Marketing Information Network (see also Acxiom)
www.minokc.com.
On-line research service for mail lists, E-mail lists, and interactive media

MyPoints.com, Inc.
100 California
San Francisco, CA 94111
Tel: 415-676-3700
www.mypoints.com
Incentive and loyalty marketing programs

Netcentives, Inc.
475 Brannan Street
San Francisco, CA 94107
Tel: 415-538-1888
www.netcentives.com
Incentive and loyalty marketing programs

Protocol
222 Rosewood Drive, Suite 301
Danvers, MA 01923
Tel: 978-762-7700
www.protocolusa.com
Marketing automation software

Response Mail Express
4517 George Road, #200
Tampa, FL 33634
Tel: 800-795-2773
www.responsemail.com
Overnight mail envelope vendor

Responsys.com
2225 E. Bayshore Road, Suite 100
Palo Alto, CA 94303
Tel: 888-219-7150
www.responsys.com
Marketing automation software

Sales Leakage Consulting
17853 Santiago Boulevard, PMB 107-339
Villa Park, CA 92861
Tel: 714-998-1737
www.salesleakage.com
Sales-lead management consulting services

Saligent, Inc. (acquired by Protocol)
1480 Garden of the Gods
Colorado Springs, CO 80907
Tel: 800-859-7104
www.saligent.com
www.protocolusa.com
Marketing automation software

SPSS, Inc.
233 S. Wacker Drive, 11th floor
Chicago, IL 60606-6307
Tel: 800-543-2185
www.spss.com
Analytical and statistical software and services

Standard Rate and Data Service (SRDS)
1700 Higgins Road
Des Plaines, IL 60018-5606
Tel: 800-851-SRDS (851-7737)
www.srds.com
Media and list source directories

Taylor Market Intelligence, Inc.
Los Angeles, CA
Tel: 310-550-1315
Focus group moderating/market research consulting

U.S. Census Bureau
Tel: 800-553-6847
www.census.gov/epcd/www/naics.html
Listing of North American Industry Classification System (NAICS) codes and U.S. Standard Industrial Classification (SIC) system codes

Ventura Associates, Inc.
1040 Avenue of the Americas
New York, NY 10018
Tel: 212-302-8277
www.sweepspros.com
Sweepstakes and promotions agency/ administrators

Vinton Marketing & Associates
Thousand Oaks, CA
Tel: 805-529-2208
Direct marketing research and consulting

WebConnect
5200 Town Center Circle
Boca Raton, FL 33486
Tel: 800-331-8102
www.webconnect.com
Internet advertising planning, placement, and tracking

WebRadio.com, Inc.
21110 Oxnard Street
Woodland Hills, CA 91367
Tel: 818-703-8436
www.webradio.com
Internet broadcast site for streaming media

SELECTED READINGS

Abraham, Jay. *Money Making Secrets of Marketing Genius Jay Abraham.* Rolling Hills Estates, CA: Abraham Publishing Group, 1997.

Backer, Bill. *The Care and Feeding of Ideas.* New York: Times Books, 1993.

Baier, Martin and Bob Stone. *How to Find and Cultivate Customers Through Direct Marketing.* Lincolnwood, IL: NTC Business Books, a division of NTC/Contemporary Publishing, 1996.

Bartlett, John. *Bartlett's Familiar Quotations: A Collection of Passages, Phrases, and Proverbs Traced to Their Sources in Ancient and Modern Literature,* 16th ed. New York: Little, Brown & Company, 1992.

Biolchini, Julia. White paper: "Cultivating Your Prospects: Sales Lead Incubation for Technology Marketers." Colorado Springs: Saligent Inc., 1999.

Bly, Robert W. *Business to Business Direct Marketing,* 2nd ed. Lincolnwood, IL: NTC Business Books, a division of NTC/Contemporary Publishing, 1998.

Bohn, Rich. "Marketing Automation: The Next Big Thing?" *Sales & Field Force Automation* (December 1998).

Booth, Emily. "Nike Takes Web Ads to the Limit." *Revolution: Business & Marketing in the Digital Economy* (March 2000).

Dillion, William R., Thomas J. Madden, and Neil H. Firtle. *Essentials of Marketing Research.* Homewood, IL: Irwin, 1993.

Direct Stock. New York: Direct-Stock, Inc., 1999.

Donath, Bob, Richard A. Crocker, Carolyn K. Dixon, and James W. Obermayer. *Managing Sales Leads: How to Turn Every Prospect into a Customer.* Lincolnwood, IL: NTC Business Books, a division of NTC/Contemporary Publishing, 1996.

Edmunds, Holly. *The Focus Group Research Handbook.* Lincolnwood, IL: NTC Business Books in conjunction with the American Marketing Association, 1999.

Evans, Dick. "Business-to-business Inquiry and Sales Lead Facts." www.adtrack.com; AdTrack Corporation, Cedar Rapids, IA, 1999.

Feinman, Jeffrey P., Robert D. Blashek, and Richard J. McCabe. *Sweepstakes, Prize Promotions, Games and Contests.* Homewood, IL: Dow Jones-Irwin, 1986.

Fink, Arlene, Linda B. Bourque, Eve P. Fielder, James H. Frey, Mark S. Litwin, and Sabine Mertens Oishi. *The Survey Kit.* Thousand Oaks, CA: Sage Publications, Inc., 1995.

Godin, Seth. *Permission Marketing.* New York: Simon & Schuster, 1999.

Hall, Doug and David Wecker. *Jump Start Your Brain.* New York: Warner Books, Inc., 1995.

Hodgson, Richard. *Direct Mail and Mail Order Handbook,* 3rd ed. Chicago: Dartnell Press, 1980.

Hopkins, Claude C. *My Life in Advertising & Scientific Advertising.* Lincolnwood, IL: NTC Business Books, a division of NTC/Contemporary Publishing, 1998.

IMT Strategies, Inc. *Permission E-mail: The Future of Direct Marketing.* 1999-2000.

Karbo, Joe. *The Lazy Man's Way to Riche$: Dyna/Psyc can give you everything in the world you really want!,*1st ed. Laguna Beach, CA: FP Publishing Co., Inc., 1973.

Khan, Mickey A. "Promotion Lowers Acquisition Costs." *iMarketing News* (June 12, 2000).

Kobs, Jim. *Profitable Direct Marketing.* Chicago: Crain Books, 1979.

Lawler, Edmund O. *Copy Chasers on Creating Business-to-business Ads.* Lincolnwood, IL: NTC Business Books, a division of NTC/Contemporary Publishing, 1994.

Levey, Richard H. "Survey: Retention-Based E-mail to Surge." *Direct* (June 2000).

McIntosh, Mac. "How to Use Relationship Marketing to Increase Sales from Leads." Direct Marketing to Business National Conference, February 1999.

Mirani, Robert. "Marketing Goes Automated." *Sales & Field Force Automation* (June 1999).

Obermayer, James W. "How to Get Stubborn, Set-in-Their-Way Salespeople to Follow-up Sales Leads." Direct Marketing to Business Conference, 1996.

———. "Internet Shortcomings Shared by Too Many Sites." *Orange County Business Journal* (September 1998).

Ogilvy, David. *Confessions of an Advertising Man.* New York: Antheneum, a division of Macmillan Publishing, 1963.

———. *Ogilvy on Advertising.* New York: Vintage Books, 1985.

Peppers & Rogers Group. *The State of OnetoOne Online: Best Practices of the top 1to1 Web Sites: Version 1.1,* 1999.

Rackham, Neil, and John R. DeVincentis. *Rethinking the Sales Force.* New York: McGraw Hill, Inc., 1999.

Rapp, Stan, and Tom Colins. *The Great Marketing Turnaround; The Age of the Individual, and How to Profit from It.* New York: Plume, 1992.

Rapp, Stan. *The New Maximarketing.* New York: McGraw Hill, Inc., 1999.

Rice, Craig S. *Strategic Planning for the Small Business.* Holbrook, MA: Adams Media Corporation, 1990.

Robert, Michel. *Strategy Pure & Simple: How Winning Companies Dominate their Competitors.* New York: McGraw Hill, Inc., 1998.

Roman, Kenneth, and Jane Mass. *How to Advertise*, 2nd edition. New York: St. Martin's Press, 1997.

Ryan, Christopher. White paper: "High Yield Marketing and Marketing Automation: A Winning Combination." Colorado Springs, CO: Saligent Inc.

Silverstein, Barry. *Business-to-business Internet Marketing: Five Proven Strategies for Increasing Profits through Internet Direct Marketing.* Gulf Breeze, FL: Maximum Press, 1999.

SRDS Business Publications Advertising Source. Des Plaines, IL: SRDS, 1999.

SRDS Direct Marketing List Source. Des Plaines, IL: SRDS, 1999.

SRDS Interactive Advertising Source. Des Plaines, IL: SRDS, 1999.

Stone, Bob. *Successful Direct Marketing Methods*, 6th ed. Lincolnwood, IL: NTC Business Books, a division of NTC/Contemporary Publishing, 1996.

Throckmorton, Joan. *Winning Direct Response Advertising.* Englewood Cliffs, NJ: Prentice Hall, 1986.

ABOUT THE AUTHOR

Russell M. Kern is a twenty-year direct response professional, recognized as one of the country's top direct marketing educators and innovators. Mr. Kern's agency, Kern Direct, Inc., located in Woodland Hills, California, is known for its sophisticated on-line and off-line lead generation campaign capabilities. Kern Direct has provided solutions for clients that include: IBM, Hewlett-Packard, Apple Computer, 3Com, Peoplesoft, Gateway Computers, Lucent Technologies, Network Associates, Citrix Systems, Banc One Mortgage, Wells Fargo Bank, as well as a host of other technology, financial, and health-care companies.

As a direct marketing innovator, Kern aggressively deploys the latest Internet marketing strategies on his clients' behalf. Under his direction, Kern Direct creates cutting-edge, value-add websites to serve as both the lead-generating offer central for clients' campaigns, as well as the platform for downstream, permission-based eNurturing communications.

Russell Kern is the creator of the S.U.R.E.-Fire® Direct Response Planning Process; a comprehensive, four-phase methodology to reduce program errors and optimize marketers' investments in lead generation campaigns. This process has been credited with increasing program results from 100 percent to 2,000 percent, and is based on the research of over 500 campaigns, $40 million in marketing investments, and 900,000 sales leads.

Kern is not new to direct marketing education. He is a frequent author of articles for industry publications such as *DM News; Sell!ng Magazine; Sales, Advertising & Marketing (SAM) Magazine; the Business-2-Business Marketer,* and *Advertising and Marketing.* His articles cover topics such as:

- The Ten Most Effective Ways to Motivate Response
- Synergistic, Value-Added, Business-to-Business Web Sites: How to Increase Value for Visitors Through Lead Generation Offers
- Four Key Elements to Increase Your Direct Marketing Success Rates
- Be Sure to Strategize, Understand, Respond, . . . and Do So Excellently
- Here's How to Get S.U.R.E.-Fire® Response Advertising
- Web Advertising Calls for Marketing 101
- The Physics and Psychology of Direct Response
- The Fundamentals of Direct Marketing

Kern is a frequent speaker at marketing industry events including the National Direct Marketing Association Conference; the Direct Marketing to Business Conference; Seattle, Phoenix, Orange County, and Los Angeles Direct Marketing Clubs; West Coast chapters of the Business Marketing Association; and national marketing meetings for companies like IBM, Apple, and Convergys Corporation.

Upon graduating from UCLA with a Bachelor of Arts Degree in Economics, Russell Kern was trained at Needham Harper & Steers (now DDB Needham). During his tenure, he gained knowledge in brand advertising, media planning, and direct marketing, while working for the agency's manufacturing, petroleum, and banking clients. Then at Doyle Dane Bernbach, Kern served as part of the account team for the multimillion-dollar launch of a major travel and entertainment credit card.

Russell Kern started his own agency in 1981 with the goal of blending the principles of brand advertising with the proven measurement techniques of direct response marketing. He has since gone on to win the prestigious Echo award from the Direct Marketing Association, and currently serves as his agency's Creative Director, responsible for the creation of hard-hitting, results-oriented, on-line and off-line campaigns.

Mr. Kern can be contacted at:

Kern Direct Marketing
20300 Ventura Blvd., Suite 210
Woodland Hills, CA 91364
800-335-4244
www.kerndirect.com (for samples of Mr. Kern's work)
www.sure-fire.net (for additonal information about *S.U.R.E.-Fire®*
    Direct Response Marketing)

INDEX